Copyright © 2021 by Sadler Media, LLC.

All Rights Reserved. No part of this book maybe used, reproduced or transmitted in any form or by any means, electronic or mechanical, including photocopying, recording or by any information storage and retrieval system without permission in writing from the author.

Published by Sadler Media, LLC

Printed in the United States of America

10 9 8 7 6 5 4 3 2 1

ISBN: 978-1-953578-15-0

Library of Congress: 2021905130

Cover photograph by Sadler Media, LLC

www.newhorizonsgroup.foundation

Also By J Stephen Sadler

Quest For The Best Series

- *Memoir* - The Story Of An Unlikely Chef Who Built An Improbable Empire From A Lost Family Recipe
- *Entrepreneurial* - Bringing Fine Dining To Small Town America
- *International Recipe Book-* The World On My Plate

Happy Garden™ Children's Books Series

- Bubba Broccoli - *Being Different is Special*
- Chuckie Carrot - *Why I Grow Low*
- Colinda Cauliflower - *Mashed Potatoes*
- Eddie Eggplant - *Being Little Is The Best*
- Paulina Potato - *Black & Brown Is Super Cool*
- Sammy Spinach - *Sammy Grows Big & Strong*
- Sidney String Bean - *With A Little Help From My Friends*
- Tanya Tomato - *The Perfect Little Fruit*

J Stephen's books are available at:
www.newhorizonsgroup.foundation,
www.jstephensgarden.com,
Amazon and other book platforms.

This book is dedicated to my friend Chef Rene Verdon who taught me that crafting a dish is like creating a fine work of art for all to remember; and to all those chef's across the world, who were willing to share their personal creations with me to bring back to my home in America.

WHAT PEOPLE ARE SAYING ABOUT CHEF J STEPHEN'S THE WORLD ON MY PLATE RECIPE BOOK

"With his world travel inspired recipe's, J Stephen's 'The World On My Plate' recipe book will be your go to guide for creatively unique dishes."

Dame Mynetta Cockerell
Executive Chef
Les Dames d' Escoffier

"A great epicurean tour of dishes from around the world. The recipes for his 400-year-old family artisan crumb cake are worth the price of the book alone. Many of his recipes bring me back to my family's Green Pastures restaurant in Austin, Texas."

Guich Koock
Storyteller, Actor & Entrepreneur
Son of one of the greatest chef's in Texas

"J Stephen has been gathering recipes for years from across the world. I have enjoyed many of them on visits to his Dallas area bistro. If you are looking for dishes that will make an impression, this book gives you access to every one of them. But it's not just his international recipes that make this book special, it's his generational family recipes that stand out. Creating family recipes has been a way for me to honor my mom as well as other family members and what joy it brings to keep them original just as they were. His sharing of the stories behind each recipe and how they were a part of special holidays and growing up is something you won't find in any other recipe book. It's the combination of unique international dishes and those wonderful family recipes that are the glue that keeps it all together making his book a recipe for success."

Chef Connie Mullins
Executive Food & Pastry Chef
www.facebook.com/ChefConnieBakes

"Cooking is like love. It should be entered into with abandon or not at all."

Harriet Van Horne

TABLE OF CONTENTS

Page 4	Dedication
Page 9	Introduction
Page 10	A World Apart
Page 17	The Right Ingredients
Page 23	Appetizers
Page 33	Soups & Salads
Page 47	Breads & Biscuits
Page 57	Breakfast & Brunch
Page 89	The Main Course
Page 127	Side Dishes
Page 137	Sandwiches
Page 146	Gravies, Sauces, Dips & Spreads
Page 163	Fillings, Frostings & Toppings
Page 178	Desserts
Page 251	Children's Recipe's
Page 261	Index
Page 268	Equivalent Measures

"Cooking is at once child's play and adult joy. And cooking done with care is an act of love."

Craig Claiborne

THE WORLD ON MY PLATE
RECIPE BOOK

Chef J Stephen Sadler

In Search of the Ultimate Dining Experience

It started with a family recipe that led to a quest to find the best dining experiences in the world.

When I was provided with my family's 400-year-old artisan crumb cake recipe, I had one simple goal in mind and that was to understand how my descendants would have made such a delicacy and where they would have sourced their ingredients. That goal led to my worldwide search for every ingredient in my family's cake. Little did I know that my goal would eventually lead to traveling the world on my quest of finding the ultimate dining experience.

My travels taught me that the crafting of a great dish involved much more than simply following a recipe. It taught me that the source of the ingredients you used were of equal importance to the actual recipe in the outcome of a dish.

"My World On A Plate" Recipe Book is not your typical recipe book that provides the how but not the why. I've made sure that you'll find all the dishes made famous at my International Bistros. But, I've also provided you with not only the ability to make each dish but also the knowledge of the specific type of ingredients to use to assure that whatever dish you craft will stand out above all others as a memorable offering.

THE STORY BEHIND IT ALL
A WORLD APART

CHILE, FRANCE, CUBA, PERU, GREAT BRITAIN, HONDURAS, GERMANY, ITALY, ARGENTINA, JAPAN, CHINA, STATES, CANADA, DENMARK, BELIZE, BELGIUM, POLAND, MEXICO, BAHAMAS, JAMAICA, URUGUAY, INDIA, BRITISH VIRGIN ISLANDS, AUSTRIA, ISRAEL, BAVARIA, SPAIN, SWITZERLAND

The selection of the offerings in my recipe book was a real challenge. There were so many dishes I have from so many countries that selecting the best was not as easy as I initially expected. There are five areas that I concentrated on. Each has its own unique merits. On the top of each recipe, you'll find the country of origin for that dish. In almost every case, I've made it exactly as I was shown in its country of origin.

Europe
Europe has some of the finest offerings in the world and Europe was where I started and to this day, is my favorite place to dine. Every country in Europe has it's great little bistro's and cafe's, each offering their own versions of all kinds of dishes. Europe is jam packed with chef's who are more than willing to share their great creations with you. Nowhere in the world will you find chef's who are more proud of their offerings.

Central America/Caribbean
Central America has its own take on great dining, it's just harder to find than in Europe or the United States. Unlike Europe, where every country has distinctly different dishes and the States where every region has its own specialty, the dishes in the Caribbean, although featuring different local spices and seasonings are mostly based on rice and beans. The challenge was to find something different, perhaps not indigent , but unique nonetheless.

South America
The key countries for varied and unique dining in South America are Peru, Argentina and Chile. Not to say the other countries are lacking in offerings , but these three countries have the most varied menu's. You'll find some really interesting dishes here from each of these countries.

Asia
Asia is still an unfinished work in progress for me. To date the only dishes I have in Asia is from Japan. Touring the rest of Asia is definitely in my plans but will have to await until I complete my tour of the America's.

North America
We are an international bistro and so, we also offer what I believe to be uniquely qualified dishes to match anything the rest of the world has to offer from the good old States. America has its own take on dishes it has created, as well as on dishes from the old world and south of the border and I wanted to feature what I believed to be the best the States had to offer.

THE STORY BEHIND IT ALL

A WORLD APART

If you like to travel and experience the world like I do, the following will be your guide to finding the great little places where so many of the recipe's in my book originate. Come along with me as we visit some of the finest dining experiences in the world.

EUROPE

BELGIUM -
Although they are available all over Belgium, I found the "Belgian" waffles we serve at a cute cafe called Desire de Lille located in Antwerp. If you're ever in Belgium, make sure you stop in and enjoy a "real" waffle." These are not your usual waffles and deserve their own story. (You can read the interesting turn of events "Belgian" waffles took to get to the States. in the next section of this chapter).

DENMARK -
I found our tuna fish recipe in the town of Aarhus, Denmark. Aarhus is about 187 kilometers northwest of Copenhagen. Aarhus is a pretty small city , but it has plenty of cafes and restaurants. Most American's know of Copenhagen, but have never heard of Aarhus. Aarhus its actually a pretty vibrant college town. If you ever get there, make sure you visit the Moesgaard Museum, it's one of my favorites.

FRANCE -
The French offerings that I chose from my recipe folder included; Parisian bruléed oatmeal that I found about 560 km southeast of Paris in the town of Annecy; A gruyere egg soufflé and two different French quiche, all found in Paris proper; and finally a French onion soup gratinée found in a little cafe about 30 minutes west of Paris in the town of Saint-Germain-en-Laye and a Grande Mariner French toast found 3 km west of Saint-Germain-en-Laye in a town called Chambourcy. Although I'm not a big fan of Paris and its people, if one ventures into the French countryside, one will find great little town's with excellent restaurants run by friendly locals.

GERMANY -
I don't believe our Freiburg grilled cheese is unique to the town of Freiburg , but as the name would imply, it came from a cafe in Freiburg. Located on the western edge of the Black Forest in the Upper Rhine region, Freiburg is surrounded by beautiful wine vineyards. If you're a wine lover, it's definitely THE place to visit in Germany.

The Story Behind It All

A world apart

EUROPE *(continued)*

ITALY -
Our Italian offerings included: Gamberaia blueberry ricotta pancakes, named after the famous Villa Gamberaia just outside of Florence, Italy (you can read my family background on these pancakes in the next section of this chapter); A Caprese salad or Inslata Caprese as Italian's call it, originating from the Isle of Capri in the Campagna region of Italy; and our roasted tomato basil soup was found in a cute little cafe in the center of Rome.

Because they are so tourist focused, I don't usually like to look for dishes in the big cities. Rome is no different, but Italy is one of the few places where you can simply rent a car and travel anywhere. Wherever you go, you'll find kind, welcoming people, manning great little cafe's, each with their own twist on Italian specialties when not on "Pausa" (think Italian for siesta - virtually all the restaurants and cafes in small towns close, so their staff can have a break). Italy is one of my favorite countries and is truly a foodies paradise.

POLAND -
I had an advantage here and didn't have to even leave my home to add this dish to my menu. My Father's mother, "little Grandma" as she was known to us, was not only famous for her family crumb cake but also for her home-cooked pierogies & kielbasa sausage. And so, this classic polish old world dish is front and center at my bistro.

NORTH AMERICA

CANADA -
My Salmon Hash & Eggs came from, of all places, a big tourist focused restaurant up the road a piece from the States in Vancouver, Canada. That's NOT the usual type of place I look to find great unique dishes, but it got such great reviews, that I tried it and it won me over.

MEXICO -
Our San Miguel Tuna Jack Nochalette's came from our friendly neighbor to the south, Mexico. Many Americans are familiar with Los Cabos or more specifically the town of Cabo San Lucas, which is a favorite vacation spot for Canadians & Americans. Our Nochalette's came, not from a cafe or restaurant, but from a little beachside stand.

THE STORY BEHIND IT ALL

A WORLD APART

NORTH AMERICA (*continued*)

States -
San Francisco and New Orleans may offer some great dishes, but in the States, if you don't start with New York City you know nothing about great food. Our New York City style egg sandwiches may not sound like much, but they are traditionally New York.

Our Jalapeño burger, Roast Pork Loin, Cranberries & Homemade Country Stuffing and our Jalapeño Biscuits and Gravy are all great breakfast and lunch dishes created by my own chef's in our home town of Dallas, Texas.

One of our most popular lunch dishes is our Impossible Burger which comes from Redwood City, California a town 27 miles south of San Francisco. We found our King Ranch Chicken Casserole in a Brownsville, Texas greasy spoon diner, all the way down about as far south as you can go in Texas, before hitting Mexico.

Our Chesapeake Bay Blue Lump Crab Soufflé came from a little cafe not far from Camden Yards in Baltimore, Maryland. And, finally our Alaskan Salmon Eggs Benedict, which may sound like it came from Alaska, but actually came from one of the many dock restaurants of Seattle.

ASIA

JAPAN -
Tokyo Japan, the largest city in the world, is not my normal hunting ground for interesting dishes. I usually like small towns, which is where you find the truly indigenous dishes. However, Tokyo is where our Japanese pancakes come from and they are a citywide favorite and unlike any pancake found in the States. If you are lucky enough to visit Japan, check out Shiawase No Pancake in the Omotesando area. That's where my pancake recipe comes from.

CHINA -
Hong Kong has some of the finest street foods in the world. My favorite is the Hong Kong Egg Waffles. If you're visiting Hong Kong, check out Tai-O Egg Waffle. Owner, 'Egg Puff Uncle' of Tai O is one of the few people left to make his egg waffles the traditional way and it's where my recipe comes from.

THE STORY BEHIND IT ALL

A WORLD APART

Caribbean/Central America

BAHAMA'S -
Most tourists visit Nassau and Paradise Island. Both offer great tourist attractions, shopping, gambling and dining. However, I'm never a tourist and I'm always looking for great dishes from the indigent people and that is where I found our South Sea's Shrimp Taco's in a beachside shack on the big Island (Andros). This little shack was on a "bight" (their term for an estuary) and it's the only thing they served (except for beverages). The dish may sound like a Tex-Mex dish , but it is true Bahamian.

BELIZE -
Belize is one of my favorite countries. The waters are blue, the topography ranges from palm-lined beaches to green mountains. I found our most popular breakfast egg dish in Placencia, Belize a peninsula located in southern Belize. My Jalapeño sausage side dish comes from Cay Caulker, in Northern Belize, a beautiful little Island that looks like a tiny fishing village that time forgot. Both dishes are absolute winners.

HONDURAS-
Roatán is the home of our most popular side dish, our Jalapeño cheese grits. Street vendors sell them wrapped in corn tortillas topped with a sauce similar to Sriracha. To me, Honduras, especially Roatán, is one of my favorite destinations. Beautiful Caribbean blue waters, palm trees and friendly locals make it a go to place for visitors from the States. This dish is a great example of what you can expect to enjoy.

JAMAICA -
Interestingly, the two dishes I found in Jamaica are not what you would think of as traditionally Jamaican dishes. My Grilled Portobello Burger, which because of the Jamaican seasoning we use could be considered Jamaican was found in Kingston, the capital. Kingston is located on the southeastern tip of Jamaica and unfortunately, is now known as the "bad" side of the Island. Not a place you would want to visit. That's a shame because Kingston has some great little restaurants.

My Banana Rum French Toast (yes I said French toast) was found in Montego Bay, a tourist town located on the northwestern side of the country. This side of Jamaica is known as the "safe" side. Although I found my French toast in a little cafe where the locals frequent, unfortunately, this is also the side where all the hotels and tourists are and as such, has lost much of its uniquely Jamaican character and dishes.

THE STORY BEHIND IT ALL

A WORLD APART

South America

PERU -
With cuisine influences from Spain, Italy, France and most recently Japan, Peru has always been, known as the culinary capital of South America. Although Ceviche is by far Peru's most popular dish, I'm not a sushi fan and so I skipped the Ceviche and went right for the Papa Rellena. That led me to Isolina Taberna Peruana on Av. San Martin in Lima where Chef Jose del Castillo serves up the finest one in Lima and this is the dish I brought home to my little bistro in Texas. It was to be one of my featured "After Hours" offerings. Unfortunately, COVID-19 nixed those nighttime dining plans, but you'll still get to taste one of the reasons Peru is a must stop for any culinary traveler visiting South America by indulging with my recipe.

CHILE -
Chile is the land of beautiful orchards and fantastic seafood. Because South America is in the southern hemisphere, its seasons are the reverse of the States. Because of this, most of the fruits and vegetables we enjoy in the winter month's come from Chile. In addition, Chile has some of the finest wines in the world. I enjoyed some of my favorite dining experiences at the vineyards. Northern Chile produces the white wines and southern Chile the reds. My favorite dining experience was at Restaurant De Viña Indómita in the Casablanca valley. Our table overlooking the vineyards and mountains behind was the perfect setting to experience their fine Chardonnay's and a wonderful assortment of octopus, pasta, and lamb dishes. I feature their Octopus Escabeche dish in this recipe book.

ARGENTINA-
On my visits to Argentina, one of the most unusual things I experienced was their unusual dining habits. Unlike in Chile, where breakfast is a big event, Argentinians choose to skip breakfast entirely. Since I'm a big breakfast person, this was a unique challenge for me. Luckily, Argentina makes some of the best empanadas I have ever eaten. Empanada literally translates to "wrapped in bread" and Argentinians know just what to wrap in these delicious stuffed dough pockets. I was able to happily exist on a large selection of meats, veggies and cheese fillings until the lunch and dinner offerings arrived. Another thing that sets Argentinians apart is their love of beef and bar-b-cue everything. This is not like the States where a good steak is appreciated and weekend bar-b-cues are common in the summer. This is like steak and bar-b-cue meats for EVERY meal. And it's understandable why. Argentine cattle live on pampas grass and this unique diet translates into steaks that taste like aged beef. If you've ever had aged beef you know what I'm talking about. There's nothing quite like it and Argentinians enjoy it for every lunch and dinner. In addition, they bar-b-cue everything not just for holidays but for every meal. You'll find every chef busy working over open flames,

Continued on the next page

THE STORY BEHIND IT ALL

A WORLD APART

Continued from previous page

ARGENTINA *(continued)* -
expertly tending to each and every dish. Since you can't get beef like that in the States, I have not included some of the great steak recipes I found there , but I have included a great Empanada recipe that I enjoyed at a cute little Empanada place called Lo Saldes. Interestingly, even though Argentina has such great steak dishes, my favorite dish came from the restaurant at the Four Seasons Hotel in Buenos Aires. It was there that Chef Maximillano Castillo treated my party to the finest Nero di Seppia Pasta (Black Squid Ink Pasta) I have ever had. You'll find that fantastic recipe in my book.

URAGUAY -
A beautiful little country that is just a one hour ferry ride across the Río de la Plata river from Buenos Aires. I was fortunate to visit the Unesco World Heritage town of Colonia del Sacramento. It's local artisan's produce beautiful pieces of jewelry from what is considered the finest Amethyst in the world. While on my visit I found a gem of a dining experience in a little bistro right on the Río de la Plata river called Charco. It was at Charco that chef Guillermo treated my party some truly excellent dishes. I chose a wonderful lamb chops with pomegranate sauce and saffron pilaf dish which you'll find the recipe in this book.

With a little help from some friends

No matter where you travel, beautifully crafted breakfast and lunch dishes are harder to find than dinner offerings. In fact, in some countries, such as Argentina for example, breakfast is never eaten at all. But, I have had the benefit of working with some great chefs who have assisted me in making EVERY dish breakfast, lunch, brunch or dinner special.

Part of what I believe made my bistros so different from other restaurants is not only the European ambiance but also the fact that I team with classically trained chef's not only for dinner but also for breakfast, lunch and brunch. You will find some fine-dining "dinner" restaurants that are manned by great chef's. Most restaurants however, have line cooks who know how to make specific dishes, but often are not schooled on what affect the varied reactions, ingredients, flavorings, and cooking practices have on a dish.

Culinary schools mainly teach their students how to make dinner NOT breakfast or lunch, (that's why I had to teach every one of my "classically trained" chef's how to make a proper egg). But you'll be hard-pressed to find a breakfast, lunch and brunch place that is served by great chef's. I always had classically trained chef's on my staff. These are the chef's that assured every dish, whether it be breakfast, lunch, brunch or dinner was always special.

What this means for the reader of my recipe book is a unique access into not only some very special dishes but also a unique take, as seen by classically trained chef's, on how they should be prepared and presented.

THE STORY BEHIND IT ALL

THE "RIGHT" INGREDIENTS

READ THIS BEFORE YOU MAKE A DISH

In my worldwide travels to find the "exact" methods and ingredients that went into my family's 400-year-old crumb cake recipe, I learned a lesson that has stayed with me for the rest of my life and that is that the "right" ingredients can often make the difference between success and failure. When most home cooks (and many "chefs") read a recipe, they pull out whatever "matching" ingredients they happen to have in their kitchen. That can be a fatal mistake. I often hear from guests who have made some of my dishes using my "exact" recipes, that their dishes just don't taste the same. This can sometimes be due to the techniques they used, but more often is due to the ingredients used.

The ingredients used in my family's crumb cake is a great example. Sour cream, eggs, vanilla, butter, flour, sugar, salt, baking powder, baking soda, dark brown sugar and cinnamon.

Sounds pretty simple right? You probably have all of those ingredients in your cupboard. HOWEVER, it's never as simple as it looks.

SOUR CREAM: Sour cream is pretty basic, as long as you NEVER use low-fat you're good to go, but from here on it gets pretty interesting.
EGGS: I only use eggs from free-roaming chickens, they taste better and are healthier for you AND for the chickens.
VANILLA: I only use Bourbon vanilla from Madagascar. It is the finest available and has a distinct depth of complex flavors that compliment my other ingredients. NEVER substitute!
BUTTER: Butter is butter right? Wrong! To control the saltiness of any of my recipes, I never use salted butter, whose salt content varies with every brand and type. AND I only use butter from Jersey or Guernsey cows. Why? Well, Butter from any other cows has A1 protein that has been linked to many ailments including Alzheimer's and asthma. Only Jersey or Guernsey cows produce butter that has A2 proteins which are not linked to any of those ailments.
FLOUR: I bet you have AP (all purpose) flour in your cupboard. That's fine for "some" dishes but never "great" for cakes. For my cakes I use a soft winter wheat European "cake" flour. Why? Cake flour is a finely milled, delicate flour with a low protein content. Because of the lower protein content, cake flour produces less gluten. In addition, because most European flours are milled differently than flours from the States, they have a lower gluten content than flours from the States. Besides the benefits of lower gluten content for those who suffer from gluten sensitivity, low gluten also makes a more tender cake. In addition, I also sift my flour which assures that my cakes are light, yet firm.

Continued on the next page

THE STORY BEHIND IT ALL

THE "RIGHT" INGREDIENTS CONTINUED

READ THIS BEFORE YOU MAKE A DISH (*Continued*)

SUGAR: You probably have a white granulated sugar in your cupboard. That's fine for some things, BUT I use the natural, unrefined sugars from the African island nation of Mauritius because they retain much of the flavor of the cane grown on soil rich with volcanic ash. In addition, I always use white Caster or superfine sugar which allows me to produce a slightly finer crumb and a lighter, more delicate crumb cake.
SALT: Most everyone uses the familiar table salt that they also use for salting their food. However, using a salt that is appropriate to the dish is actually quite important. I use a kosher salt in my crumb cake mixes because it has a different texture and flavor burst and is also less likely to contain additives like anti-caking agents and iodine. For my Caramel Sea Salt Topped cakes, I use a Fleur de Sel French Sea Salt because it has a much higher amount of moisture than common salt (up to 10% as compared to 0.5% for common salt). This allows the crystals to stick together in snowflake-like forms which makes it taste even saltier than table salt. That's the perfect salt for a salty/sweet combination. There are still other dishes where the typical table salt works best.
BAKING POWDER/BAKING SODA: Although they are both leaveners (which means they both generate gas that helps your cake rise), they are chemically different. Why do I use both? Simple, baking powder needs heat to activate. Baking soda needs liquid too activate. However, like a carbonated beverage, the bubbles created by both only last so long. Have you ever noticed that most recipes have you create the "dry" ingredients first and then add the "liquid" ingredients. That's done to make sure you don't activate the baking soda. With my cakes, I want the maximum rise and so I add baking soda which kicks in as soon as I mix my cakes and just as those bubbles are dying down, the heat from the oven, as my cakes are baking, activates the baking powder which continues the rise. By the way, if your baking powder has been sitting around for over 6-month's throw it out, it's no longer good. This is not a problem with baking soda which will last indefinitely.
DARK BROWN SUGAR: I use dark Muscovado Sugar because it has a fine, moist texture, high molasses content, and a strong lingering flavor that blends well and adds to the depth and richness of my crumbs. There is no other dark brown sugar that even comes close.
CINNAMON: In every other part of the world, "cinnamon" means Ceylon cinnamon. Unfortunately, the States uses a bolder, spicier species of cinnamon known as Cassia. The subtle complexity of flavor and texture of Ceylon cinnamon from Vietnam, is far superior to Cassia. It builds gradually into a complex symphony of rich floral flavors and aromas that compliment rather than overwhelm as Cassia does. Although expensive and often hard to find, Ceylon cinnamon also known as Saigon cinnamon should be a essential part of your basic ingredient set..

Continued on the next page

THE STORY BEHIND IT ALL

THE "RIGHT" INGREDIENTS CONTINUED

All this may sound very complicated, but I've made it easier by highlighting in blue and underlining where you can purchase any of the special ingredients in each of my recipes. I've also provided you with a handy reference chart explains why the ingredient is so special. BTW, I make $-0- on the companies I recommend.

INGREDIENT	WHY IT'S SPECIAL
Baking Powder Where you can get it Amazon	(1) To prevent a metallic taste in your baked goods and to eliminate one more chemical from your diet, always use aluminum-free baking powder. (2) Always keep your baking powder in an air-tight container and because it loses it's strength over time, never keep it over 6 month's
Butter Where you can get it Lucky Layla Farms	(1) Since the salt content varies with every brand and type, always use unsalted butter to control the saltiness of your recipes. (2) Always use butter from Jersey or Guernsey cows. Butter from any other cows has A1 protein that has been linked to many ailments including Alzheimer's and asthma. Only Jersey or Guernsey cows produce butter that has A2 proteins which are not linked to any ailments.
Cheese Where you can get it Parmigiano - igourmet Mozzarella - Mozzarella Company Brie - Gourmet Food Store Camembert Fromagerie Durand	There are hundreds of cheeses. These are the ones I use the most. (1) Parmesan - Always use FRESH Parmigiano Reggiano cheese. If it says "Parmesan", (note the spelling difference), it's an imitation version of "REAL" Parmigiano Reggiano cheese and as with all "imitation" anythings, it leaves a lot to be desired. The best Parmigiano Reggiano is Parmigiano Reggiano Stravecchio. (2) Brie - The finest Brie cheese comes from Brie France. It is a soft and creamy cheese and heats beautifully. (3) Gruyere - Imported gruyère (It MStatesT be imported) is a sweet but slightly salty hard cheese that puts Swiss cheese to shame. (4) Mozzarella - A traditionally southern Italian cheese made from Italian buffalo's milk. A great cheese for pasta dishes and salads (5) Camembert - A soft, buttery cheese that is creamy and spreadable. This is one of my little known (outside of France, where it's the most popular cheese) cheese tray must haves. **Bottom line... Spend the money and get a "Quality" cheese for your cheese trays, soups and salads. It will make the difference between a "Good" dish and a "Great" dish.**
Chocolate Where you can get it Olive Nation	There are hundreds of different chocolates, each with a different flavor characteristic. I NEVER use the standard "Baking Chocolate" found at the grocery stores. It's of the lowest quality and your dish will reflect that fact. Callebaut Chocolate makes most of the chocolates for all the "fine" chocolate brands. Use one of their good 60% or higher dark chocolates.
Cinnamon Where you can get it My Spice Sage	(1) Always use Saigon cinnamon. Most cinnamon sold in the States is an inferior Cassia cinnamon that provides overpowering spikes in taste. The subtle complexity of flavor and texture of Ceylon cinnamon from Vietnam, is far superior. It builds gradually into a complex symphony of rich floral flavors and aromas that compliment rather than overwhelms as Cassia does. Although expensive and often hard to find, Ceylon cinnamon, also known as Saigon cinnamon, should be a vital part of your basic ingredient set.
Dark Brown Sugar Where to get it India Tree	(1) Choose dark Muscovado Sugar because of its fine, moist texture, high molasses content, and a strong lingering flavor that blends well and adds to the depth and richness of your dish. There is no other dark brown sugar that comes close to its rich, full-bodied taste.

The Story Behind It All

The "Right" Ingredients Continued

INGREDIENT	WHY IT'S SPECIAL
Flavor Extracts Where to get it Olive Nation	If you can't find a fresh natural flavoring (usually because of seasonal availability), always use a Natural Flavor extract. Be careful, extracts are much more robust than the real deal. Use them carefully.
Flours Where you can get it King Arthur	You probably have AP (all purpose) flour which will work okay for most baking, "OKAY" is the key word here. You'll get much better results if you use the correct flour for the task. (1) Bread Flour is ideal for bread because it's high in protein and gluten. Gluten provides elasticity for doughs to expand and hold large amounts of air which produces a high rise.(2) Cake Flour is a low protein, low gluten flour that is perfect for cakes, muffins, biscuits and most other baked goods. (3) Whole Wheat Flour has a slightly nutty flavor. It's a whole grain flour with high protein and low gluten properties which produces a dryer but more nutritional end product. (4) Pastry flour strikes the ideal balance between flakiness and tenderness, making it perfect for pies, tarts and most cookies. ***Bottom Line… Use bread flour for your breads, Cake flour for your cakes and pastries and whole grain flours for whole grain fiber breads."***
Fruit Fillings Where you can get it Apricot - B&R Farms. Lemon or Lime Curd - See my recipes	We use many fruit fillings in our cakes. There is a great difference in the ones you use. (1) Apricot - By far, the best apricot filling/jam/puree is made from Blenheim apricots from California. We get ours from B&R Farms." (2) Lemon or Lime Curd- make your own curds. They're easy to make and unmatched by store purchased. (3) Raspberry - With it's fresh fruit all natural flavor, I use Hungarian Lekvar. It's hard to find and it's availability is often limited, so you'll have to search, but it's well worth the effort. Whatever flavor you choose, make sure it is all natural not only for health reasons but also for the purity of your recipe (added sugar, in any form, changes the composition and mouth feel of your dish.)
Honey Where to get it Find a local producer near you	You have a choice to choose locally farmed or shipped in raw or pasteurized honey. (1) Pasteurization removes the bee pollen and propolis. Bee pollen and propolis has antioxidant properties, anti-inflammatory effects, antibacterial, anti-cancer and antiulcer action and antifungal action pain-relieving properties. (2) Because bees use pollen from the same flowers and trees in your area that make you sneeze and sniffle, local honey helps you build up immunity to these allergens. ***Bottom line… Definitely choose raw unfiltered honey that is made from bees that live within 50 miles of your home.***
Vanilla Where to get it My Spice Sage	NEVER use imitation vanilla. The chemical composition of imitation vanilla is different than "real" vanilla and interacts differently with creations. The finest vanilla is Madagascar bourbon vanilla pure vanilla extract. I use Nielson-Massey because of their cold extraction process, which draws out over 300 flavor compounds from the vanilla bean.

The Story Behind It All

The "Right" Ingredients Continued

INGREDIENT	WHY IT'S SPECIAL
Oils Where you can get it Olive Oil - Formaggio Kitchen Avocado Oil - La Tourangelle	(1) Vegetable Oil - It's not made from vegetables and is not healthy. DON'T use it! (2) Canola Oil - Because of its high "smoke point" it's a good oil to use when you're cooking especially when using high-temperatures. (3) Olive Oil - "un-refined, early harvest, extra virgin olive oil is one of the healthiest and tastiest oils you can consume. However, because of a low "smoke point," it's not a good cooking oil. (4) Corn Oil, Grape Seed Oil & Sunflower Oil - All are rich in omega 6 (which lowers blood cholesterol) (5) Sesame Oil, Walnut Oil & Pistachio Oil - Because they are great sources of monounsaturated fat, anti-inflammatories and antioxidants, they are healthy oils. However, all have low "smoke points" and are not good for high heat cooking. (6) Palm Oil - Since Palm Oil farms are one of the prime causes of deforestation, NEVER use it. (7) Coconut Oil - Because it has high saturated fat content, I don't recommend its use. (8) Flaxseed Oil, Hemp Seed Oil & Pumpkin Seed Oil - All have high amounts of omega-3 fatty acids which have been shown to decrease inflammation and control blood pressure levels. Because of this, these three oils are some of the healthiest oils you can consume. (9) Avocado Oil - I've saved the best for last. Avocado oil is extremely high in oleic acid, which protects you against heart disease, diabetes, obesity, and high blood pressure. Although olive oil has the best flavor profile of all the oils, because avocado oil offers the same oleic acid benefits, robust anti-inflammatory qualities AND has a relatively high "smoke point", it should be your every day oil of choice. ***Bottom line... Save your "un-refined, early harvest, extra virgin" olive oil for your dressings, dips, spreads and marinades and choose your avocado oil for all your cooking.***
Salts Where to get it Saltworks	Use different salt's for different purposes. Use a kosher salt if you're looking for robust flavor burst. It is also less likely to contain additives like anti-caking agents and iodine. Use a Fleur de Sel French Sea Salt because of its much higher amount of moisture than common salt (up to 10% as compared to 0.5% for common salt). This allows the crystals to stick together in snowflake-like forms which makes it taste even saltier than table salt. It's the perfect salt for a salty/sweet combination. Common table salt is fine for most other offerings. ***Bottom line... don't automatically grab the table salt. Instead, use the salt that fits the dish.***
White Sugars Where to get it India Tree	(1) Most homes have white granulated sugar. Kind of like AP (all purpose flour), it can be used for most dishes BUT, choose the natural, unrefined sugars from the African island nation of Mauritius because they retain much of the flavor of the cane grown on soil rich with volcanic ash. (2) If you're looking to produce a a slightly finer, lighter, more delicate cake, always use white Caster or superfine sugar. Since it dissolves so easily, its also ideal for simple syrup. (3) Since it doesn't melt during the baking process, use a Belgium Pearl sugar if you want to create a gooey cinnamon roll or Liege waffle. (4) Because they retain much of their rich flavors, Turbinado sugar is great for your teas and coffees. (5) Confectioners Sugar, also referred to as powdered sugar is a type of white sugar that has been ground into a fine powder. It also has a small amount of cornstarch blended in to prevent clumping. Confectioners sugar easily dissolves in liquid, and is perfect for making icings and frostings, as well as decorating baked goods. ***Bottom line... There's a sugar for every use, choose the best fit for what you hope to accomplish.***

"Cooking is not difficult. Everyone has taste, even if they don't realize it. Even if you're not a great chef, there's nothing to stop you understanding the difference between what tastes good and what doesn't."

Gerard Depardieu

APPETIZERS

"Similar to what movie trailers are to movies, appetizers set the pace for what comes next. In many cases, appetizers are actually stand-alone meals. In fact, it is now common at many restaurants for diner's to order only from the appetizer menu. TGI Fridays® was one of the first restaurants to introduce a separate appetizer menu and it became an instant hit. Today, many social events and private parties feature appetizers and desserts only. With that in mind, this is the area where you can shine. Where you can create fancy designs and unique combinations.

Because they are usually so easy to make and hard to screw up, even the worst chef's in the world, can find several appetizers that they can craft that will impress their guests. In many cases, without even going close to the oven!

In my bistro's we made the most interesting appetizers for private events and parties. In those cases, people like to offer something that stands out. Something that will have their guests talking for years. But, don't save this great segment of the dining experience to a special event. You can enjoy appetizers for a family dinner, a picnic or simply when you have a few friends over for drinks. So, drop the crackers and cheese, nuts and dip's. You can easily whip up a great appetizer that will wow them every time."

Chef J Stephen

FRANCE

Camembert with Pistachio Crust

SERVES 15, PREP 10MIN, TOTAL 10MIN

Ingredients

½ cup pistachio nuts
1 Camembert cheese round (about 10 ounces)
1 Tablespoon honey
½ cup dried cranberries
Crackers, for serving (sturdy)

Chef Secrets

"Make sure you use fresh pistachios. The finest pistachios come from the tiny village of Bronte, in Sicily. Since they're near impossible to find in the States, I suggest you choose Setton Farms gourmet pistachios."

"If you can find it online, choose one of the last Camemberts made with raw milk by the farmer-producer who raises his own cattle. named Fromagerie Durand from the village of Camembert"

Instructions

Process your pistachio's in a food processor until they are chopped into small pieces (do not over-process)

For your Camembert, you can leave the crust on or scrape it off (your preference.) If you choose to scrape the crust off, do it gently

Brush the top and sides of your cheese with fresh locally grown honey

Sprinkle a layer of your pistachio nuts over the top and pat the nuts by hand along the entire sides of the cheese. Press the nuts in with your hands to make sure they stay on the sides

Place the remaining nuts on the center of your serving platter and place your cheese on top

Sprinkle your dried cranberries around your cheese

Serve at room temperature with sturdy crackers

Chef J Stephen

MEXICO

NOCHALETTE'S

SERVES 5, PREP 15MIN, TOTAL 20MIN

INSTRUCTIONS

In a medium mixing bowl, place one can (5 ounces) of drained Albacore tuna. Break apart your tuna by hand to assure there are no large chunks

Add 2 tablespoons of mayonnaise and mix thoroughly. This tuna may look a bit dry, but you do not want a wet tuna (which will make your chips soggy)

Place ten tortilla chips on a lined sheet pan. Allow for plenty of space between the chips. To make sure the liner doesn't cover the chips when baking, make sure a chip is placed by each corner of your pan liner

Using a tsp, place 1 tsp of your tuna mix on each tortilla. Top with 1 tsp of sour cream and top that with Monterey Jack Cheese. Cheese should completely cover each chip. Don't worry if some goes off the sides, when it's done, that will be the best part

Place in an oven for approx. 7-10 min at 375° (until cheese browns)

Top each chip with a pickled, sliced jalapeño. Make sure you add a bit of the pickled jalapeño juice, it's key to finishing off the great taste of this appetizer

INGREDIENTS

10 Large tortilla chips
5 ounces Albacore tune in water - drained
2 tablespoons mayonnaise
⅓ cup sour cream
¾ cup shredded Monterey Jack cheese
10 pickled jalapeños (sliced)

CHEF SECRETS

"Always use Albacore tuna for the most vibrant tuna taste. Make sure its not in oil as that will make your chips soggy and add a subtle flavor that you don't want."

"I usually choose fresh over canned or processed, but in this case, make sure you use pickled jalapeños. The key to this dish is not only the "pickled" jalapeño taste but also the dribble of jalapeño juice on each of the Nochalette's."

Chef J Stephen

POLAND

ŚMIETANKA TOAST

SERVES 6, PREP 10MIN, TOTAL 20MIN

INGREDIENTS

8 slices white bread (you can substitute for any bread you like)
3 tbsp mayonnaise
8 ounces cream cheese
Pinch of black pepper
½ tsp grated white onion
Pinch of salt
3 tbsp grated Parmesan cheese
1 tsp paprika
Drizzle virgin olive oil

INSTRUCTIONS

In a medium mixing bowl, add your mayonnaise, cream cheese and onions. Mix thoroughly

Spread approx. ¼" thick layer of your mix across each slice of bread

Sprinkle your parmesan cheese and paprika across the top's of your bread

Set your oven to broil

Place your slices of bread on a lined sheet pan in oven for approx. 2 minutes (watch closely) until tops have turned a light brown

Lightly top with salt and black pepper and a light drizzle of virgin olive oil

Cut each slice in half

Plate and serve hot from the oven

CHEF SECRETS

"I never cheap out on the mayonnaise choosing to always use Hellmans and NEVER use Miracle Whip."

"Your bread needs to be firm but soft and definitely not crisp. In fact many in my family choose to trim the crusty edges off their bread."

"Choose 'early harvest' olive oil in a dark bottle (a dark bottle preserves your oil longer). Early harvest olive oil is oil squeezed from the olive before the olive is ripe. An unripe olive yields much less olive oil but much higher quality oil, so it will be expensive but well worth the price. You can find a great early harvest olive oil [Formaggio Kitchen](.)."

"I always use Parmigiano Reggiano Stravecchio cheese, that I grind myself. You can find a good one at [igourmet](.). If you can't find that, most any Parmigiano Reggiano are not quite as good but will work fine. Get a quarter of a wheel and store it. It will keep well."

Chef J Stephen

INDIA

Cucumber Vases

SERVES 4, PREP 10MIN, TOTAL 20MIN

Instructions

Using a mandolin (or vegetable slicer if you don't own a mandolin), slice your cucumber in 9 long strips. discard the first cut. This will leave you with 8 cucumber strips

Wrap your 8 sliced cucumbers into vases as pictured

Gather ½ cup of spring salad mix and fill each cucumber vase

Sprinkle your spring mix with a pinch of kosher salt, pinch of black pepper and a sprinkle of olive oil

Top with a dollop of sour cream

Garnish with a mint leaf

Ingredients

1 seedless cucumber
½ cup spring salad mix
2 ounces sour cream
4 mint leaves
1 pinch kosher salt
1 pinch black ground pepper
2 tsp olive oil

Chef Secrets

"As with all your fruit and vegetables, you want to choose your cucumber from the farmers market"

"Most people have a vegetable peeler, but you should really use a mandolin. They're inexpensive and they give you much greater control over the slices you make."

"Choose 'early harvest' olive oil in a dark bottle (a dark bottle preserves your oil longer). Early harvest olive oil is oil squeezed from the olive before the olive is ripe. An unripe olive yields much less olive oil but much higher quality oil, so it will be expensive but well worth the price. You can find a great early harvest olive oil Formaggio Kitchen"

"You'll notice that on some of my recipe's I call for kosher salt, others simply salt and still others Fleur de Sel: (French sea salt). There is a difference. kosher salt is a larger flake and on some dishes, I wan't the salt to jump out, on others where I want a more subtle marriage. I'll choose regular salt. Finally, where I want the salt to lightly melt in your mouth, I'll choose Fleur de Sel. You can find a great Fleur de Sel at Saltworks. As with so many ingredients, when the recipe calls for 'salt', you need to know, what you're trying to accomplish before you choose your salt."

Chef J Stephen

FRANCE

HONEY ALMOND BAKED BRIE

SERVES 6, PREP 10MIN, TOTAL 20MIN

INSTRUCTIONS

Preheat oven to 350 °

Place your Brie cheese on a small lined sheet pan

Bake for approx. 10-12 minutes or until softened

Remove from the oven and let cool for about 5 minutes

Brush the top and sides of your cheese with your fresh locally grown honey

Sprinkle a layer of your slivered, toasted almonds over the top and pat the almonds by hand along the entire sides of the cheese. Press the almonds in with your hands to make sure they stay on the sides

For additional color and flavor, you can chop some dried apricots and place around the base of your cheese

INGREDIENTS

1 (8 ounce) round Brie cheese
¼ cup locally grown honey
½ cup slivered roasted, salted almonds
8 sliced toasted baguettes (can substitute with crackers)

CHEF SECRETS

"The finest Brie comes from Brie France. You can purchase a good one at Gourmet Food Store. If you can't wait for a delivery from France, choose your Brie from a cheese store not a grocery store."

"Always choose raw locally grown honey. Raw honey has anti-bacterial, anti-viral, and anti-fungal properties, and promotes digestive health. Raw, local honey also contains a blend of local pollen, which can strengthen a person's immune system, and reduce pollen allergy symptoms."

"The best almonds come from California. Choose organic if you can. I like the quality of Tierra Farms Almonds. You'll have to toast and salt them but it will be worth it."

"Stay away from the usual "Turkish" apricots found in most grocery stores. They are definitely inferior to Blenheim apricots from California. We get ours from B&R Farms."

Chef J Stephen

FRANCE

Streusel Wrapped Scallops & Bacon

Serves 6, Prep 20min, Total 30min

Instructions

Streusel
Cut your unsalted butter into 4" squares

Into a large mixing bowl, combine your cake flour, dark brown Muscovado sugar and Saigon cinnamon

Mix until all the lumps are gone

Add your unsalted butter to the mix. Mix until fully incorporated (It will be course and granular)

You'll have extra streusel, but never fear, you can freeze your extra streusel for future use

Bacon
Since your bacon browns up much slower than your scallops, pre-cook your bacon first. Don't cook it all the way. Instead, cook it to ¾ the way you normally cook bacon.

In a large sauté pan, cook your bacon over medium heat until golden brown, BUT it should still be soft and pliable

Scallops

Pat your scallops dry with a paper towel

In a small bowl, mix your sea salt, black pepper, and garlic and then sprinkle this mix generously over scallops

Wrap each scallop with ½ of your bacon strip and secure it to the scallop using a toothpick

Continued on next page

Ingredients

Bacon Wrapped Scallops
4 strips of thick bacon. You'll use a half slice of bacon for each scallop.
2 tbsp unsalted butter
1 lb fresh deep sea scallops
1 tsp sea salt
1 tsp pepper
1 tsp garlic powder
1 tsp ginger

Streusel
1 lb unsalted butter
½ cup cake flour (you can substitute A/P flour)
1 lb dark brown Muscovado sugar
2 tbsp Saigon cinnamon

Chef Secrets

"The natural, unrefined dark Muscovado Sugars from the African island nation of Mauritius are particularly special because they retain much of the flavor of the cane grown on soil rich with volcanic ash. Because of its fine, moist texture, high molasses content, and a strong lingering flavor it blends well with the smokey floor of your bacon. You can find a great dark brown Muscovado sugar at India Tree."

" Because I want my bacon to have a rich deep flavor and I like it thicker than any 'thick bacon' offered from the grocery store, I always purchase my bacon from my local butcher. Try it, you'll be surprised by the difference."

Continued on next page

FRANCE

STREUSEL WRAPPED SCALLOPS & BACON
CONTINUED

In another small bowl, mix your streusel mix and ginger

Sprinkle ¼ tsp per scallop of your streusel ginger mix over your scallops

Melt your unsalted butter in a large sauté pan

Add your scallops to the pan and cook on medium high heat

Flip after 5 minutes flip your scallops and sprinkle with another ¼ tsp per scallop of your streusel ginger mix

Make sure you lightly brown each side, and pay attention to the middle of the scallop. When the scallop turns bright white and opaque it is cooked. DON'T OVERCOOK

Garnish with some chopped chives

Serve immediately

CHEF SECRETS (CONTINUED)

"Scallops are under appreciated mainly because most people don't know how to cook them. Either too chewy or too fishy usually has a lot to do with how they're prepared and overcooking is usually the culprit."

"Because wet scallops don't crisp up as well as dry scallops, always pat dry your scallops. I always use unsalted butter to fry them. When you cook your scallop, to assure they don't get tough or fishy tasting (both of which happens when you overcook), DON'T OVERCOOK with too high a flame and DON'T OVERCOOK by cooking too long! Did I make the part about DON'T OVERCOOK clear enough? I hope so."

Chef J Stephen

BELIZE

BELIZEAN CRAB CAKES

SERVES 6, PREP 35MIN, TOTAL 1HR 15MIN

INGREDIENTS

Crab Cakes
1 lb blue lump crabmeat
6 tbsp panko bread crumbs
1 ¼ tsp Dijon mustard
1 ounce old bay seasoning
1 ¼ tsp Worcestershire sauce
1 ½ tsp fresh parsley (chopped)
1 cup mayonnaise
1 large egg
1 tbsp kosher salt
1 tbsp black pepper
¼ tsp clear corn syrup
¾ tsp lime juice
2 tbsp bread flour
¾ tsp black pepper
6 tbsp water
1 sprig fresh rosemary (per serving)

Sun-dried Tomato Aioli
1 ½ medium garlic cloves
3 large sun dried tomatoes
1 cup mayonnaise
2 tbsp lemon juice
¼ tsp kosher salt
½ tsp black pepper

Avocado Dip
1 fresh, ripe avocado
1 tbsp plain greek yogurt
1 tbsp Tahini Sauce
1 tbsp fresh squeezed lime juice
¾ minced garlic
½ tsp sea salt
1 ⅓ tsp water

Continued on next page

INSTRUCTIONS

Crab Cakes
Mix warm water and your crab base in a small bowl to create your "Base". Mix until fully dissolved and then set aside

Line a sheet pan

Chop your fresh parsley

Place your lump blue crabmeat in mixing bowl. Break up all lumps (remove any shell fragments)

In another mixing bowl add your Dijon mustard, Worcestershire sauce, fresh parsley, mayonnaise, large egg, Key West lime juice, Old Bay seasoning, clear corn syrup, and black pepper. Once you mix it thoroughly, add your crabmeat, bread flour and Panko breadcrumbs to the mix. Combine thoroughly

Add your water & crab base mixture to this mix and mix thoroughly

Cover with clear wrap and refrigerate for a minimum of 2-hrs (for the best results refrigerate overnight)

After refrigeration, form into 1 ounce (about the size of a large meatball) crab cake patties

You can use your patties immediately, refrigerate for 1 week or freeze for 30 days

Dipping Sauces

Sun-dried Tomato Aioli
Chop your medium garlic clove fine

Continued on next page

BELIZE

BELIZEAN CRAB CAKES

CONTINUED

Chop your medium sun dried tomato into small diced pieces

Place your mayonnaise, chopped sun dried tomatoes, lemon juice, sea salt, black pepper, and chopped garlic into your blender

Mix on high until puree'd

You can refrigerate for 5 days

Avocado Dip
Remove the pit and scoop out your avocado. Discard the skin

Mince and mash your garlic into a paste

Combine your avocado, yogurt, Tahini sauce, lime juice, minced garlic paste, water and sea salt into a food processor

Pulse until smooth. Scrape the sides as you pulse as necessary

You can refrigerate for 5 days

French Moutarde
Place your mayonnaise, horseradish and spicy mustard in a medium mixing bowl

Mix by hand, thoroughly

You can refrigerate for 5 days

INGREDIENTS (CONTINUED)

French Moutarde
¾ cup mayonnaise
2 tbsp spicy deli mustard
1 tsp horseradish

CHEF SECRETS

"I found this great dish in a little cafe on the beach on the island of Caye Caulker in Belize. You can enjoy them so many ways. At my bistros I serve them as part of a delicious Eggs Benedict. The dish you're looking at here is served as an appetizer for my 'after hours' dining guests (see my Catalina Isles Egg Benedict recipe). Either way, they are a delightfully light tropical experience."

"Make sure you use the large lumped blue crab from your local seafood vendor and don't substitute regular breadcrumbs for Panko breadcrumbs. Panko breadcrumbs are readily available at your grocery store."

Chef J Stephen

Soups & Salads

"There's nothing like a great soup on a cold winter day or a light refreshing salad on a hot summer day. Unlike appetizers, which are often stand alone offerings, your soups and salads should be designed to compliment the main course.

"The soups and salads I have included in my recipe book are by far the most popular offered at my bistros. They provide a variety of different dishes to assure you find the right one for your main course."

"As with every dish, but even more so with soups and salads, fresh, fresh, fresh is of utmost importance. This is the prime area where any sophisticated guest will immediately taste the difference between store purchased croutons, inexpensive cheeses and packaged dressings."

Chef J Stephen

Italy

Caprese Salad

Serves 6, Prep 40min, Total 2hrs 30min

Ingredients

- 3 Slices fresh Mozzarella
- 1 Heirloom Tomato
- 1 pinch kosher salt
- 1 pinch black pepper
- ½ tsp balsamic vinegar
- 1 tsp virgin olive oil

Chef Secrets

"Fresh Mozzarella is a must and the best in the States is from a little company in Dallas, TX called The Mozzarella Company. For your tomatoes, always choose Heirloom tomatoes. They offer interesting colors and a great 'Old world' tomato taste that can no longer be found with our current tomatoes."

"Choose 'early harvest' olive oil in a dark bottle (a dark bottle preserves your oil longer). Early harvest olive oil is oil squeezed from the olive before the olive is ripe. An unripe olive yields much less olive oil but much higher quality oil, so it will be expensive but well worth the price. You can find a great early harvest olive oil Formaggio Kitchen."

Instructions

In a small (2 ounce) ramekin, mix your fresh pesto with the virgin olive oil

Slice and layer 3 slices of fresh buffalo mozzarella, 3 slices, and heirloom tomatoes as shown

Top with virgin olive oil, balsamic vinegar and your pesto/olive oil mix

Garnish with fresh basil

Place on a chilled salad plate and chill in freezer for 10 minutes prior to serving

Chef J Stephen

Mexico

Caesar Salad

Serves 6, Prep 10min, Total 20min

Instructions

Chop together anchovy fillets, the garlic and the pinch of kosher salt to form a paste

Whisk in the egg yolks, lemon juice, and mustard

Gradually whisk in the olive oil and then the avocado oil

Whisk until your dressing is thick and glossy

Whisk in your parmesan cheese

Rinse thoroughly 6 romaine hearts leaves

Top with 3-4 slices shaved parmesan cheese (shave with a vegetable peeler), 5 anchovy fillets, pinch of salt, pinch of ground pepper, and a spritz of fresh squeezed lemon juice

Ingredients

6 anchovies in oil, drained
1 garlic clove
1 pinch kosher salt
2 large egg yolks
2 tbsp fresh lemon juice
¾ tsp Dijon mustard
2 tbsp olive oil
½ cup avocado oil
3 tbsp grated parmesan
1 pinch ground black pepper
6 romaine hearts leaves
3-4 slices (peeled with a mandolin or vegetable peeler) parmesan cheese
5 anchovy fillets

Chef Secrets

" *Yes, Caesar Salad actually comes from Mexico not France. And a REAL Caesar Salad ALWAYS has fresh anchovies and is made with anchovy paste. As with all your fruit and vegetables, you want to choose your romaine lettuce and lemon from the farmers market.*"

"*I always use Parmigiano Reggiano Stravecchio cheese, that I grind myself. You can find a good one at igourmet. If you can't find that, most any Parmigiano Reggianos are not quite as good but will work fine. Get a quarter of a wheel and store it. It will keep well.*"

"*Choose 'early harvest' olive oil in a dark bottle (a dark bottle preserves your oil longer). early harvest olive oil is oil squeezed from the olive before the olive is ripe. An unripe olive yields much less olive oil but much higher quality oil, so it will be expensive but well worth the price. You can find a great early harvest olive oil Formaggio Kitchen.*"

Chef J Stephen

BRITISH VIRGIN ISLANDS

Marina Bay Salad

Serves 5, Prep 20min, Total 30min

Ingredients

Salad:
7 ½ ounces romaine hearts (1 ½ ounce per dish)
8 ½ ounces toasted coconut (1 ½ ounce per dish)
¾ cup of toasted walnuts
¼ cup of toasted slivered almonds (2 ounce per serving)
1 ¼ cups mandarin oranges (3 ounce per serving)
30 cherry tomatoes (6 per serving)
1 ¼ tsp of black pepper (¼ tsp per serving)
10 ounces salad dressing (2 ounce per serving)
5 ounces virgin olive oil (1 ounce per serving)
2 ½ garlic cloves (½ clove per serving)
2 ½ pounds uncooked shrimp (¼ lb per serving)

Dressing:
⅓ cup wine vinegar
1 tsp kosher salt
1 ½ tsp white granulated sugar
1 tsp brown spicy mustard
1 tsp greek seasoning
⅓ cup safflower oil
½ cup Hellmans mayonnaise

Chef Secrets

"A wonderfully light tropical Island salad that I enjoyed at the British Virgin Island of Virgin Gorda. As with all your fruit and vegetables, you want to choose your romaine lettuce from the farmers market. In addition, always use the hearts of the romaine lettuce. The hearts are the center leaves. They are smaller, a bit more yellow, but much sweeter, with a delicious flavor and crispness that you won't find with the romaine leaves."

Chef J Stephen

Instructions

Dressing:
Combine in your food processor, all your ingredients except for your virgin olive oil and mayonnaise

Mix for 30 seconds

Slowly add to your dressing, your virgin olive oil and mayonnaise

Mix for 30 seconds

Salad:
Mince your garlic cloves

Sauté your shrimp in virgin olive oil for 5 minutes

Slice your shrimp horizontally to double the amount of shrimp

Combine all your ingredients in a salad mixing bowl

Toss gently

Add your salad dressing

Toss gently, assuring that ample amounts of ingredients remain on top of salad

Sprinkle with your black pepper

Chill in freezer for 10 minutes prior to serving

UNITED STATES

SPINACH SALAD

SERVES 6, PREP 10MIN, TOTAL 20MIN

INGREDIENTS

Salad:
½ cup of fresh baby spinach
½ tbsp raspberry vinaigrette
¼ cup of toasted walnuts
¼ cup of dried cranberries
6 parmesan croutons
1 pinch of salt
1 pinch of black pepper

Parmesan Croutons:
32 ounces (1 loaf) bread
4 ounces unsalted butter
⅔ cup parmesan cheese

Toasted walnuts:
½ cup water
4 tbsp white sugar
1 tsp Saigon cinnamon
5 cups shelled walnuts
½ cup dark brown Muscovado sugar

CHEF SECRETS

"Why make a blah lettuce, tomatoes and cucumber side salad when, with a little effort you can make an exquisite start to any meal."

"If you wan't your dish to be special, NEVER use store bought accompaniments. It's a lot easier to craft your own and the effort will be rewarded when your guests wonder just how your salad tastes so much better than theirs."

Continued on next page

INSTRUCTIONS

Salad:
Remove the stems from your fresh baby spinach

Place in small mixing bowl. Add your raspberry vinaigrette and toss

Plate your tossed spinach salad on a chilled salad plate

Top with your toasted walnuts, dried cranberries, parmesan croutons, a pinch of salt and a pinch of black pepper

Chill in freezer for 10 minutes prior to serving

Croutons:
Cube 1 loaf of bread into ½" squares and store extra cube's in your freezer for future use. Any bread (including stale bread) will do

To prepare for your salads, melt 4 ounce unsalted butter

Place your cubed bread into a large mixing bowl. Add your melted butter and toss until coated

Add your freshly ground parmesan cheese and toss again

Place your croutons on a lined sheet pan and bake at 375° for 5-10 minutes (until brown)

Continued on next page

UNITED STATES

SPINACH SALAD
CONTINUED

Toasted Walnuts:
Combine in a medium sauce pan, on low-medium heat, your water, sugar and Saigon cinnamon

Add your walnuts making sure to coat completely

Stir until mixture thickens

Spread your coated walnuts across a lined sheet pan and sprinkle evenly with dark brown Muscovado sugar over top

Bake for approx. 4 minutes @ 375°

Toss and bake for an additional 3 minutes

You can store unused croutons and walnuts in your freezer

Croutons:
Cube 1 loaf of bread into ½" squares and store extra cube's in your freezer for future use. Any bread (including stale bread) will do

To prepare for your salads, melt 4 ounce unsalted butter

Place your cubed bread into a large mixing bowl. Add your melted butter and toss until coated

Add your freshly ground parmesan cheese and toss again

Place your croutons on a lined sheet pan and bake at 375° for 5-10 minutes (until brown)

Chill in freezer for 10 minutes prior to serving

CHEF SECRETS (CONTINUED)

"As with all your fruit and vegetables, you want to choose your romaine lettuce from the farmers market. In addition, always use baby spinach in your salads. The flavor of baby spinach is much milder than that of mature spinach."

"I always use Parmigiano Reggiano Stravecchio cheese, that I grind myself. You can find a good one at igourmet. If you can't find that, most any Parmigiano Reggianos are not quite as good but will work fine. Get a quarter of a wheel and store it. It will keep well."

Chef J Stephen

Denmark

Tuna Salad

Serves 2, Prep 20min, Total 30min

Instructions

Tuna
In a medium sized bowl, combine the lemon juice, Saigon cinnamon, salt, and pepper. Mix by hand

Add the cranberries, sour cream, and mayonnaise. Combine by hand

Remove the skin from your apple and peel into thin strips with a potato peeler

Add your apple strips to the mix. Combine by hand

Chop your celery into small pieces and add to your mix. Combine by hand

Drain your cans of tuna and break apart by hand to assure there are no large chunks

Add your tuna to your salad mix, combine well

Plate your tuna salad over a bed of romaine lettuce hearts

Top with your toasted walnuts, dried cranberries, parmesan croutons, a pinch of salt and a pinch of black pepper

Chill in freezer for 10 minutes prior to serving

Ingredients

- 2 cans (6 ounce ea) Albacore tuna in water
- 1 small Granny Smith apple
- ½ cup fresh celery
- ¼ cup dried cranberries
- ¼ cup mayonnaise
- ¼ cup sour cream
- 1 tsp lemon juice
- 1 pinch salt
- 1 pinch black pepper
- ¾ tbsp powdered Saigon cinnamon
- 3 fresh Romain lettuce hearts

Chef Secrets

"Not your typical tuna salad. I found this in Aarhus, Denmark where they don't like fish to taste fishy. If you're like them, and you are looking for an interesting non-fishy tuna salad or sandwich, you'll love this recipe."

"As with all your fruit and vegetables, you want to choose your romaine lettuce from the farmers market. In addition, always use the hearts of the romaine lettuce. The hearts are the center leaves. They are smaller, a bit more yellow, but much sweeter, with a delicious flavor and crispness that you won't find with the romaine leaves."

"Always use Albacore tuna for the most vibrant tuna taste. Make sure its not in oil as that will conflict with the combined flavors of your tuna salad."

Chef J Stephen

ITALY

TOMATO BASIL SOUP

SERVES 12, PREP 60MIN, TOTAL 90MIN

INGREDIENTS

Tomato Basil Soup
8 lbs fresh Roma tomatoes
2 tbsp +2 tsp vegetable stock
24 ounce tomato paste
32 ounce heavy cream
3 tbsp salt
46 ounces tomato juice
2 tbsp black pepper
16 ounces cold water
8 ounces basil butter*

Garnish
2 fresh basil leaves per cup of soup, 3 per bowl of soup
3 croutons per cup of soup, 6 per bowl of soup
1 tbsp fresh ground parmesan cheese per cup of soup, 2 tbsp per bowl of soup

Croutons
1 loaf of bread (any bread including your stale bread will work fine)
4 ounces unsalted butter
4 tbsp fresh fresh ground parmesan cheese

* *"Look for my Basil Butter recipe"*

Chef J Stephen

INSTRUCTIONS

Remove the stem ends off each Roma tomato

Place your Roma tomatoes in a large stock pot. Fill your pot with cold water to just cover tomatoes

Add 1 ½ tbsp of salt (this will help in the skinning process)

Cook on a medium/low flame to just prior to boil (you will see the skin pulling away) approx. 15 minutes

Remove the tomatoes with a slotted spoon and drop in a large bowl of ice water. Make sure you immerse completely to halt the cooking process. Put aside

Drain the water from the cooking pot (not your ice water)

Place your tomato paste, tomato juice, vegetable base and remaining salt in your pot. Mix well

Remove your tomatoes one by one from ice water

Skin your tomatoes (hold in hand, pull back skin)

Add your skinned tomatoes to the pot with the other ingredients

Measure out 16 ounces of the ice water. This will be used to cool your tomatoes

Remove all the leftover skins

Add your ice water to your ingredients in the pot

Continued on next page

ITALY

TOMATO BASIL SOUP
CONTINUED

CHEF SECRETS

"There is definitely a difference between canned soup and homemade soup. As with all your fruit and vegetables, you want to get your Roma tomatoes if at all possible from the farmers market. You can make your own vegetable stock, but I find that there is little difference in flavor between homemade and store bought vegetable stock."

"When you pick your Roma tomatoes, make sure they are fully ripened. Fully ripened Roma's are easier to peel and taste better than partially 'hard' Roma's."

"Since tomato basil soup stores well in the fridge or freezer, I usually double this recipe to make enough soup for several meals. Basil is easy to care for as long as it's watered and gets a bit of sun. Nowadays, you can get live Basil plants at any grocery store. Plant one and pick the leaves for your dishes. It really will make a difference."

"Garnishing with your home-made croutons, fresh basil and freshly grated Parmigiano Reggiano will really set your tomato basil soup apart from all others."

"I always use Parmigiano Reggiano Stravecchio cheese, that I grind myself. You can find a good one at [igourmet](). If you can't find that, most any Parmigiano Reggianos are not quite as good but will work fine. Get a quarter of a wheel and store it. It will keep well."

Chef J Stephen

Place your pot on your range on medium flame for 30 minutes, stirring occasionally to prevent burning

Remove your pot from the range. Add your basil butter mix, black pepper, and the remaining salt

Mix your soup in the pot (if you have an immersion blender, this is the time to pull it out). Mix until smooth

Add your heavy cream, folding your cream into your pot with a spatula, until fully incorporated

Cool to room temperature for approx. 30 minutes. Place in a storage container

You can store your soup in your refrigerator or even your freezer until ready for use

Croutons:
Cube 1 loaf of bread into ½" squares and store extra cube's in your freezer for future use. Any bread (including stale bread) will do

To prepare for your salads, melt 4 ounce unsalted butter

Place your cubed bread into a large mixing bowl. Add your melted butter and toss until coated

Add your freshly ground parmesan cheese and toss again

Place your croutons on a lined sheet pan and bake at 375° for 5-10 minutes (until brown)

FRANCE

FRENCH ONION SOUP

SERVES 12, PREP 40MIN, TOTAL 46MIN

INGREDIENTS

Soup Broth
64 ounces of beef broth
3 cups of water
6 cups red Cabernet wine
2 bay leaves
1 tsp dry thyme
2 tsp kosher salt
1 tsp ground black pepper

Onions
2 white onions
1 ounce unsalted butter

Garnishments
12 ounces imported gruyere cheese
1 loaf French baguette bread
4 ounces unsalted butter
4 fresh chives (chopped)

CHEF SECRETS

"Most restaurants in the States 'cheap out' when making French onion soup. They use Swiss cheese instead of gruyere cheese, cooking sherry or even no wine at all instead of a good Cabernet and pre-made baguettes. Don't make the same mistake! To make a GOOD French soup, you must make it like they make it in France."

*"You can use an empty regular tea bag or a soup tea bag available at most grocery stores, to hold your seasoning.".

Continued on next page

INSTRUCTIONS

Soup Broth
Place your thyme and bay leaves in a tea bag*. Staple the top closed (this will create your seasoning bag)

In large pot combine your beef broth, water, wine and the seasoning bag you created

Heat on medium for 30 minutes

Add your kosher salt and black pepper

Let cool and place in your refrigerator when cool. Your french onion soup will store for several days in a refrigerator

Caramelized Onions
Peel and slice (julienne style) your white onions

Place your butter in large skillet. Set to med/high

When your butter is melted, add your sliced onions. Stir continually while sautéing to assure even browning without burning. (Caramelized onions should be brown but not burned)

Let cool and place in your refrigerator when cool. Your caramelized onions will store for several days in a refrigerator

Gruyere Cheese
Slice your gruyere cheese into ¼" thick slices (your choice of one or two slices per bowl)

Continued on next page

FRANCE

FRENCH ONION SOUP
CONTINUED

Toasted Baguettés
Pre-heat your oven to 375°

Melt your unsalted butter in a microwave or on medium heat in a sauté pan

Slice your loaf of French baguette bread (on the bias - at a 45° angle). Each slice should be about ¼" wide

Place your sliced bread in a large mixing bowl and add your melted butter. Toss to coat your bread

Place each slice of your bread flat on a lined sheet pan or cookie sheet and place in your oven for approx. 10 minutes or until brown

You can use your toasted baguettes immediately or store for future use

Serving Preparation
Pre-heat your oven to 375°

In a ramekin soup bowl, place ¼ cup of your caramelized onions and your French soup broth leaving room for your baguette and cheese

Add one toasted baguette and top with one or two ¼" thick slices of gruyere cheese (if you choose to use two slices of cheese)

Place in your oven for approx. 20 minutes or until your cheese is completely melted and a bit brown on the top

Garnish with a pinch of fresh chopped chives

Serve Immediately

CHEF SECRETS (CONTINUED)

"Making your own French baguettes is easy to do. It only involves a good French bread, butter and an oven."

"Do not substitute your wine for cooking sherry. The French ALWAYS use a good Cabernet and you should too. It will make a world of difference. You don't have to spend a lot, a $9-$12 bottle will do just fine."

"Through the years, I have had many discussions with my bistro guests about the difference between 'imported' gruyere and 'domestic' gruyere. Trust me, although it will be the most expensive ingredient in your soup, the difference is like night and day. I ALWAYS use an 'imported' gruyere from France or Switzerland and you should too. You can find an excellent gruyere cheese at the [gourmet food store](.)"

"You'll notice that I have no problem using a pre-made beef broth. I usually use [Swanson's](.) but most any will do. Why? Because I find the amount of effort for the average home cook to make a beef broth from scratch is not worth the effort. Stick to the pre-mades and you'll do just fine."

"When topping your French onion soup, I leave it up to you on the amount of cheese to use. Some people prefer gob's of cheese, while others like a lighter touch. I'm in the more cheese group, especially when it involves imported gruyere, but you can decide which touch you prefer."

Chef J Stephen

FRANCE

LOBSTER BISQUE
BISQUE DE HOMARD

SERVES 6, PREP 40MIN, TOTAL 60MIN

INSTRUCTIONS

Lobster
Dip the head of each lobster in boiling water holding the lobster by the tail for a few seconds. Cut off and crack the claws. Insert a knife in the abdomen and cut the shell from the abdomen up towards the head. Then proceed to cut towards the tail. Separate the lobster. Cut the tail and the four pieces crosswise. Remove the stomach from the head and discard along with the intestinal track. Keep the juice of the lobster as well as the green tomalley or "roe" in the females

Bisque
Place your butter in a large skillet on medium heat. Once melted, add your onions, carrots, celery, garlic and shallots until partially cooked. Turn the heat to high and add the lobster, cooking until the shells turn bright red

Pouring half of your Cognac and *Flambé

Remove your lobster from the pan and add your tomato paste, white wine, fish stock, small green leak, and peppercorns. Simmer

While your mix is simmering, remove the meat from the shells and the claws of your lobster. Crush all the lobster shells in a processor and then simmer your crushed shells in the stock for about 20 minutes. When done strain out with a sieve and add your uncooked rice and whisk in the tomalley

Cook on low heat until the rice is soft (about 20 minutes). Purée in a blender and strain through a cheesecloth

Continued on next page

INGREDIENTS

Bisque
1 or 2 live lobsters total weight four pounds
5 tablespoons butter or vegetable oil
1 cup of heavy cream
1 sprig of thyme, 1 bayleaf and 1sprig of parsley wrapped in the green skin of your leek and tied
1 cup finely chopped white onions
1 cup finely chopped carrots
1 cup finely chopped celery
1 clove of minced garlic
4 finely chopped shallots
1 top (only) of a small green leek
6 tbsp's of Cognac
2 ½ cups of dry white wine
6 parsley sprigs
1 tbsp tomato paste
5 cups of fish stock
2 tbsp's black peppercorn
2 tbsp's raw rice (cooked plain rice can be substituted)

Beurre Manié (optional)
2 ½ cups all purpose flour
12 ounces unsalted butter

CHEF SECRETS

"I love a good Lobster bisque and my favorite recipe from René is his Bisque de Homard. This is it, in all it's glory."

Continued on next page

FRANCE

LOBSTER BISQUE
BISQUE DE HOMARD

CONTINUED

Bring your bisque back to a boil.

Lower your heat and add the remaining 3 tbsp's of Cognac and a half cup of the remaining lobster (cut into small and and large pieces and cream

If you like a thick bisque, you can add a bit of cornstarch or if you want to keep your bisque traditionally French, use beurre manié

Beurre Manié (option)
In a large bow place your unsalted butter, AP (all purpose) flour

Mix together until a paste is formed

Roll into 4 ounce balls and wrap in plastic wrap

Store in your freezer for future use

CHEF SECRETS (CONTINUED)

"This is probably the most challenging soup in my recipe book BUT, it's also the finest tasting and most gratifying to make. Don't let the steps deter you. The end result will be well worth the effort."

"There is nothing better than a well made bisque and so few restaurants, let alone home cooks make it the traditional French way. THIS recipe is as traditional as it gets."

"You can use this same recipe to make a crab or fish bisque by simply substituting the lobster. You'll should also have extra lobster left over from this recipe. Use it to make a great lobster salad or lobster roll."

*The term flamb [flahm-BAY] is a French word meaning "flaming" or "flamed." Flambe means to ignite foods that have liquor or liqueur added. This is done for a dramatic effect and to develop a rich flavor of the liqueur to the foods without adding the alcohol.

Chef J Stephen

CUBA

CUBAN BLACK BEAN SOUP

SERVES 4, PREP 40MIN, TOTAL 60MIN

INSTRUCTIONS

Soak your beans overnight in a 6 quart heavy pot with 10 cups of water

Place your bacon and chorizo in a sauté pan. Cook to render fat (Not Crispy). Remove meat and chorizo

Add your bell pepper, white onion, garlic cloves, and virgin olive oil to a sauté pan with bacon fat. Sauté on medium heat to soften vegetables. Do Not Overcook.

Add your sofrito, bacon, chorizo bell pepper, white onion, garlic cloves, virgin olive oil and dried bay leaf to your beans

Bring to a boil in the same soaking water

Lower the heat to medium and simmer your beans until just tender, checking regularly and skimming the foam that forms on top for approx. 45 to 60 minutes

Garnish with chopped parsley

INGREDIENTS

Soup
1 pound dried black beans (rinsed well)
1 large Bell pepper (stemmed seeded and diced)
½ large white onion (diced)
4 large garlic cloves (peeled and lightly crushed)
1 tbsp virgin olive oil
1 dried bay leaf
¼ pound bacon (4 strips)
¼ pound chorizo
10 cups water
2 pieces parsley (chopped)
2 tbsp sofrito

CHEF SECRETS

"A stick to your ribs hearty winter soup that is a main dish in Cuba. It takes time to soak your black beans but the end result is well worth the effort."

"By sautéing your veggies in the bacon chorizo fat, you add a delicious undercurrent of flavors that enhances your soup beyond the norm."

Chef J Stephen

Breads & Biscuits

"When my family would dine out at restaurants, my dad would always say that you can tell how good the main course will be by the quality of the salad and bread. If the restaurant cheap's out on the bread or salad, you can bet they'll cheap out on the main dish as well. That's a rule of thumb that I have always used whenever I dine out and it has always proven to be true. A restaurant that is unwilling to spend the money on the bread or salad is often cutting corners everywhere they can, and that includes the main course and desserts."

"The same thing is true for the home cook. In the case of your breads and biscuits, although it would be great if you baked your own, most of us don't have the time to become expert bakers. However, you should always purchase your bread from a bakery, not the grocery store."

"With that said, the Bread & Biscuits section of my recipe book does not include recipes of how to make either. That would be an entirely separate book on its own. Instead, it provides recipes of what to do with the great breads and biscuits you can purchase for your meal."

Chef J Stephen

FRANCE

Parmesan Crouton's

Serves 20, Prep 15min, Total 20min

Instructions

Cube 1 loaf of bread into ½" squares and store extra cube's in your freezer for future use

To prepare for your salads, melt 4 ounce unsalted butter

Place your cubed bread into a large mixing bowl. Add your melted butter and toss until coated

Add your freshly ground parmesan cheese and toss again

Place your croutons on a lined sheet pan and bake at 375° for 5-10 minutes (until brown)

Ingredients

4 ounces unsalted butter
1 loaf French baguette bread
4 tbsp fresh fresh ground parmesan cheese

Chef Secrets

"Having a supply of toasted croutons for your salads, soups and cheese boards is always a great idea and so easy to do. This is one time you don't have to worry about the bread you use. In fact, any bread (including stale bread) will work just fine."

"The key to a great crouton is the parmesan cheese. I always use Parmigiano Reggiano Stravecchio cheese, that I grind myself. You can find a good one at igourmet. If you can't find that, most any Parmigiano Reggianos are not quite as good but will work fine. Get a quarter of a wheel and store it. It will keep well. Make sure your Parmesan has 'Reggiano' in its name. If you have the room, get a quarter of a wheel and store it. It will keep well and you'll use it on so many great dishes."

Chef J Stephen

FRANCE

ESCARGOT BREAD

SERVES 6, PREP 15MIN, TOTAL 20MIN

INSTRUCTIONS

Pre-heat your oven to 450°

Mince and mash your garlic into a paste

Add with ⅛ teaspoon kosher salt into your paste

Beat together your unsalted butter, shallots, garlic paste, parsley, your remaining ¼ teaspoon kosher salt, and black pepper in a small mixing bowl with an electric mixer until it's combined well

Add your dry white wine and combine well

Place your Escargot butter into the oven until your Escargot butter is completely melted approx. 4 minutes

Slice your French baguette bread on the bias - at a 45° angle into approx. 11 slices ½" wide

Remove your heated Escargot butter from the oven, dip both sides of each slice of your bread into the Escargot butter with tongs

Serve immediately

INGREDIENTS

2 small garlic cloves
¾ tsp kosher salt
8 ounces unsalted butter, softened
3 tsp finely minced shallots
2 tbsp finely chopped fresh flat-leaf parsley
½ tsp black pepper
2 tbsp dry white wine
1 loaf French baguette bread

CHEF SECRETS

"So many people love the taste of Escargot but are intimidated by the dish. Still others would never think of eating a snail in any form whatsoever. For those who have enjoyed this great French delicacy, you know that the garlicky sauce used to make this dish is almost as delicious as the Escargots themselves. Part of the enjoyment of eating Escargot is the dipping of the crusty bread into the luxurious 'snail butter'. With that in mind, my Escargot bread recipe solves both issues. You don't have to make the actual dish, your finicky friends can see what its like to enjoy the great Escargot butter and your experienced Escargot fans can all enjoy a fantastic dipping bread."

Chef J Stephen

France

Toasted Baguette's

Ingredients

4 ounces unsalted butter
1 loaf French baguette bread

Serves 6, Prep 15min, Total 20min

Instructions

Pre-heat your oven to 375°

Melt your unsalted butter in a microwave or on medium heat in a sauté pan

Slice your loaf of French baguette bread (on the bias - at a 45° angle) into approx. 22 slices ¼" wide

Place your sliced bread in a large mixing bowl

Add your melted butter

Toss your sliced bread to coat

Place each slice of your bread flat on a lined sheet pan or cookie sheet

Place in your oven for 10 minutes

Remove and let cool

Store for future use in salads, soups or your cheese

Chef Secrets

"Having a supply of toasted baguettes for your salads, soups and cheese boards is always a great idea and so easy to do. The key to making a great baguette is using a fresh loaf of French baguette bread from a bakery. Don't cheap out by buying your bread at the grocery store. Grocery stores use a different type of dough that won't provide the crisp crust and chewy interiors of a great French Baguette."

"Always buy your French baguette bread at the last minute. French baguettes are made with a lean dough that has flour, water, yeast and salt. There are no additives, bread improvers or chemical preservatives. That's the reason baguettes go stale so quickly. Conversely, sandwich breads, even home baked ones, are made with enriched dough which lasts much longer."

Chef J Stephen

UNITED STATES

BUTTERMILK BISCUITS

SERVES 12, PREP 20MIN, TOTAL 35MIN

INSTRUCTIONS

Preheat your oven to 425°

Place your unsalted butter in your freezer

Beat 2 of your eggs in small bowl

Place the remaining egg and 2 tbsp of buttermilk in a separate small bowl. Beat to fully incorporate

In a large mixing bowl, place your self rising-flour, baking powder, baking soda, and salt. Mix until fully incorporated

Grate your frozen unsalted butter (use the largest side of your grater)

Add your grated butter into your dry mix. *(Do not over mix by trying to fully incorporate the butter. You want the butter to remain separate - see my "Chef Secrets" section)*

Add your 2 beaten eggs to your dry mix with a spoon until just combined (don't over mix)

Add the rest of your buttermilk. Mix by hand to form a sticky dough

Sprinkle your flour LIGHTLY on your counter top

Place your dough on a floured surface

Continued on next page

INGREDIENTS

7 ¼ cups of self rising flour
3 tbsp baking powder
1 ½ tsp baking soda
12 ounces unsalted butter
½ tbsp salt
4 ¾ cups buttermilk
3 large eggs

CHEF SECRETS

"The reason my recipe asks that you place your butter in the freezer prior to making your biscuits is to assure a flaky biscuit. When partially incorporated pieces of butter melt as the biscuits bake, they release steam and create pockets of air. Those pockets make the biscuits airy and flaky on the inside while remaining crisp on the outside. The key to making a light and fluffy biscuit is to never overwork your dough. If you overwork your dough, you will end up with tough, hard and flat biscuits."

"If you want your biscuits to rise beautifully, don't twist your pastry cutter when cutting your biscuits. Twisting your cutter seals the dough on the edges which prevents your biscuits from rising."

Continued on next page

UNITED STATES

BUTTERMILK BISCUITS
CONTINUED

To prevent the dough from sticking on your hands, sprinkle some flour LIGHTLY on your hands

Fold your dough over 5 times then flatten to approx. 1¼" height

Form your biscuits using a pastry cutter 4" W x 1¼" H

To prevent your dough from sticking to your pastry cutter, dip your pastry cutter in flour between each cut

Place your cut out biscuits on a lined sheet pan or cookie sheet

Leave 1" between each biscuit to allow your biscuits to spread

Brush each biscuit with your egg buttermilk mix

Bake at 425° for 15 minutes or until golden brown

Although your biscuits will last in the refrigerator for up to 6 days and in the freezer up to 90 days, they are always best enjoyed hot out of the oven

CHEF SECRETS (CONTINUED)

"If you want beautifully high biscuits (the best to eat stand-alone with butter, honey or jam), place them closely together on your sheet pan. If you prefer a wider, flatter biscuit (ideal for sausage, egg and biscuit sandwiches or biscuits and gravy), space your biscuits apart."

"Be careful when shopping for your buttermilk. It's not as easy to find, but always use 'regular' buttermilk. 'Low fat' buttermilk is what you usually see in the grocery store but it's best left right there. You need the fat content in regular buttermilk to finish your biscuits properly."

"Although I don't include it in my recipe book as a stand alone recipe, if you make my buttermilk biscuits and top them with my Jalapeño Sausage Gravy (see my Gravies, Sauces, Dips & Spreads section of my book), you'll have one fantastic breakfast. I offered this dish as a special at my bistros and it was always a big hit, selling out within the first couple of hours."

Chef J Stephen

ENGLAND

Yorkshire Pudding

SERVES 4, PREP 10MIN, TOTAL 45MIN

Instructions

Preheat your oven to 450°

Sieve your flour into a bowl and add your salt

Gradually add your whole milk until you've reached a thick consistency. Leave to stand for at least 1 ½ hours

Prior to placing in the oven, whisk your eggs and then add to the mixture. Continue to whisk until your batter is creamy and smooth

Pour your beef drippings into a "thin" 12" X 14" roasting pan and pre-heat in your pre-heated oven

When your beef drippings are hot, approx. 15 minutes, add your batter

Make sure you spread your batter evenly across the pan

Place in the oven and cook for 25-30 minutes or until your pudding has risen, looks golden brown and crisp.

Cut into squares and serve (preferably with your prime ribs, quartered potatoes, french string beans and gravy)

"Instead of offering bread, you can also make Yorkshire Pudding as a delicious popover with any meal by making them in a muffin pan. This is an excellent way to make any dish special. Popovers always provide that 'wow' factor to any meal."

Ingredients

1 cup AP (all purpose) flour
½ tbsp salt
1 cup whole milk
2 large eggs (beaten)
½ cup pan beef drippings *

Chef Secrets

"Yes all you folks from the 'States', this is NOT what you would think of as a pudding, BUT in my opinion, it's the greatest dish to come out of England! The name comes from the area of the same name in northern England. It was used to distinguish the light and crispy nature of the batter puddings made in this region from batter puddings created in other parts of England."

"My wife is Scottish/English and accordingly, this is her family's recipe. In England, it is traditionally made alongside prime ribs, quartered potatoes and string beans, along with a brown gravy to finish it off. And that is exactly what my family enjoys each year as our traditional Christmas dinner."

"Yorkshire pudding is traditionally cooked in a large, shallow tin and then cut into squares to be served, rather than the individual popovers that are most common today. My recipe is made the traditional way."

* *"You'll notice in my ingredients list above, one of the key ingredients is the pan drippings from the roast beef. A perfect Yorkshire Pudding mixture needs to be light and airy, with the fat in the bottom of the cooking dish needing to be as hot as possible in order for it to rise."*

Chef J Stephen

UNITED STATES

CRANBERRY NUT BREAD

SERVES 8, PREP 40MIN, TOTAL 1 HR 40MIN

INSTRUCTIONS

Preheat your oven to 350°

Spray, with pan spray, the bottom only, of a 7"x3" loaf pan

In a mixing bowl, whisk your eggs

In a separate bowl, mix with a whisk, your flour, castor sugar, baking powder, table salt, and baking soda to fully incorporate

Add your fresh orange juice, shortening, and whisked eggs to your dry mix

Mix until well fully blended

Add your chopped cranberries and chopped nuts

Mix briefly to incorporate

Pour into your greased loaf pan

Bake for approx. 55 to 60 minutes (or until loaf is golden brown)

Check the center of your loaf with a toothpick to assure it is cooked throughout

INGREDIENTS

4 cups AP (all purpose) flour
2 cups castor sugar
3 tsp baking powder
2 tsp table salt
1 tsp baking soda
4 tbsp shortening
1 ½ cups fresh orange juice
2 large eggs (beaten)
2 cups fresh cranberries (chopped)
1 cup walnuts (chopped)

CHEF SECRETS

"My two favorite loaf breads are the cranberry nut and banana bread. Originating in the New England area in the 1700's, they are the ideal snack bread to enjoy with a slab of homemade butter."

"Use a toothpick to the center to assure your cranberry nut bread is cooked throughout."

Chef J Stephen

UNITED STATES

BANANA NUT BREAD

Serves 8, Prep 40min, Total 1 hr 40min

Instructions

Preheat your oven to 350°

Spray with pan spray, the bottom only, of a 7"x3" loaf pan

In a mixing bowl, with a whisk, cream your unsalted butter

Add your castor sugar and beat well. Then add eggs and beat well again

Add your baking soda into your cup of buttermilk

Add to your mix alternately with your flour while continuing to mix

Add your bananas, pecans, and vanilla to the mix

Mix briefly to incorporate

Pour into your greased loaf pan

Bake for approx. 55 to 60 minutes (or until loaf is golden brown)

Check the center of your loaf with a toothpick to assure it is cooked throughout

Ingredients

2 cups AP (all purpose) flour
1 ½ cups castor sugar
3 tsp baking powder
2 tsp table salt
1 ½ tsp baking soda
4 ounces unsalted butter
1 tsp Madagascar bourbon vanilla
2 large eggs (beaten)
2 fresh ripe bananas (mashed)
½ cup pecans (chopped)
1 cup buttermilk

Chef Secrets

"My two favorite loaf breads are the cranberry nut and banana bread. Originating in the New England area in the 1700's, they are the ideal snack bread to enjoy with a slab of homemade butter."

"Use a toothpick to the center to assure your banana nut bread is cooked throughout."

Chef J Stephen

"To eat is a necessity, but to eat intelligently is an art."

François de la Rochefoucauld

Fall In Love With Breakfast Again
Breakfast & Brunch

"Breakfast has always been my favorite meal. There is just something special about waking up with a hot tea and one of my favorite dishes. Catching up with friends and family, perusing the news and most of all, getting in touch with the world. When I say getting in touch with the world, I don't mean the man-made world, but nature. Mornings are when I sit on my patio and breath in the fresh air and feel the breeze as it drifts through the trees. Mornings are also where family gets together to enjoy the start of each day. Most, but not all of my breakfast recipes are from my Crumbzz bistro in Dallas. Some came from my Upper Crust cafes in New York."

"For me, brunch is always filled with memories of family and friends gathering together to celebrate not only great food but also great company. Some of my brunch dishes were special dishes, offered on holidays, or other special occasions, others were daily offerings, but ALL were special!"

"Except for the dishes I grew up enjoying with my family, all my dishes came from my travels to different countries around the world. Because so many came from such a wide expanse of the world, all are unique offerings that you won't commonly find anywhere in the States. Enjoy perusing through them all, but most of all, enjoy creating them and wowing your guests and family members."

Chef J Stephen

FRANCE

MUSHROOM SPINACH QUICHE

Serves 6, Prep 1hr, Total 1 hour 45min

INGREDIENTS

Shell (makes 3 shells)
30 ounces AP (all purpose) flour
½ tbsp kosher salt
12 ounces unsalted butter
8 ounces water

Filling
4 large eggs
2 cups heavy whipping cream
¾ tsp black pepper
¾ tsp kosher salt
¼ lb button mushrooms (sliced)
1 white onion (Julianne)
2 ½ ounces baby spinach
1 tbsp unsalted butter

Garnish
1 fresh strawberry
6 medium red grapes
1 slice fresh orange

CHEF SECRETS

"You'll notice I have you making three pie shells, even though you'll only be using one per 6 servings. That's because it's a bit of a chore making shells and since you've committed to the task and once frozen, you can use them for a multitude of dishes, it makes sense to knock them out all at once."

"You can make multiple quiche and freeze them for up to 30 days (Good luck having them last that long!)"

Continued on next page

INSTRUCTIONS

Dough
Ice your water
Cut your unsalted butter into ½" cubes

In a mixer, on slow speed, combine your AP flour and kosher salt. Add your unsalted butter while your mixer is running

Remove the ice from your water and add your de-iced water, slowly, until your dough is tacky and malleable

Shape your dough into 3 even pieces (weight approx.13 ounce per dough ball)

Create Quiche Shells
Lightly flour your rolling surface
Roll out to approx. 12" wide
Form into a shell crimping the tops with your fingers (see photo) in a 10" pie pan
Cover with freezer wrap and place in freezer overnight

You will use one shell for your quiche and keep the two other shells in your freezer for up to 120 days for future use for pies or quiche

Filling
In large mixing bowl, combine your large eggs, heavy whipping cream, salt and black pepper

Whisk until fully combined

In a medium sauté pan, slice and sauté your button mushrooms and white onions

Remove all the baby spinach stems from your baby spinach

Continued on next page

FRANCE

CHEF SECRETS (CONTINUED)

"It may be a bit of work, but there is absolutely no comparison between a homemade quiche and a store purchased frozen quiche. Once you make one you will be hooked forever."

"This quiche is creamier than most so, don't be fooled into thinking it's not cooked enough."

Chef J Stephen

MUSHROOM SPINACH QUICHE
CONTINUED

Quiche Preparation
Take out your pre-made frozen pie shell from freezer

Pre-heat your oven to 375°

Line the bottom of your pie shell with half of your baby spinach (cover the bottom of the shell completely)

Place a layer your sautéed onions on top of your baby spinach

Layer the remaining ½ baby spinach on top of your sautéed onions

On top of this layer of sautéed onions, place a layer of your sautéed mushrooms

Top your multi-layers with your filling

Place your quiche on the middle rack and bake for 43 minutes and then rotate your quiche and bake for another 43 minutes

Let cool for 2 hours at room temperature and then refrigerate overnight

Serving
Remove your quiche from the refrigerator

(For single servings) place each slice in a pie pan and place in a pre-heated oven at 400° for 16 minutes

(For full quiche) place in a pre-heated oven at 400° cook for 30 minutes (test the center to assure your quiche is heated throughout)

Plate and garnish with a fresh strawberry, grapes and slice of orange

FRANCE

HAM & ASPARAGUS QUICHE

SERVES 6, PREP 1HR, TOTAL 1 HOUR 45MIN

INGREDIENTS

Shell (makes 3 shells)
30 ounces AP (all purpose) flour
½ tbsp kosher salt
12 ounces unsalted butter
8 ounces water

Filling
4 large eggs
2 cups heavy whipping cream
¾ tsp black pepper
¾ tsp kosher salt
¼ lb fresh baby asparagus
2 ounces Taylor ham (chopped)
1 ¾ ounces gruyere cheese (shredded)
1 ounce Monterey jack cheese (shredded)
1 tbsp unsalted butter

Garnish
1 fresh strawberry
6 medium red grapes
1 slice fresh orange

CHEF SECRETS

"You'll notice I have you making three pie shells, even though you'll only be using one per 6 servings. That's because it's a bit of a chore making shells and since you've committed to the task and once frozen, you can use them for a multitude of dishes, it makes sense to knock them out all at once."

"You can make multiple quiche and freeze them for up to 30 days (Good luck having them last that long!)"

Continued on next page

INSTRUCTIONS

Dough
Ice your water
Cut your unsalted butter into ½" cubes

In a mixer, on slow speed, combine your AP flour and kosher salt. Add your unsalted butter while your mixer is running

Remove the ice from your water and add your de-iced water, slowly, until your dough is tacky and malleable

Shape your dough into 3 even pieces (weight approx.13 ounce per dough ball)

Create Quiche Shells
Lightly flour your rolling surface
Roll out to approx. 12" wide
Form into a shell crimping the tops with your fingers (see photo) in a 10" pie pan
Cover with freezer wrap and place in freezer overnight

You will use one shell for your quiche and keep the two other shells in your freezer for up to 120 days for future use for pies or quiche

Filling
In large mixing bowl, combine your large eggs, heavy whipping cream, salt and black pepper

Whisk until fully combined

In a medium sauté pan, slice and sauté your chopped baby asparagus and your (¼") chopped) Taylor ham

Continued on next page

FRANCE

HAM & ASPARAGUS QUICHE

CONTINUED

Quiche Preparation
Take out your pre-made frozen pie shell from freezer

Pre-heat your oven to 375°

Line the bottom of your pie shell with half of your Taylor Ham and asparagus (cover the bottom of the shell completely)

Add all your cheese

Top with your filling

Lift up all your ingredients with your hands to mix all your ingredients evenly throughout your quiche

Place your quiche on the middle rack and bake for 43 minutes and then rotate your quiche & bake for another 43 minutes

Let cool for 2 hours at room temperature and then refrigerate overnight

Serving
Remove your quiche from the refrigerator

(For single servings) place each slice in a pie pan and place in a pre-heated oven at 400° for 16 minutes

(For full quiche) place in a pre-heated oven at 400° cook for 30 minutes (test the center to assure your quiche is heated throughout)

Plate and garnish with a fresh strawberry, grapes and slice of orange

CHEF SECRETS (CONTINUED)

"You'll notice I have you making three pie shells, even though you'll only be using one per 6 servings. That's because it's a bit of a chore making shells and since you've committed to the task and once frozen, you can use them for a multitude of dishes, it makes sense to knock them out all at once.

You can make multiple quiche and freeze them for up to 30 days (Good luck having them last that long!)"

Chef J Stephen

MEXICO

JALAPEÑO BACON BROCCOLINI QUICHE

Serves 6, Prep 1hr, Total 1 hour 45min

INGREDIENTS

Shell (makes 3 shells)
30 ounces AP (all purpose) flour
½ tbsp kosher salt
12 ounces unsalted butter
8 ounces water

Filling
4 large eggs
2 cups heavy whipping cream
¾ tsp black pepper
¾ tsp kosher salt
¼ lb fresh broccolini
2 ounce Jalapeño bacon
1 ounces gruyere cheese (shredded)
1 ounce Monterey jack cheese (shredded)
1 ounce mild cheddar cheese
1 tbsp unsalted butter

Garnish
1 fresh strawberry
6 medium red grapes
1 slice fresh orange

INSTRUCTIONS

Dough
Ice your water
Cut your unsalted butter into ½" cubes

In a mixer, on slow speed, combine your AP flour and kosher salt. Add your unsalted butter while your mixer is running

Remove the ice from your water and add your de-iced water, slowly, until your dough is tacky and malleable

Shape your dough into 3 even pieces (weight approx.13 ounce per dough ball)

Create Quiche Shells
Lightly flour your rolling surface
Roll out to approx. 12" wide
Form into a shell crimping the tops with your fingers (see photo) in a 10" pie pan
Cover with freezer wrap and place in freezer overnight

You will use one shell for your quiche and keep the two other shells in your freezer for up to 120 days for future use for pies or quiche

Filling
In large mixing bowl, combine your large eggs, heavy whipping cream, salt and black pepper

Whisk until fully combined
Blanch your Broccolini for 2 minutes. Remove and place in ice water to stop cooking. Drain.

Continued on next page

MEXICO

JALAPEÑO BACON BROCCOLINI QUICHE

CONTINUED

Quiche Preparation
Take out your pre-made frozen pie shell from freezer

Pre-heat your oven to 375°

Line the bottom of your pie shell with your broccolini and jalapeño bacon (cover the bottom of the shell completely)

Add all your cheese

Top with your filling

Lift up all your ingredients with your hands to mix all your ingredients evenly throughout your quiche

Place your quiche on the middle rack and bake for 43 minutes and then rotate your quiche & bake for another 43 minutes

Let cool for 2 hours at room temperature and then refrigerate overnight

Serving
Remove your quiche from the refrigerator

(For single servings) place each slice in a pie pan and place in a pre-heated oven at 400° for 16 minutes

(For full quiche) place in a pre-heated oven at 400° cook for 30 minutes (test the center to assure your quiche is heated throughout)

Plate and garnish with a fresh strawberry, grapes and slice of orange

CHEF SECRETS

"You might be tempted to use regular broccoli, but broccolini is much more tender and because of its size (smaller) they don't intrude on the crazy bite feel of your quiche"

"Using jalapeño bacon versus jalapeños provides a more even, distributed taste profile to your quiche."

Chef J Stephen

FRANCE

BLUE LUMP CRAB SOUFFLÉ

Serves 3, Prep 30min, Total 50min

INGREDIENTS

Filling
6 ounces Monterey jack cheese (shredded)
1 ounces Romano parmesan cheese (grated)
½ tsp seafood seasoning
1 ½ tsp lemon zest
6 ounces blue lump crab
1 tsp dried thyme
⅛ tsp crab base

Béchamel
2 tbsp unsalted butter
2 tbsp AP (all purpose) flour
1 ¼ cups (heated) whole milk
½ tsp kosher salt
½ tsp ground black pepper

Shallots
1 small fresh shallot (chopped)
1 tbsp unsalted butter

Soufflé
2 large eggs

CHEF SECRETS

"My favorite seafood seasoning is from Old Bay which you should be able to find at your local grocery store or online on Amazon."

Continued on next page

INSTRUCTIONS

Shallots
Place your unsalted butter in a small frying pan on medium heat

Chop your small shallot into small pieces

Place your shallots into your small frying pan and sauté for approx. 12 minutes (do not brown). Put aside

Béchamel
Heat your whole milk

Melt your unsalted butter in a medium saucepan

Add your flour and cook, on medium heat stirring continually for approx. 2 minutes until your sauce starts to bubble, do not let it brown

Add your heated milk, continuing to stir as your sauce thickens. Bring to a boil

Add your salt and pepper, lower the heat, and continue to cook, stirring for approx. 3 minutes. Remove from the heat

You can refrigerate your leftover Béchamel for 7 days or freeze for 90 days

Filling
*Zest your lemon

In a bowl, place your shredded Monterey jack cheese, grated Romano parmesan cheese, seafood seasoning, dried thyme, blue lump crab, lemon zest, and crab base

Continued on next page

FRANCE

BLUE LUMP CRAB SOUFFLÉ

INGREDIENTS (CONTINUED)

Soufflé Bowl
1 ½ ounces unsalted butter
1 ½ ounces grated parmesan cheese

CHEF SECRETS (CONTINUED)

"I use Minor's crab base for my Blue Lump Crab soufflé's. Unfortunately, I believe it only comes in 16 ounce sizes which is a lot for a home cook. You might find other smaller sized crab bases online or at your local grocer, but since I haven't used them I hesitate to recommend any brand, so you're on your own here."

"So many people are afraid to make a soufflé because they've been told that they're so hard to make. That's far from true if you follow a few simple steps. Soufflé's don't like to be disturbed. Once you put your soufflé' in the oven, don't jostle it around or keep opening the door to peak. Instead, turn on your oven light. Make sure your egg whites are finished in stiff peaks. If you're having issues make stiff peaks it's usually because you're using a plastic bowl or a bowl that has a bit of oily residue or you haven't separated your eggs properly and have a bit of egg yolk in your mix. Use a 'clean' stainless or glass bowl to whip your egg whites. Lastly, Soufflé's quickly lose the air that hold them up so, serve them immediately after they come out of the oven."

*"Zest - scrape off the outer colored part of the peel of (a piece of citrus fruit) for use as flavoring. Make sure you don't scrape too deep to prevent bitterness."

Chef J Stephen

CONTINUED

Pre-heat your oven to 400°

Soufflé
Separate your eggs

Place your egg whites in a mixing bowl and beat on high speed until stiff peaks are formed. Put aside

Place 6 ounces of your béchamel in a small plastic bowl and heat in your microwave for 60 seconds

Ramekin Bowl Preparation
Coat the entire inside of your three large ramekin bowls with approx. ½ ounces unsalted butter (per bowl)

Sprinkle approx. ½ ounce (per bowl) of your grated parmesan cheese into each ramekin bowl (Make sure your parmesan cheese covers evenly all areas of sides and bottom)

Place your filling into your heated béchamel, add your egg yolks and sautéed shallots

Mix thoroughly to assure your eggs have thoroughly combined and your cheese has creamed into the mix

Fold in your beaten egg whites

Place your combined mix into the parmesan/butter coated soufflé ramekin bowls

Bake in your pre-heated oven for 20 minutes or until your soufflé has risen and browned (see photo)

Serve IMMEDIATELY

FRANCE

Gruyère Egg Soufflé

SERVES 3, PREP 30MIN, TOTAL 50MIN

Ingredients

Filling
6 ounces imported gruyère cheese (grated)
1 ounce Romano parmesan cheese (grated)
1¼ tsp cayenne pepper
⅛ tsp fresh nutmeg (ground)

Béchamel
2 tbsp unsalted butter
2 tbsp AP (all purpose) flour
1¼ cups (heated) whole milk
½ tsp kosher salt
½ tsp ground black pepper

Shallots
1 small fresh shallot (chopped)
1 tbsp unsalted butter

Soufflé
2 large eggs

Soufflé Bowl
1 ½ ounces unsalted butter
1 ½ ounces grated parmesan cheese

Chef Secrets

"Since the heat of a soufflé keeps it high and fluffy, you must <u>serve your quiche immediately</u> or it will drop and flatten out!"

Continued on next page

Instructions

Shallots
Place your unsalted butter in a small frying pan on medium heat

Chop your small shallot into small pieces

Place your shallots into your small frying pan and sauté for approx. 12 minutes (do not brown). Put aside

Béchamel
Heat your whole milk

Melt your unsalted butter in a medium saucepan

Add your flour and cook, on medium heat stirring continually for approx. 2 minutes until your sauce starts to bubble, do not let it brown

Add your heated milk, continuing to stir as your sauce thickens. Bring to a boil

Add your salt and pepper, lower the heat, and continue to cook, stirring for approx. 3 minutes. Remove from the heat

You can refrigerate your leftover Béchamel for 7 days or freeze for 90 days

Filling
In a bowl, place your grated gruyère cheese, grated Romano parmesan cheese, cayenne pepper, and fresh ground nutmeg

Continued on next page

FRANCE

GRUYÈRE EGG SOUFFLÉ

CHEF SECRETS (CONTINUED)

"Always use FRESH Parmigiano Reggiano cheese. If it says 'Parmesan', (note the spelling difference), it's an imitation version of 'REAL' Parmigiano Reggiano cheese and as with all 'imitation' anythings, it leaves a lot to be desired. The best Parmigiano Reggiano is Parmigiano Reggiano Stravecchio."

"Through the years, I have had many discussions with my bistro guests about the difference between 'imported' gruyere and 'domestic' gruyere. Trust me, although it will be the most expensive ingredient in your soup, the difference is like night and day. I ALWAYS use an 'imported' gruyere from France or Switzerland and you should too. You can find an excellent gruyere cheese at the [Gourmet Food Store.](#)"

"So many people are afraid to make a soufflé because they've been told that they're so hard to make. That's far from true if you follow a few simple steps. Soufflé's don't like to be disturbed. Once you put your soufflé' in the oven, don't jostle it around or keep opening the door to peak. Instead, turn on your oven light. Make sure your egg whites are finished in stiff peaks. If you're having issues make stiff peaks it's usually because you're using a plastic bowl or a bowl that has a bit of oily residue or you haven't separated your eggs properly and have a bit of egg yolk in your mix. Use a 'clean' stainless or glass bowl to whip your egg whites. Lastly, Soufflé's quickly lose the air that hold them up so, serve them immediately after they come out of the oven."

Chef J Stephen

CONTINUED

Pre-heat your oven to 400°

Soufflé
Separate your eggs

Place your egg <u>whites</u> in a mixing bowl and beat on high speed until stiff peaks are formed. Put aside

Place 6 ounces of your béchamel in a small plastic bowl and heat in your microwave for 60 seconds

Ramekin Bowl Preparation
Coat the entire inside of your three large ramekin bowls with approx. ½ ounce unsalted butter (per bowl)

Sprinkle approx. ½ ounce (per bowl) of your grated parmesan cheese into each ramekin bowl (Make sure your parmesan cheese covers evenly all areas of sides and bottom)

Place your filling into your heated béchamel, add your egg <u>yolks</u> and sautéed shallots

Mix thoroughly to assure your eggs have thoroughly combined and your cheese has creamed into the mix

Fold in your beaten egg <u>whites</u>

Place your combined mix into the parmesan/butter coated soufflé ramekin bowls

Bake in your pre-heated oven for 20 minutes or until your soufflé has risen and browned (see photo)

Serve IMMEDIATELY

FRANCE

GRAND MARINER FRENCH TOAST

SERVES 5, PREP 25MIN, TOTAL 45MIN

INSTRUCTIONS

24-hours prior to serving
Line a large sheet pan

*Zest your oranges to produce your orange zest

Place your large eggs in a large mixing bowl and stir with a whisk to thoroughly break down eggs

Add your heavy cream, Grand Mariner, castor sugar, and orange zest

Dip your slices of bread in your mix (fully saturate)

Place your saturated bread on your lined sheet pans

Refrigerate for two hours and then turn over your bread

Cover with clear wrap and refrigerate overnight

Orange Butter
Soften your unsalted butter to room temperature

*Zest your medium oranges and juice them to get your 1 ounce of orange juice

Place your butter, orange juice, Grand Mariner and orange zest in mixing bowl. Whisk on high speed for approx. 25 seconds or until fluffy (if your butter separates, don't worry, it will still taste perfectly)

You can refrigerate your orange butter for 2 weeks or freeze it or 90 days

INGREDIENTS

French Toast
3 cups heavy cream
3 large eggs
3 ounces Grand Mariner liqueur
¼ cup white castor sugar
2 tbsp orange zest
10 slices French Brioche bread
7 tbsp confectioners sugar

Orange Butter
2 medium oranges
1 ounce fresh squeezed orange juice
3 ounces unsalted butter
2 tbsp Grand Mariner

Fruit Macerate
¼ cup fresh strawberries
¼ cup fresh blueberries
¼ cup fresh blackberries
¼ cup fresh raspberries
1 ounce white granulated sugar
1 ounce of fresh squeezed lemon juice

CHEF SECRETS

"This was a delightfully light spring time favorite at my bistros. It takes a bit of work, but it's worth it. The fresh fruit and the start orange is a wonderful marriage that will brighten any morning."

Continued on next page

Continued on next page

FRANCE

GRAND MARINER FRENCH TOAST
CONTINUED

Fruit Macerate
Wash your fruit thoroughly and pat dry

Slice off the tops of your strawberries, slice in half and place in a medium bowl

Add your blueberries and blackberries (hold off on adding your raspberries until morning)

Sprinkle your caster sugar over the top of your fruit

Add your lemon juice

Mix your fruit gently to assure equal coverage

Refrigerate overnight

Serving Day
Pre-heat your oven to 400°

Turn over your slices of bread and dip in any mix that remain on your sheet pan

Place your bread onto a new sheet pan and bake for 15 minutes

Place your orange butter in your microwave to soften

Add your raspberries to your your fruit macerate, mix and place in your microwave to warm

Drain most of the liquid from your macerate

Spread your orange butter over your baked french toast

Top with your fruit macerate and sprinkle with powdered sugar

CHEF SECRETS (CONTINUED)

"By letting your bread soak overnight, your french toast is thoroughly infused with the delicious orange batter. Notice that I use castor sugar for this recipe. French toast made with caster sugar results in a softer, lighter, and more buttery flavor than French Toast made with regular sugar. Conversely, in my fruit macerate, I use a white granulated sugar. I can never say it enough but the 'type' of ingredients you use often make the difference between a 'good' dish and a 'great' dish."

*"Zest - scrape off the outer colored part of the peel of (a piece of citrus fruit) for use as flavoring. Make sure you don't scrape too deep to prevent bitterness."

Chef J Stephen

Jamaica

Jamaican Rum French Toast

Serves 3, Prep 35min, Total 55min

Ingredients

Batter (Makes 24 ounces)
3 cups heavy whipping cream
3 large eggs
1 ½ ounces Grand Mariner liqueur
½ ounce dark spiced rum
½ ounce banana liqueur
1 ¼ tsp natural banana extract
¼ tsp ground nutmeg

Syrup (Makes 16 ounces)
1 cup Jamaican Rum batter
2 ounces unsalted butter
½ cup dark brown Muscovado sugar
2 tbsp banana liqueur
½ tbsp ground nutmeg
½ cup dark spiced rum

Banana Butter
2 ounces unsalted butter
½ ounce Monin banana syrup
¼ tsp kosher salt

French Toast
3 cups Jamaica Rum French toast batter
6 slices French Brioche bread
3 ounces Jamaica Rum French toast syrup
2 fresh bananas (sliced)
3 ounces Banana Butter

*The term flamb [flahm-BAY] is a French word meaning "flaming" or "flamed." Flambe means to ignite foods that have liquor or liqueur added. This is done for a dramatic effect and to develop a rich flavor of the liqueur to the foods without adding the alcohol.

Instructions

Batter
Mix all your ingredients in a large mixing bowl

You can refrigerate your batter for 4 days

Syrup
Place your unsalted butter in a medium sauce pan on medium heat

Add your ground nutmeg, dark brown Muscovado sugar, and banana liqueur to your melted butter. Stir continuously until dissolved approx. 4 minutes and then remove from heat

Add your dark spiced rum and place back on medium heat. *Flambé until all your alcohol burns off

Continue to heat to thicken (reduce) until a nap forms on your ladle and then cool in the sauce pan. (*A nap is when your liquid thickens but still slowly slides off your ladle.*)

Once cooled, combine in equal parts your French Toast Syrup and French Toast batter BOTH MIXES MStatesT BE THE SAME TEMP

You can refrigerate your syrup for 30 days

Continued on next page

JAMAICA

JAMAICAN RUM FRENCH TOAST
CONTINUED

Banana Butter
Soften your unsalted butter to room temperature.

Place in a mixing bowl and whisk on high speed until fluffy

Add your banana syrup and kosher salt

Whisk on high speed for approx. 15 seconds or until fluffy

You can refrigerate for 2 weeks or freeze for 90 days

French Toast
Pre-heat your oven to 375°

Line a sheet pan

Dip each slice in your Jamaican Rum French toast batter (fully saturate)

Place your bread onto your lined sheet pan

Bake for 8 minutes and flip. Bake for another 8 minutes (or until golden brown)

Slice your bananas into ⅛" slices (see photo)

Place a small amount (approx. 3 ounces) of your Jamaica rum french toast syrup in the microwave to warm

Remove your French toast from oven when golden brown and spread your heated banana butter on each slice

Top with your sliced fresh banana slices and the warmed Jamaican banana rum syrup

CHEF SECRETS

"You would think this dish would be French, but that's not where I found it. I found this dish in of all places, Kingston, Jamaica! My question to the chef was, you're making a French dish in Jamaica? It's just one of the things I love about traveling the world to find little gems in the most unusual places!"

"There are many types of banana syrup available at most grocery stores. I prefer Monin which you can find locally or online at their Monin website."

"Make sure you use 'spiced' rum for this recipe. If you will only be using your rum for baking purposes, no need to spend the extra money for 100 proof."

"Choose dark Muscovado Sugar because of its fine, moist texture, high molasses content, and a strong lingering flavor that blends well and adds to the depth and richness of your dish. There is no other dark brown Muscovado sugar that comes close to the rich, full-bodied taste. You can find this type of sugar online at India Tree."

"If you need to use an extract because the natural juices are not seasonally available, always use a natural organic extract. You can find a good orange extract online at Olive Nation."

Chef J Stephen

Japan

Japanese Pancakes

Serves 3, Prep 7min, Total 17min

Ingredients

Crème Anglaise (Makes 4 servings)
½ cup heavy whipping cream
½ cup whole milk
½ tsp Madagascar bourbon vanilla
3 tbsp white granulated sugar
3 large egg yolks

Orange Butter
2 medium oranges
1 ounce fresh squeezed orange juice
3 ounces unsalted butter
2 tbsp Grand Mariner

Pancakes
2 large eggs
1 cup buttermilk
6 tbsp white granulated sugar
1 tsp Madagascar bourbon vanilla
1 tsp sea salt
1 ½ cups AP (all purpose) flour
1 tsp baking powder
¼ tsp baking soda
1 ½ tsp natural orange extract
2 tbsp orange butter
6 fresh blueberries
3 fresh strawberries
1 orange slice
¼ tsp avocado oil
2 tbsp Crème Anglaise

Instructions

Crème Anglaise
Combine your milk and heavy whipping cream in a medium saucepan

Add your Madagascar bourbon vanilla. Bring to a simmer and then remove from heat

Whisk your egg yolks and sugar in a medium mixing bowl to blend

Slowly whisk in your heated milk/cream/Madagascar bourbon vanilla mixture into your yolk/sugar mixture

Return this combined mix to your saucepan. Stir over low heat until your Crème Anglaise thickens (should hold to the back of a spoon) approx. 5 minutes (do not boil)

Transfer to a bowl

You can refrigerate for 2 days

Orange Butter
Soften your unsalted butter to room temperature.

*Zest your medium oranges and juice them to get your 1 ounce of orange juice

Place your butter, orange juice, Grand Mariner, and orange zest in mixing bowl. Whisk on high speed for approx. 25 seconds or until fluffy (if your butter separates, don't worry, it will still taste perfectly)

You can refrigerate your orange butter for 2 weeks or freeze it or 90 days

Continued on next page

Japan

Japanese Pancakes

Continued

In a mixing bowl, place your AP flour, baking powder, baking soda, and sea salt. With a whisk, blend until fully combined

Place your large eggs, orange extract, buttermilk, white granulated sugar, and Madagascar Bourbon vanilla in another bowl. Mix to fully incorporate

Add your wet mix to your dry mix and blend until doughy

Pan spray the insides of your English muffin moulds

Coat a flat pan skillet with your avocado oil and place on medium heat

Place your your english muffin moulds on your skillet pan

Pour your pancake batter into your english muffin moulds until half full

Cook for 3 minutes or until bubbles start to form on top. Flip each of your moulds with a spatula

Cook for an additional 3 minutes, or until golden brown on both sides (center of pancake should be moist, like a soufflé, but not runny)

Place your Crème Anglaise and orange butter in your microwave to warm

Top your pancakes with your melted orange butter, and Crème Anglaise

Garnish with your sliced strawberries, blueberries and orange slice (see pict)

Chef Secrets

"One of the few dishes I have brought back from Asia and it's a beauty. Japanese pancakes are like mini soufflé's (don't overcook, the centers which should be moist) that can't make up their minds if they're a breakfast or a dessert. To prevent a metallic taste in your pancakes and to eliminate one more chemical from your diet, always use aluminum-free baking powder. Always keep your baking powder in an air-tight container and because it loses it's strength over time, never keep it over 6 month's"

"NEVER use imitation vanilla. The chemical composition of imitation vanilla is different than 'real' vanilla and interacts differently with creations. The finest vanilla is Madagascar bourbon vanilla, pure vanilla extract. I use Nielson-Massey because of their cold extraction process, which draws out over 300 flavor compounds from the vanilla bean. You can find it online at My Spice Sage. If you need to use an extract because the natural juices are not seasonally available, always use a natural organic extract. You can find a good orange extract online at Olive Nation."

"It's hard to find 'regular' buttermilk in the grocery stores. They usually offer only non-fat. Go the extra mile and find 'regular' buttermilk. you need the fat in the buttermilk to provide the smooth mouthfeel that is such a vital part of this dish."

*"Zest - scrape off the outer colored part of the peel of (a piece of citrus fruit) for use as flavoring. Make sure you don't scrape too deep to prevent bitterness."

Chef J Stephen

ITALY

GAMBERAIA BLUEBERRY RICOTTA PANCAKES

SERVES 6, PREP 55MIN, TOTAL 1HR 15MIN

INGREDIENTS

Lemon Curd (Makes 4 servings)
The zest of 1 lemon
⅔ cup fresh lemon juice
1 cup white granulated sugar
2 large egg yolks
2 large eggs
3 ounces unsalted butter
⅛ tbsp sea salt

Lemon Butter
2 medium oranges
1 ounce fresh squeezed orange juice
3 ounces unsalted butter
2 tbsp Grand Mariner

Pancakes
3 eggs (yolks)
½ cup ricotta cheese
2 cups buttermilk
¾ cup white granulated sugar
1 ¼ tsp Madagascar bourbon vanilla
¾ tsp sea salt
1 ½ cups AP (all purpose) flour
1 ½ tsp baking powder
2 large lemons
2 tbsp lemon butter
7 frozen blueberries (per pancake)
7 fresh blueberries (per pancake)
¼ tsp avocado oil
6 ounces lime seltzer
1 tsp confectioners sugar (per pancake)
1 ½ tbsp unsalted butter

INSTRUCTIONS

Lemon Curd
In a large mixing bowl, add your butter and sugar and whisk for approx. 2 minutes.

Slowly add your eggs and yolks. Whisk for 1 minute. Add your lemon juice. Don't worry about curdled look, it will smooth into a curd as it cooks

In a medium saucepan, cook your curd over low heat until it becomes smooth. Raise the heat to medium and cook, stirring continually, until the curd thickens, approx. 15 minutes (should hold to the back of a spoon). Do not boil.

Remove your curd from the heat and stir in your lemon zest. Transfer your curd to a bowl. Cover with plastic wrap on the surface of the curd and chill in the refrigerator. The curd will thicken further as it cools

You can refrigerate for 1 week or freeze for 90 days

Lemon Butter
Soften your unsalted butter to room temperature

Place your butter in a mixing bowl and whisk on high speed until fluffy

Add your lemon curd and whisk on high speed for approx. 15 seconds or until fluffy

You can refrigerate for 2 weeks or freeze for 90 days

Continued on next page

ITALY

CHEF SECRETS

"These are the lightest pancakes you will ever have. Notice that there is no syrup in my recipe. Interestingly, unless its a tourist restaurant catering to Americans, I almost never syrup for pancakes or waffles. Most of the world has other ways to sweeten these dishes and this recipe does just that. Believe me you won't miss your syrup (and the calories that go with it) with the confectioners sugar and lemon butter."

"To prevent a metallic taste in your pancakes and to eliminate one more chemical from your diet, always use aluminum-free baking powder. Always keep your baking powder in an air-tight container and because it loses it's strength over time, never keep it over 6 month's"

"NEVER use imitation vanilla. The chemical composition of imitation vanilla is different than 'real' vanilla and interacts differently with creations. The finest vanilla is Madagascar bourbon vanilla, pure vanilla extract. I use Nielson-Massey because of their cold extraction process, which draws out over 300 flavor compounds from the vanilla bean. You can find it online at [My Spice Sage](). You can find a good orange extract online at [Olive Nation](). It's hard to find 'regular' buttermilk in the grocery stores. Their offerings are usually limited to non-fat. Go the extra mile and find 'regular' buttermilk. you need the fat in the buttermilk to provide the smooth mouthfeel that is such a vital part of this dish.

*"Zest - scrape off the outer colored part of the peel of (a piece of citrus fruit) for use as flavoring. Make sure you don't scrape too deep to prevent bitterness."

Chef J Stephen

GAMBERAIA BLUEBERRY RICOTTA PANCAKES
CONTINUED

Pancakes
Place your AP flour, baking powder, granulated sugar, and sea salt in mixing bowl. *Zest your lemons and add your zest to your mix. Mix with a paddle on slow speed until fully incorporated

Melt your unsalted butter in your microwave

Separate your egg yolks (save your egg whites for later). Add your egg yolks, ricotta cheese, and vanilla to your dry mix. Set your mixer with paddle on slow speed. Add your lime seltzer, buttermilk, and melted unsalted butter. Fully incorporate

Place your avocado oil in a large square skillet on low heat

Place ¾ cup of your pancake batter in a separate medium mixing bowl.

Place ½ cup egg whites in a separate mixing bowl and mix with a whisk on high until peaks are high and firm approx. 1 ½ minutes

Fold your egg whites into pancake batter and incorporate fully

Ladle into 3 pancakes on pre-heated square skillet approx. 5 ½" wide X 1 ¼" high

Place evenly 7 frozen blueberries (per pancake)

Cook your pancakes for approx. 6 minutes on the first side and 4 minutes on the second side. Your pancakes should be light brown when done

Top with confectioners sugar and garnish with your lemon butter and 7 fresh blueberries

AUSTRIA

Gaufre Liege Waffles

Serves 6, Prep 3hr 7min, Total 3hr 11min

Instructions

Streusel
Cut your unsalted butter into 4" squares

Into a large mixing bowl, combine your cake flour, dark brown Muscovado sugar, and Saigon cinnamon. Mix until all the lumps are gone

Add your unsalted butter to the mix. Mix until fully incorporated (It will be course and granular)

You'll have extra streusel, but never fear, you can freeze your streusel for up to 6 months

Waffle Butter
Soften your unsalted butter to room temperature. Place in a mixing bowl and whisk on high speed until fluffy. Add your homemade streusel and fold in with spatula

You can refrigerate for 2 weeks or freeze for 90 days

Waffles
Separate your bread flour into 2 ⅔ cups and 1 cup amounts

Combine your whole milk and water in a small saucepan and heat until lukewarm. Do Not Overheat (should be around 110°)

Place your large eggs and activated dry yeast into a mixer bowl. Mix on slow speed with a paddle. Add your milk/water mix while continuing to mix on slow speed. Stop your mixer and add your 2 ⅔ cups of bread flour to your mix

Turn your mixer back on slow speed and continue to mix until your dough is a tacky dough consistency. Stop your mixer

Ingredients

Streusel (Makes 11 servings)
1 lb unsalted butter
½ cup cake flour (you can substitute A/P flour)
1 lb dark brown Muscovado sugar
2 tbsp Saigon cinnamon

Waffle Butter (Makes 20 servings)
½ cup homemade streusel
8 ounces unsalted butter

Waffles
¼ cup water
½ cup whole milk

2 large eggs
2 ¼ tsp activated dry yeast

2 tbsp muscovado dark brown Muscovado sugar
3 ⅔ cups bread flour
1 tbsp Madagascar bourbon vanilla
1 tsp kosher salt
7 tbsp unsalted butter (softened)
1 cup pearl sugar - large granular (no substitutions)
3 tbsp pure honey
1 ¼ cups streusel

AUSTRIA

GAUFRE LIEGE WAFFLES

CONTINUED

<u>Top</u> your dough mix with your remaining 1 cup of bread flour. DO NOT INCORPORATE. Cover your bowl with clear wrap and let it rest at room temperature for 2-hours

Place your dark brown Muscovado sugar, kosher salt, honey and vanilla in a medium bowl. Mix occasionally to make sure it stays fully incorporated

Once your dough has rested for the 2 hours, add your dark brown Muscovado sugar/kosher salt/honey/vanilla mix to your to dough and then add your <u>softened</u> unsalted butter to dough

Set your mixer with paddle on slow speed and incorporate for 1 minute. Stop your mixer and pull the dough off your paddle. Set your mixer on medium speed and mix for 8 minutes

Turn off your mixer and let your dough rest for 2 minutes. Turn your mixer back on for an additional 4 minutes on medium speed. Stop your mixer and pull the dough off your paddle. Set your mixer on slow speed and add in your pearl sugar and streusel. Mix on slow speed until fully incorporated, approx. 2 minutes

Cover your mix with clear wrap. Place your clear wrap directly on dough to prevent it from drying out. Cover your mixing bowl with another layer of clear wrap. Wrap should have two levels of clear wrap, one on mix itself, one on top of mixing bowl

Store overnight in your refrigerator

Remove your dough from your refrigerator and separate into 4 ounce portions (about the size of an oversized meatball). Place your dough balls into a pre-heated Belgium waffle iron. When finished, top with either your waffle butter or fresh fruit and whipped cream

You can refrigerate for 1 week or freeze for 30 days

CHEF SECRETS

"These waffles are unlike any waffle you've ever had. They may be a challenge to make but are well worth the effort."

"I always use artisanal Muscovado dark brown from the island of Mauritius. This unrefined brown baking sugar has a fine, moist texture, a high molasses content that provides a rich, lingering flavor that is unlike any other. You can find it online here at [India Tree](.)."

"NEVER use imitation vanilla. The chemical composition of imitation vanilla is different than 'real' vanilla and interacts differently with creations. The finest vanilla is Madagascar bourbon vanilla, pure vanilla extract. I use Nielson-Massey because of their cold extraction process, which draws out over 300 flavor compounds from the vanilla bean. You can find it online at [My Spice Sage](.)."

"You can't substitute your pearl sugar. It's vital to the finished dish. You can find a good pearl sugar locally or online at [My Panier](.)."

Chef J Stephen

ISRAEL

CORNED BEEF HASH & EGGS

SERVES 6, PREP 30MIN, TOTAL 45MIN

INSTRUCTIONS

Corned Beef
Place your corned beef in a crock pot

Add water to completely cover the meat (approx. 6" above meat)

Add the provided seasoning package

Set your crock pot on low for 8 hours

When corned beef is finished cooking, slice your corned beef into ¼" ½" cubes

Potatoes
Wash your Russet potatoes and slice into ¼" - ½" cubes. Place in a large pot of salted boiling water. Boil until fork tender

Preparation
Shred your carrots, mince your garlic cloves, and chop your onions

Place your unsalted butter, and chopped Russet potatoes, in 8" skillet on medium flame

Add your Greek seasoning, shredded carrots, dried thyme and chopped onions. Cook for approx. 5 minutes on medium flame

Add your cubed corned beef and minced garlic to the skillet. Cook for 2-3 minutes on medium flame

Continued on next page

INGREDIENTS

2 lbs corned beef
5 large Russet potatoes
¼ tsp salt
2 tbsp unsalted butter
1 large white onion
½ tsp black pepper
¼ tsp dried thyme
2 cups water
¼ tsp Greek seasoning
3 tbsp hollandaise sauce
¼ clove fresh garlic
2 tbsp fresh chopped parsley
1 large carrot

Hollandaise
3 large eggs yolks
4 ounces unsalted butter
1 tsp Key Lime juice
¼ tsp Dijon mustard
¼ tsp Tabasco sauce

Poached Eggs
2 large eggs
2 tbsp white vinegar
1 tsp salt

Continued on next page

ISRAEL

CORNED BEEF HASH & EGGS
CONTINUED

Hollandaise
Melt your butter in a microwave or sauté pan. Butter MStatesT be fully melted and hot

Place 3 egg yolks, Dijon mustard, Key Lime juice, and tabasco sauce into a blender

Set your blender on high speed

While the blender is running, add your melted butter through the lid. Hollandaise should set up quickly. If runny, run until creamy

Poached Eggs
Place your white vinegar and salt in a medium sauté pan. Add water ¾ of the way up the pan

Set on medium/high heat. When water is boiling, gently add two eggs

Cook until eggs are white and semi firm (approx. 2-minutes) Don't overcook. Remove eggs with a slotted spoon and place on top of your hash browns

Garnish with a pinch of chopped parsley

CHEF SECRETS

"Homemade corned beef and hash is a great breakfast dish and making your own corned beef hash and topping it with your homemade hollandaise sauce is the crown on your masterpiece."

"Because of it's well deserved reputation for being hard to make, most home cooks stay away from making hollandaise, but my recipe for hollandaise sauce is so simple and easy to do you'll make it over and over again for, not only your poached eggs, but also your vegetables and fish dishes."

"There are two keys to a good hollandaise. (1) Don't over-blend your mix. An over-blended mix becomes more of a paste than a sauce; and (2) <u>Never</u> substitute any of the ingredients. The toughest ingredient to find is the Key West lime juice. It's best to use fresh Key West limes, but Key West limes are hard to find. If you can't find Key West limes, you can use a bottled Key West lime juice. The best is Nellie & Joes, which you can find online at <u>Walmart</u>. <u>Never</u> substitute Key West lime juice with regular lime juice or lemon juice. It simply won't work."

"It might seem odd to put vinegar and salt into your poached egg water but they achieve two different things. The salt not only seasons the eggs but also helps the water come to a boil. The vinegar makes sure your poached eggs stay together. Don't worry, you won't taste the vinegar when you enjoy your eggs."

Chef J Stephen

FRANCE

PARISIAN OATMEAL

SERVES 1, PREP 14MIN, TOTAL 20MIN

INSTRUCTIONS

Streusel
In a medium mixing bowl, combine your AP flour, dark brown Muscovado sugar and Saigon cinnamon. Mix by hand to remove any lumps

Add your unsalted butter to the mix. Mix by hand until the mix becomes course and granular

Oatmeal
In a small pot, combine your whole milk, streusel and Madagascar bourbon vanilla. Mix to fully incorporate

Add your whole oats

Set on medium/high flame

Slice 1 fresh strawberry in half for garnishment on the top (see photo)

Chop the remaining fresh strawberry into quarters

Place your chopped fresh strawberry and 7 fresh blueberries in bottom of your serving cup

Cook your oatmeal (stirring continually to prevent scalding) to the proper consistency (moist but not runny)

Place your cooked oatmeal over the chopped fresh strawberry and 7 fresh blueberries in serving cup

Top your oatmeal with the white sugar and caramelize using a torch

Garnish your oatmeal with the other sliced fresh strawberry and the remaining 7 fresh blueberries

INGREDIENTS

Oatmeal
6 ounces whole milk
1 tbsp streusel
½ tsp Madagascar bourbon vanilla
⅓ cup whole oats
1 tbsp white granulated sugar
2 fresh medium sized strawberries
14 fresh blueberries
½ tbsp unsalted butter

Streusel
5 tbsp unsalted butter
1 tbsp unsifted AP (all purpose) flour
¾ tsp Saigon cinnamon
¾ cup muscovado dark brown Muscovado sugar

CHEF SECRETS

"You can choose whatever whole oats you like. You can purchase fresh whole oats from stores like Whole Foods or . If you can't find fresh whole oats, try Silver Palate's Thick & Rough® Oatmeal it's my favorite."

"Make extra of my family's 400-year-old streusel recipe. You'll not only use it in your oatmeal but also in my cakes and my Crumbler™ ice cream topping"

"I always use artisanal muscovado dark brown Muscovado sugar from the island of Mauritius. This unrefined brown baking sugar has a fine, moist texture, a high molasses content that provides a rich, lingering flavor that is unlike any other. You can find it online here at India Tree."

Chef J Stephen

FRANCE

SALMON EGGS BENEDICT

SERVES 3, PREP 10MIN, TOTAL 20MIN

INGREDIENTS

Poached Eggs
1 tbsp of white vinegar
½ tsp table salt
2 cups water

Salmon
3 - 4 ounce salmon filets
3 tbsp virgin olive oil
1 tbsp kosher salt
1 tbsp black pepper

Hollandaise
3 large eggs
¼ tsp Dijon mustard
1 tsp key lime juice
¼ tsp tabasco sauce
4 ounces unsalted butter

Garnish
6 fresh cherry tomatoes
½ tbsp paprika
6 sprig's of dill

CHEF SECRETS

"You can use fresh or frozen salmon. Believe it or not, unless you live in an area where fresh salmon are fished, quality frozen salmon will taste just as good."

Continued on next page

INSTRUCTIONS

Preheat your oven to 350°

Place 1 tbsp of virgin olive oil in a medium sauce pan on medium heat

In a poached egg pan (preferably) or a small sauce pan if you don't have a poached egg pan, pour your white vinegar and table salt. Add your water and set on high heat. Bring to a boil

Slice each of your salmon filets horizontally in half. Rub each with your remaining 2 tbsp of virgin olive oil, black pepper, kosher salt, and place on your pre-heated medium sauce pan. Sear each side for 1 minute. Set aside

Slice horizontally and place 3 biscuits (see my biscuit recipe) on a lined sheet pan or cookie sheet in your pre-heated oven

Place 6 large eggs (2 per salmon) in your boiling water. Set a 4 minute timer

Hollandaise
Separate your eggs. Place the 3 egg yolks in a blender. Add your Dijon mustard, key lime juice and tabasco sauce. Do NOT turn on your blender just yet

Melt your unsalted butter in the microwave (or sauté pan. YOUR BUTTER MStatesT BE FULLY MELTED & HOT

Set your blender on high speed. Pour your melted butter into the egg yolk mixture in a thin stream through open lid. Your sauce should thicken in approx.10 seconds

Continued on next page

FRANCE

SALMON EGGS BENEDICT

CONTINUED

Crown your 6 cherry tomatoes

Remove your biscuits from the oven

Remove your poached eggs with a slotted spoon upon 4-minute timed alarm

Place your seared salmon on your biscuits and top your salmon with your poached eggs

Top each with your hollandaise Sauce

Top each egg with a pinch of paprika sprinkled and a sprig of dill

Garnish with your crowned cherry tomatoes

CHEF SECRETS (CONTINUED)

"Although it will not taste near as good, you can use pre-made biscuits that you simply pop in the oven."

" Although you can get away with pre-made biscuits, you should ALWAYS make your own hollandaise. It's actually quite easy to do and really makes a big difference in the taste of the finished dish."

"Don't use regular lime juice or God forbid lemon juice in this recipe. If you can't find 'real' Key Limes, you can purchase a pretty good 'natural' Key Lime juice locally or online from [Nellie & Joe's](.)."

Chef J Stephen

BELIZE

CATALINA ISLES EGGS BENEDICT

Serves 6, Prep 55min, Total 1hr 15min

INGREDIENTS

Poached Eggs
1 tbsp of white vinegar
½ tsp table salt
2 cups water
6 large eggs

Crab Cakes (Makes 12 crab cakes)
1 lb blue lump crabmeat
6 tbsp panko bread crumbs
1¼ tsp Dijon mustard
1 ounce old bay seasoning
1¼ tsp Worcestershire sauce
1½ tsp fresh parsley (chopped)
1 cup mayonnaise
1 large egg
1 tbsp kosher salt
1 tbsp black pepper
¼ tsp clear corn syrup
¾ tsp lime juice
2 tbsp bread flour
¾ tsp black pepper
6 tbsp water

Hollandaise
3 large eggs
¼ tsp Dijon mustard
1 tsp key lime juice
¼ tsp tabasco sauce
4 ounces unsalted butter

Garnish
1 sprig chives (chopped)
⅛ tsp cayenne

INSTRUCTIONS

Crab Cakes
Mix your warm water and crab base in a small bowl to create your "Base". Mix until fully dissolved

Set aside

Line a sheet pan

Chop your fresh parsley

Place your lump blue crabmeat in mixing bowl. Break up all lumps (remove any shell fragments)

In another mixing bowl add your Dijon mustard, Worcestershire sauce, fresh parsley, mayonnaise, large egg, Key West lime juice, Old Bay seasoning, clear corn syrup, and black pepper. Once you mix it thoroughly, add your crabmeat, bread flour and Panko breadcrumbs to the mix. Combine thoroughly

Add your water & crab base mixture to this mix and mix thoroughly

Cover with clear wrap and refrigerate for a minimum of 2-hrs (for the best results refrigerate overnight)

After refrigeration, form into 1 ounce (about the size of a large meatball) crab cake patties

You can use your patties immediately, refrigerate for 1 week or freeze for 30 days

Continued on next page

BELIZE

CATALINA ISLES EGGS BENEDICT

CONTINUED

Preheat your oven to 375°

Spray a small baking pan with pan spray

Place two of your crab cakes in your pan and bake for 10 minutes

While crab cakes are baking, create your hollandaise, and poach your two large eggs

Hollandaise
Separate your eggs. Place the 3 egg yolks in a blender. Add your Dijon mustard, key lime juice, and tabasco sauce. Do NOT turn on your blender just yet

Melt your unsalted butter in the microwave (or sauté pan. YOUR BUTTER MStatesT BE FULLY MELTED & HOT

Set your blender on high speed. Pour your melted butter into the egg yolk mixture in a thin stream through open lid. Your sauce should thicken in approx.10 seconds

Finishing Your Dish
Remove your crab cakes from the oven and plate

When your eggs are poached, top each crab cake with a poached egg

Top your poached eggs with your hollandaise sauce and sprinkle a pinch of cayenne and chopped chives on top of the hollandaise sauce

Serve immediately

CHEF SECRETS

"Don't use regular lime juice or heaven forbid, lemon juice in this recipe. If you can't find 'real' Key Limes, you can purchase a pretty good 'natural' Key Lime juice locally or online from [Nellie & Joe's](). "

"You'll notice that I put salt and vinegar in your poached egg water. The salt helps speed up the boiling point of your water and the white vinegar helps keep your egg together. Don't worry about tasting the white vinegar. You won't taste it when your eggs are done."

"Don't worry about making the hollandaise sauce. Everyone freaks out over making hollandaise sauce. You'll find that my recipe makes it quite easy with little fuss or muss."

Chef J Stephen

BELIZE

JALAPEÑO SAUSAGE GRAVY & BISCUITS

INGREDIENTS

Gravy
1 pound jalapeño sausage*
1 slice thick cut butcher bacon
3 tbsp AP (all Purpose) flour
1 tsp table salt
½ tsp black pepper
4 cups whole milk
3 tbsp unsalted butter

Biscuits
7 ¼ cups of self-rising flour
3 tbsp baking powder
1 ½ tsp baking soda
12 ounces unsalted butter
½ tbsp salt
4 ¾ cups buttermilk
3 large eggs

CHEF SECRETS

"The reason my recipe asks that you place your butter in the freezer prior to making your biscuits is to assure a flaky biscuit. When partially incorporated pieces of butter melt as the biscuits bake, they release steam and create pockets of air. Those pockets make the biscuits airy and flaky on the inside while remaining crisp on the outside. The key to making a light and fluffy biscuit is to never overwork your dough. If you overwork your dough, you will end up with tough, hard and flat biscuits."

Continued on next page

INSTRUCTIONS

Create Gravy
Slice your bacon into thirds. Place in bottom of a sauté pan. Cook both sides on medium heat until cooked through (not crispy). Remove your bacon, but leave bacon fat

Add your jalapeño sausage (break up your sausage while cooking (on medium/high heat) into ½" pieces. Turn flame down to medium heat and add your unsalted butter. Do not brown butter

Whisk in your AP flour. Whisk until fully incorporated for approx. 2 minutes

Add your whole milk, ⅓ at a time, while continuously stirring

Cook for approx. 6 minutes until thickened to a gravy consistency

Remove from flame

Add your salt and black pepper. Stir in with a whisk until fully incorporated

Create Biscuits
Preheat your oven to 425°

Place your unsalted butter in your freezer

Beat 2 of your eggs in small bowl

Place the remaining egg and 2 tbsp of buttermilk in a separate small bowl. Beat to fully incorporate

In a large mixing bowl, place your self-rising flour, baking powder, baking soda, and salt. Mix until fully incorporated

Continued on next page

UNITED STATES

JALAPEÑO SAUSAGE GRAVY & BISCUITS
CONTINUED

Grate your frozen unsalted butter (use the largest side of your grater)

Add your grated butter into your dry mix (do not over mix by trying to fully incorporate the butter. You want the butter to remain separate - see my "Chef Secrets" section)

Add your 2 beaten eggs to your dry mix with a spoon until just combined

Add the rest of your buttermilk. Mix by hand to form a sticky dough

Sprinkle your flour LIGHTLY on your counter top

Place your dough on a floured surface

To prevent the dough from sticking on your hands, sprinkle some flour LIGHTLY on your hands

Fold your dough over 5 times then flatten to approx. 1¼" height

Form your biscuits using a pastry cutter 4" W x 1¼" H

To prevent your dough from sticking to your pastry cutter, dip your pastry cutter in flour between each cut

Place your cut out biscuits on a lined sheet pan or cookie sheet

Leave 1" between each biscuit to allow your biscuits to spread

Brush each biscuit with your egg buttermilk mix

Bake at 425° for 15 minutes or until golden brown

Continued on next page

CHEF SECRETS (CONTINUED)

"If you want your biscuits to rise beautifully, don't twist your pastry cutter when cutting your biscuits. Twisting your cutter seals the dough on the edges which prevents your biscuits from rising."

"If you want beautifully high biscuits (the best to eat stand-alone with butter, honey or jam), place them closely together on your sheet pan. If you prefer a wider, flatter biscuit (ideal for sausage, egg and biscuit sandwiches or biscuits and gravy), space your biscuits apart."

"Be careful when shopping for your buttermilk. It's not as easy to find, but always use 'regular' buttermilk. 'Low fat' buttermilk is what you usually see in the grocery store but it's best left right there. You need the fat content in regular buttermilk to finish your biscuits properly."

"Although I don't include it in my recipe book as a stand alone recipe, if you make my buttermilk biscuits and top them with my Jalapeño Sausage Gravy (see my Gravies, Sauces, Dips & Spreads section of my book), you'll have one fantastic breakfast. I offered this dish as a special at my bistros and it was always a big hit, selling out within the first couple of hours."

"Although your biscuits will last in the refrigerator for up to 6 days and in the freezer up to 90 days, they are always best enjoyed hot out of the oven."

Chef J Stephen

Belize

Jalapeño Sausage

SERVES 12, PREP 27MIN, TOTAL 35MIN

Instructions

Place your pork breakfast sausage meat in a large mixing bowl

Add your thyme, kosher salt, fresh sage, pickled jalapeño juice, and large diced jalapeño's

Mix by hand until fully incorporated

Form individual 4 ounce patty's

Place your unsalted butter in a medium sized skillet on medium heat

Cook each jalapeño sausage patty for approx. 6 minutes (or until browned) flipping to assure both sides have browned. DO NOT OVER COOK

Wrap each patty individually in freezer baggies (if freezing) or in clear wrap if refrigerating

You can refrigerate for up to 10 days and freeze for up to 90 days

Ingredients

2 ½ lbs of pork breakfast sausage meat
1 tbsp of thyme
¼ tbsp kosher salt
1 ½ tbsp fresh sage
4 ounces pickled jalapeño juice
1 ounces large diced jalapeño's
2 tbsp unsalted butter

Chef Secrets

"This is our most popular breakfast meat at my bistros and is a great twist on your usual breakfast sausage. I found this dish at a little cafe in Placencia Belize. Although pre-made uncooked pork sausage meat will work, if possible, to assure your dish is really special, get your pork sausage from a butcher."

Chef J Stephen

CANADA

ONTARIO CANDIED BACON

SERVES 10, PREP 10MIN, TOTAL 23MIN

INGREDIENTS

Streusel
1 lb unsalted butter
½ cup cake flour (you can substitute A/P flour)
1 lb dark brown Muscovado sugar
2 tbsp Saigon cinnamon

Bacon
½ tbsp black pepper
1 ¾ ounces pancake syrup
1 tsp chipotle chili powder
¼ tsp cayenne
20 slices bacon (thickly sliced)
9 ounces streusel

CHEF SECRETS

"I found this great bacon recipe in a little cafe in Ontario Canada. This specialty bacon is a big hit at my bistros and is a unique twist on your typical bacon dish. One of the keys here is to buy thickly sliced bacon from a butcher. You can't really get a good 'thickly' sliced bacon at your local grocery store. In addition, butcher supplied bacon has no preservatives."

"If you end up with extra streusel, don't worry, you can refrigerate and freeze it for extended periods of time and there are plenty of dishes in my recipe book that call for it."

Chef J Stephen

INSTRUCTIONS

Streusel
Cut your unsalted butter into 4" squares

Into a large mixing bowl, combine your cake flour, dark brown Muscovado sugar, and Saigon cinnamon. Mix until all the lumps are gone. Add your unsalted butter to the mix. Mix until fully incorporated (It will be course and granular)

You'll have extra streusel, but never fear, you can freeze your extra streusel for up to 6 month's for future use

Candied Bacon
Pre-heat your oven to 350°

Place parchment paper on a sheet pan or cookie sheet. Cover your parchment paper with a rack to prevent your bacon from sitting in grease while cooking

In a medium bowl, place your streusel, pancake syrup, chipotle chili powder, and cayenne. Mix thoroughly with a spatula

With your small spatula, spread your candied bacon mix over top of each slice of bacon making sure to cover each slice of bacon entirely

Place your bacon on your racked sheet pan. Bake for approx. 16 minutes

Remove from the oven and cool on your racked sheet pan for approx. 15 minutes

Place your cooled bacon on parchment paper, placing a sheet of parchment paper between the slices so they don't stick to each other

You can refrigerate for up to 10 days and freeze for up to 90 days

THE MAIN COURSE

"Now that you have wetted their appetite with anticipation with your wonderful appetizers, soups, salads and breads, it's time to move on to the main attraction, your entrees. There are so many different entrees to choose from and they can be made in so many different ways that oftentimes it can be overwhelming to the home cook who doesn't entertain often. But never fear, as with most everything that's new, once you get the hang of it, you quickly realize that your fear was more in your head than in the task at hand."

"All the recipes in my recipe book were offered at my bistros at one time or the other. Some were special dishes, offered on holidays or other special occasions, others were daily offerings. All came from my travels to different countries around the world. Most, but not all, of my main dish recipes are from my Upper Crust Bistros in New York some are from my Crumbzz 'After Hours' offerings in Dallas. Because so many came from such a wide expanse of the world, all are unique offerings that you won't commonly find anywhere in the States. Enjoy perusing through them all, but most of all, enjoy creating them and wowing your guests and family members."

Chef J Stephen

British Virgin Islands

Pelican Cay Crêpe's

SERVES 4, PREP 60MIN, TOTAL 1HOUR 10MIN

Instructions

Vegetables
Cut your diced pineapple cubes in half

Chop your fresh garlic into small 1/16" pieces

Slice your bell peppers and onions into 2" long x ¼" wide slices (see photo)

Place your unsalted butter in medium stock pot over med/high flame. When butter is melted, add your sliced bell peppers, sliced onions, kosher salt, black pepper, Jamaican Jerk seasoning, and fresh lime juice

Sauté for approx. 8 minutes

Add your chopped garlic and pineapple chunks

Sauté for approx. 5 minutes

You will use 4 ounces of vegetables for each crêpe. You can store any extra finished vegetables for up to 3-month's in individual freezer bags

Sauce
Cut your diced pineapple cubes in half

Place your coconut milk, heavy cream, fresh lime juice, Jamaican Jerk seasoning, kosher salt, black ground pepper, and pineapple diced cubes into a medium sauce pan

Continued on next page

Ingredients

Vegetables
½ cup pineapple diced cubes
1 large white onion
2 large bell peppers (assorted colors)
1 tsp fresh garlic
1 tsp Jamaican Jerk seasoning
½ tsp kosher salt
½ tsp black ground pepper
1 tbsp fresh lime juice
2 tbsp unsalted butter

Sauce
1 ½ cups coconut milk
¾ cup heavy cream
1 tbsp fresh lime juice
1 tsp Jamaican Jerk seasoning
1 tsp kosher salt
½ tsp black ground pepper
¼ cup pineapple diced cubes

Continued on next page

British Virgin Islands

Pelican Cay Crêpe's

Continued

Set your flame on medium and bring to a soft boil, continuously stirring (to reduce) for 10-15 minutes

You can store any extra crêpe sauce in your refrigerator for 4-6 days

Crêpe
In a large mixing bowl, whisk together the flour and the eggs. Gradually add in the milk and water, stirring to combine. Add the salt and butter; beat until smooth

Lightly oil a sauté pan and place over medium/high heat.

Pour your batter onto the pan, using approx. ¼ cup for each crepe. Tilt the pan with a circular motion so that the batter coats the surface evenly. Cook the crepe for about 2 minutes, or until the bottom is light brown. Loosen with a spatula, turn and cook the other side.

Preparation
Slice your fresh shrimp horizontally (to double your pieces of shrimp). Place your sliced shrimp (6 sliced shrimp per crêpe) in a sauce pan. Add ½ ounce unsalted butter.

Sauté your shrimp on medium heat. Add your vegetables (¼ cup per crêpe). Heat on med/high flame for approx. 2 minutes

Fill each crêpe shell with ¼ cup of vegetables per crêpe and (6 sliced shrimp per crêpe). Fold your crêpe shell's to close (see photo)

Top with your crêpe sauce and toasted coconut

Garnish with a slice of fresh lime

Serve Immediately

Ingredients (continued)

Crêpe
½ cup AP (all purpose flour)
1 large egg
¼ cup whole milk
¼ cup water
⅛ tsp salt
1 tbsp unsalted butter (melted)

Preparation
4 crêpe shells
12 fresh shrimp
4 fresh lime slices
4 tbsp toasted coconut
1 ounce chopped chives

Chef Secrets

"A wonderfully light tropical dish that I found many years ago in the British Virgin Islands. You can choose to buy a store bought crêpe, or make your own. If you make your own, you can use a sauté pan but if you find that you are making crêpe's often, pick up a crêpe pan. They're easier to work with and your crêpe's will come out better."

Chef J Stephen

UNITED STATES

NEW ORLEANS CRAWFISH ROLL

Serves 4, Prep 45min, Total 1 hour 15min

INGREDIENTS

1 tbsp lemon juice
1 cup mayonnaise
⅓ stalk fresh celery (minced)
1 tsp seafood seasoning
1 large fresh lemon
1 ½ lb pre-cooked crawfish tails
4 lobster rolls
4 tbsp unsalted butter
⅓ tsp Louisiana hot sauce
1 tsp fresh parsley

INSTRUCTIONS

If your crawfish is frozen, defrost at room temperature

*Zest your large lemon and then juice your lemon

Place in a large bowl, your mayonnaise, Louisiana hot sauce, seafood seasoning, lemon zest, and lemon juice. Mix thoroughly

Wash throughly your stalk of fresh celery and mince

Butter your lobster rolls on both sides

Place your buttered lobster rolls on a flat pan skillet. Flip from side to side to brown both sides of the roll

When your rolls are browned, remove from your skillet and fill with your crawfish mix

Top with fresh chopped parsley

Lobster and crawfish rolls are traditionally eaten cold (except for the toasted roll). If you prefer your crawfish roll hot, feel free to heat your crawfish tails and mix in the microwave prior to serving

CHEF SECRETS

"Most everyone has had a lobster roll at one time or the other BUT, few have had a crawfish roll! My recipe comes from a great little restaurant located in the heart of the Bourbon Street area of New Orleans where crawfish is king! To make sure your crawfish roll authentic, you must use a toasted 'lobster roll.' Any other way is sacrilegious! You should be able to find them in your local grocery store and online at [Main Lobster Now](). If you have any rolls left over, never fear, they're so delicious that you'll use them for your hot dogs as well."

"Although fresh crawfish tails are the best, you can use frozen crawfish tails as well. You can find frozen crawfish at most grocery stores and online at [Cajun Grocer]()."

"My favorite seafood seasoning is from Old Bay which you should be able to find at your local grocery store or online on [Amazon]()."

*"Zest - scrape off the outer colored part of the peel of (a piece of citrus fruit) for use as flavoring. Make sure you don't scrape too deep to prevent bitterness."

Chef J Stephen

UNITED STATES

CRAWFISH VOL-AU-VENT

SERVES 5, PREP 15MIN, TOTAL 1 HOUR 30MIN

INGREDIENTS

Roux
1 ¼ tbsp unsalted butter
1 ¼ tsp AP (all purpose) flour
2 cups whole milk
¾ tsp kosher salt
1 tbsp tabasco sauce
¼ tsp black pepper

Sauce
1 tbsp virgin olive
1 tbsp creole seasoning
1 lb crawfish tails
2 tbsp shallots (minced)
1 tbsp fresh garlic
1 tbsp Worcestershire

10 pastry shells
¼ tbsp fresh chives (chopped)
¼ cup green onions (chopped)

CHEF SECRETS

"Although fresh crawfish tails are the best, you can use frozen crawfish tails as well. You can find frozen crawfish at most grocery stores and online at Cajun Grocer."

"My favorite creole seasoning is from Tony Chachere's which you should be able to find at your local grocery store or online on Amazon."

Chef J Stephen

INSTRUCTIONS

Preheat your oven

Roux
Place your unsalted butter in large saucepan. Melt over medium heat

Add your AP flour. Whisk until fully combined
Allow your mix to slow oil for 1-2 minutes DO NOT BROWN

Gradually add, while stirring, your whole milk Continue to stir until fully incorporated. Allow your mix to slow boil for approx. 5 minutes (until slightly thickened). Add your kosher salt and black pepper. Stir and remove from flame

Pastry Shells
Place your pastry shells in your oven (follow package directions)

Sauce
Mince your shallots and garlic

Place your virgin olive oil in a large sauce pan over medium heat. Add your minced shallots and garlic.

Sauté for approx. 4 minutes stirring continually (to prevent your garlic from burning)

Add your crawfish tails and creole seasoning
Sauté for approx. 5 minutes

Add your tabasco sauce, Worcestershire, chopped green onions, and prepared roux

Place your heated crawfish sauce in and on your pastry shells

Garnish with your chopped chives

UNITED STATES

CHICKEN POT PIE

SERVES 6, PREP 45MIN, TOTAL 1 HOUR 15MIN

INSTRUCTIONS

Pastry
In a large bowl, mix together your AP flour and kosher salt. Using a pastry blender (or two knives if you don't have a pastry blender), cut your unsalted butter into your AP flour until coarse crumbs have formed

In a separate small bowl, beat together your eggs and cold water

Add your eggs/cold water mix to your AP flour mix

Mix lightly until a soft dough forms. Shape your dough into a round shape, wrap your shaped dough in plastic wrap and chill in your refrigerator for one hour

INGREDIENTS

Pastry
3 cups AP (all purpose) flour
2 tsp kosher salt
5 ½ ounces unsalted butter (cut into cubes)
2 large eggs
6 tbsp water (cold)
1 large egg (lightly beaten - for glaze)

Filling
4 cups chicken (cooked and cubed)
¼ cup white wine (dry)
1 tbsp unsalted butter
4 tbsp AP (all purpose) flour
½ lb fresh mushrooms (sliced)
4 fresh carrots
1 cup celery (sliced)
1 cup frozen peas
3 cups heavy whipping cream
3 tsp paprika
1 ¼ tsp kosher salt
1 ¼ tsp black pepper
1 ½ cup chicken broth
2 cups Yukon Gold potatoes

Filling
Preheat your oven to 400°

Slice your mushrooms

In a small skillet, over low heat, melt your unsalted butter. Once your butter is melted, add your mushrooms. Increase your heat to medium/high. Cook until browned (all your liquid should have evaporated), approx. 5 minutes

Add your dry white wine. Cook until most of the liquid has evaporated, approx. 2 minutes

Peel and slice your carrots, wash, peel and cube your potatoes, and celery

In a large sauce pan combine your potatoes, carrots, peas, and celery. Add water to cover and boil for 15 minutes. Remove from heat, drain. Stop cooking process by rinsing with cold water. Drain off water. Set aside.

CHEF SECRETS

"Since you're making the chicken for this dish, you can make your own chicken broth. I'm always a big fan of making everything from scratch, but on occasion, if I don't see a big difference in the finished offering, I'll suggest the use of a pre-made ingredient. That's exactly the case for pot pies."

Continued on next page

Continued on next page

UNITED STATES

CHICKEN POT PIE

CONTINUED

In a medium sauce pan, set to low heat, with a whisk, add your heavy whipping cream, AP flour, paprika, kosher salt, and black pepper. Cook until thickened, approx. 5 minutes. Whisk in your chicken broth. Cook for an additional 1 minute on medium heat. Remove from heat

Add your mushroom mix, your chicken and vegetable mix and fold gently to combine

Build your pot pie
Cut your dough into two pieces. On a lightly floured surface, using a lightly floured rolling pen, roll one piece of your dough to fit the bottom of a 2-quart casserole dish (including sides) and one piece to fit the top of your casserole

Place the bottom piece of your rolled dough in your casserole dish. Push to corners and up sides. Add your filling making sure your chicken pieces are distributed evenly

Place the top of your dough on top of your casserole. Trim and seal the edges of your dough

You'll have extra dough (the trimmed off portions). You can use these to make your pot pie look really professional. To do this, roll out the trimmings. Cut out leaves or flowers or whatever design you choose. Brush the top of your pot pie with your egg glaze. Add your decorations and brush again with your glaze

Place your pot pie in your pre-heated oven and bake until the filling is bubbly and the crust is browned approx. 25 - 30 minutes

Transfer to a wire rack to cool slightly

Serve hot. Can be stored in freezer bag or container for up to 120 days for future use

CHEF SECRETS (CONTINUED)

"Since you're working hard making your own dough, this is a time to save a bit of work by using a pre-made chicken broth. Don't feel guilty, I promise, they'll never know. I think Swanson makes as good a broth as there is. You can find it at most any grocery store or online at Target."

"If you still want to make your own chicken broth, check out my recipe."

Chef J Stephen

Italy

Steak Pizzaiola

SERVES 4, PREP 30MIN, TOTAL 50MIN

Instructions

Concasse

Fill a large bowl with ice cubes and water

Bring a large pot of water to a boil

Cut an X in the bottom of each tomato. Place into pot of boiling water for approx. 30 seconds (until skins begin to peel off). Remove your tomatoes from the boiling water and place into your bowl of iced water. When cool, peel off skin, cut your tomatoes in half (crosswise) and remove all the seeds. Finely dice the flesh

Steak

Heat your oil in a large sauce pan over high heat

Season your steaks on both sides with a pinch each of your black pepper and table salt

Add your steaks to your heated pan and sear until browned, approx. 2 minutes on each side. Remove your steaks but keep your oil in your pan

Place your unsalted butter and mushrooms into the pan and season again with a pinch of table salt. Cook and stir until your mushrooms are lightly brown, approx. 5 minutes

Reduce the heat to medium and add your sweet peppers. Cook while stirring until softened, about 2 minutes. Add your garlic while continuing to stir for approx. 1 minute.

Pour in your vermouth and your dried oregano. Increase the heat to medium-high and cook until the vermouth is evaporated, approx. 3 minutes

Add your tomato concasse and simmer for approx. 4 minutes until your tomatoes are fully cooked. Add your balsamic vinegar, and red pepper, fresh oregano. and your steaks to the pan and cook for approx. 6-8 minutes

Ingredients

Concasse
6 tomatoes (cored)
6 cups water (iced)

Steak
4 personal sized beef chuck steaks (1 lb, cut into 4 medallions)
1 tbsp your choice avocado or olive oil (see Chef Secrets below)
½ cup bread crumbs (see my breadcrumb recipe)
4 ¾ tsp fresh garlic (chopped)
3 tbsp sweet vermouth
1 tsp balsamic vinegar
¼ tsp dried oregano
2 tbsp fresh oregano (chopped)
¼ tsp black pepper
¼ tsp table salt
¼ tsp red pepper flakes
1 cup sweet peppers
1 cup fresh mushrooms (sliced)

Chef Secrets

"Since we will be heating your skillet on high heat, you'll need to be careful you don't burn your oil. Although olive oil has the best flavor profile of all the oils, because avocado oil offers the same oleic acid benefits, robust anti-inflammatory qualities AND has a relatively high 'smoke point', you may want to choose this oil, but it's your choice."

Chef J Stephen

UNITED STATES

King Ranch Casserole

Serves 6, Prep 40min, Total 1hr 30min

Instructions

Pre-heat your oven to 350°

Bake your chickens for 75 minutes or if you prefer you can purchase pre-cooked chickens from your grocery store. Let cool

Shred your baked chicken

Drain 5 ounces only of the Rotel diced tomatoes and green chili's

Tear your corn tortillas into small 1" pieces

Layer the bottom of the pan with the torn tortillas

Top the tortilla layer with 5 ounces of the undrained Rotel diced tomatoes and green chili's

In a large mixing bowl, place your Cream of Chicken soup, the remaining DRAINED 5 ounces Rotel diced tomatoes and green chili's, your shredded chicken, and your sour cream. Mix to fully incorporate

Top your Rotel diced tomatoes and green chili's layer with this mix

Mix your cheddar and Monterey Jack cheese together

Top your casserole evenly with the combined cheese mix

Place your pan in the oven at 350° for 40-50 minutes. Slice in 6 square pieces and plate. Top with a sprig of cilantro

Serve immediately

Ingredients

22.6 ounces cream of chicken soup (1 family size Campbells soup can)
10 ounces Rotel diced tomatoes & green chilies (1 can)
10 - 6" corn tortillas
2 cups sour cream
1 - 3 pound rotisserie chickens (cooked)
16 ounces shredded Monterey Jack cheese
16 ounces shredded cheddar cheese
2 pieces cilantro (for garnish)

You'll also need 1 - 12"x10" aluminum pan for this recipe

Chef Secrets

"This is an old-time Texas favorite that is great as a fresh made or re-heated dish."

"This is one of the dishes where homemade chicken doesn't really matter. It's also one of the dishes where the taste value of homemade soup and chilies is not significant enough to spend the time. The nature of a casserole, where everything is blended together, aptly fits the saying… The whole is greater than the sum of its parts."

"I only recommend brand names if they are superior and I use them myself. You can get other cans of tomato and green chilies but Rotel is the best. You can find it online at many places including Walmart."

Chef J Stephen

UNITED STATES

LEMON CHICKEN

Serves 6, Prep 20min, Total 1hr 5min

Instructions

Trim off fat from your chicken cutlets

Place in a large mixing bowl

*Zest your 1 large lemon

Squeeze the juice from your 3 large lemons into a 1 cup measuring cup. It should make approx. ½ cup lemon juice

Place your bread crumbs in a medium bowl

Place half (1½ ounces) of your unsalted butter in a large sauce pan. Set on medium heat

Place each one of your chicken cutlets in your breadcrumb mix and flip to cover chicken cutlet completely

Once your butter has melted, place your breaded chicken cutlets in the pan. Sear (for color) on both sides

Remove chicken cutlets and place in baking dish

Place the remaining 2 ½ ounces of your unsalted butter in your large sauce pan. Set on medium heat. Add your chopped garlic. Cook for 1 minute.

Add your lemon zest, vermouth, lemon juice and white granulated sugar. Stir while cooking for approx. 2 minutes (until sugar completely dissolves)

Pour over your chicken cutlets. Bake for approx. 30 minutes at 350°

Serve immediately

Ingredients

Chicken
2 ½ lbs chicken cutlets
1 large fresh lemon (*zest)
3 large fresh lemons (½ cup lemon juice)
1 cup bread crumbs
5 ounces unsalted butter
1 tsp fresh garlic (chopped)
½ tsp vermouth
1 tsp fresh parsley (for garnish)
1 tsp Parmesan
1 tsp white granulated sugar

Breadcrumbs
1 cup AP (all purpose) flour
1 tsp paprika
½ tsp table salt
½ tsp black pepper
Breadcrumbs recipe - makes 2 cups

Chef Secrets

"Make your own bread crumbs with stale bread with a food processor. They will taste much better and you'll never again freak out over your bread going stale. Best of all, any bread will do. I always use Parmigiano Reggiano Stravecchio cheese, that I grind myself. You can find a good one at [igourmet](). If you can't find that, most any Parmigiano Reggianos are not quite as good, but will work fine. Get a quarter of a wheel and store it. It will keep well."

"Zest - scrape off the outer colored part of the peel of (a piece of citrus fruit) for use as flavoring. Make sure you don't scrape too deep to prevent bitterness."

Chef J Stephen

CHINA

HONG KONG EGG WAFFLES

SERVES 1, PREP 25MIN, TOTAL 35MIN

INSTRUCTIONS

Pre-heat your egg waffle pan to 150°

Place all your ingredients except for your avocado oil (AP flour, tapioca starch, large eggs, 1 baking powder, vanilla, custard powder, granulated white sugar, evaporated milk, and water) in a large bowl

Mix with whisk until only small lumps remain

Set your batter in the refrigerator for 1 hour to cool

Lightly brush your avocado oil into your pre-heated egg waffle pan

Pour 6 ounces of the batter into the middle of your egg waffle pan, close and immediately flip the pan, making sure to hold the pan together tightly so batter doesn't leak out sides

Cook for 2 minutes, then flip to other side and cook for another 2 minutes

Remove your waffle carefully from pan with waffle fork

Fill your waffle with a filling of your choice (see my Chef Secrets) roll your waffle around the filling

Top with a topping of your choice

Serve while still warm, immediately upon filling

INGREDIENTS

2 large eggs
¾ cup granulated white sugar
1 cup AP (all purpose) flour
1 tsp baking powder
¼ tsp kosher salt
1 tsp Madagascar bourbon vanilla
1 tbsp avocado oil
½ tbsp tapioca starch
1 tbsp custard powder
2 tbsp evaporated milk
¾ cup water

CHEF SECRETS

"This is one of the most versatile dishes I know. This is one of the most popular street foods in Hong Kong. I've had it as a dessert with ice cream, berries and whipped cream, bananas and peanut butter, or as a savory dish as a pizza, eggs and ham, avocado, tomato & lettuce and BLT. If you can think of it, you can probably make it."

"If you don't have an egg waffle pan, they're available locally for under $50 at many stores (they are also known as bubble waffle makers) or online at [Hammacher Schlemmer.](#)"

"In some parts of the country custard powder may be hard to find. You can find it online at [World Market.](#) If you can't find tapioca powder locally you can find it online at [nuts.com](#). Specialty stores, especially asian markets will almost always carry both."

Chef J Stephen

ARGENTINA

BISTECCA MORSI STEAK

SERVES 2, PREP 10MIN, TOTAL 55MIN

INGREDIENTS

Steak
2 tbsp virgin olive oil
½ tbsp kosher salt
½ tbsp black pepper
1 ounce unsalted butter
¼ tsp red pepper
4 cloves of fresh garlic
1 tbsp fresh parsley
2 twelve ounce sirloin steaks
2 tsp baking soda
1 cup of water
¼ ounce Parmesan cheese

Mornay Sauce
3 cups whole milk
4 ½ tbsp unsalted butter
6 tbsp AP (all purpose) flour
1 ounce grated gruyere cheese
½ tsp salt
⅛ tsp black pepper
⅛ tsp fresh grated nutmeg

CHEF SECRETS

"You have three keys here. (1) Make sure you purchase a good sirloin from a butcher shop if possible. You would be surprised at the variance in quality you'll find with steaks in general and especially with sirloin steaks in particular. (2) Make sure your sliced parmesan is a high quality parmesan. I always use Parmigiano Reggiano Stravecchio cheese, (igourmet has a great one) that I grind myself.

Continued on next page

INSTRUCTIONS

Mornay Sauce
Melt your unsalted butter in a large saucepan over moderately low heat

When your butter is completely melted, add your flour and cook over low heat. Make sure you whisk continually for approx. 3 minutes

Add your milk slowly while you continue to whisk

Continue to whisk and bring to a boil

Set your heat on low and simmer while whisking occasionally for approx. 10 minutes

Remove from heat and add your gruyere cheese, while whisking, until melted, then whisk in your salt, black pepper, and grated nutmeg

Steak
Mince your cloves of fresh garlic

Chop your fresh parsley

Chop your sirloin steaks into bite size pieces (see photo)

Fully dissolve your baking soda into a cup of water

Soak your steak pieces in the baking soda water for 15 minutes

Remove your steak pieces from their baking soda bath and lightly pat dry

Add to your steaks, your black pepper and kosher salt. Mix to fully incorporate

Continued on next page

ARGENTINA

BISTECCA MORSI STEAK

CONTINUED

Place your virgin olive oil into a large cast iron skillet. Heat your skillet over high heat (400°-500°) YOUR SKILLET MStatesT BE FULLY HEATED TO ALLOW SEARING

Place your steaks into your skillet. Cook for approx. 2 minutes before flipping to assure your steaks sear on each side. Remember… you are searing NOT cooking. DO NOT OVERCOOK

Place your steaks into a mixing bowl

Turn your skillet down to medium heat

Add your unsalted butter to the skillet

When melted, add the cloves of chopped garlic and the red pepper

Cook your butter garlic, while continually stirring for 30 seconds (garlic should turn light brown)

Pour your garlic butter over your steak bits, toss to assure even coverage

Place your Mornay dipping sauce in a 1 ounce ramekin. Serve along side your steak

Slice, directly over your steaks, with a mandoline, 3 pieces (per steak) of your parmesan cheese. Your cheese should be thinly sliced (opaque)

Garnish with chopped fresh parsley

CHEF SECRETS (CONTINUED)

If you can't find that, most any Parmigiano Reggianos will work fine. However, make sure your Parmesan has 'Reggiano' in its name. If you have the room, get a quarter of a wheel and store it. It will keep well and you'll use it on so many great dishes. (3) To assure you have an exquisitely tasting, oh so creamy Mornay sauce, always use an imported gruyere cheese. Through the years, I have had many discussions with my bistro guests about the difference between 'imported' gruyere and "domestic" gruyere. Trust me, although it is more expensive than domestic gruyere cheese, the difference is like night and day. I ALWAYS use "imported" gruyere from France or Switzerland and you should too. You can find an excellent gruyere cheese online at the Gourmet Food Store."

SECRET TO A GREAT STEAK…
"Dissolve baking soda in water (for every 12 ounces of meat, use 1 tsp of baking soda and ½ cup of water). Soak your steak in the solution for at least 15 minutes. Remove and rinse. Cook as desired."

"You won't believe the difference this one chef's secret makes."

Chef J Stephen

FRANCE

BLACK CURRENT DUCK

SERVES 2, PREP 30MIN, TOTAL 1HR

INSTRUCTIONS

Duck
Pre-heat your oven to 375°

*Remove the wings from your duck by cutting through the breast bone to cut the duck in half. Turn your duck over and cut out the backbone from each side. Remove the thigh and leg. Then remove the shoulder bone from the breast. Don't remove the rib cage. Trim off the neck bone. Remove the keel bone

*(You can buy your duck pre-cut from your butcher and save the work

In an oven ready skillet, sauté your two duck bone breasts for 3 minutes per side. Start with the skin side down to cook off the fat

Move your duck to your pre-heated oven and roast for 8 minutes. Remove from the oven and season with your kosher salt and black pepper

Remove your duck from the skillet and cover to keep warm

Pour the fat from your skillet and place over medium heat

Add your dark brown Muscovado sugar, black current liqueur, raspberry vinegar, black currents and brown sauce

Bring to a boil just prior to serving

Detach the rib bones from your cooked duck breast meat and carve ¼" slices on the diagonal

Pour your black current sauce over your sliced duck

Continued on next page

INGREDIENTS

Duck
1- 6 to 8 lb Muscovy or Moulard duck
1 tsp sea salt
1 tsp black pepper

Black Current Sauce
2 tbsp kosher salt
2 tbsp raspberry vinegar
2 cups dark brown Muscovado sugar
1 cup fresh black currents (use canned if you can't find fresh)
2 tbsp black current liqueur
2 cups brown sauce

Risotto
32 ounces unsalted chicken stock
1 tbsp unsalted butter
1 tbsp avocado oil
1 cup arborio rice
¼ tsp kosher salt
¼ cup parmigiano-reggiano cheese (grated)
¼ cup gruyere cheese (shredded)

CHEF SECRETS

"Brown Sauce is a British sauce that is used on many meat dishes. Don't confuse it with Chinese Hoisin sauce. You can find it in specialty grocers and online at [The British Food Depot.](.)"

Continued on next page

FRANCE

BLACK CURRENT DUCK

CONTINUED

Risotto

In a medium saucepan over medium heat, bring your chicken stock to a simmer. Reduce the heat to low to keep warm

In a large skillet heat your unsalted butter and avocado oil. Once the butter has melted and the oil/butter combo is hot, add your arborio rice

Stir to assure an even coating of your rice, approx. 2 minutes

Add ½ cup of your warm chicken broth while continuing to stir. Once it has thoroughly mixed, let it rest while the broth is mostly absorbed, approx. 3 minutes

Once absorbed, stir while adding another cup of your warm chicken broth, while continually stirring

Cook (do not stir) until the chicken broth is entirely absorbed

Repeat this procedure until approx. ½ cup of your chicken broth remains (total cook time should be approx.15 minutes)

Turn off heat

Add your kosher salt, whatever remains of your chicken broth, and your grated parmesan and gruyere cheese

Stir gently to fully incorporate the cheese assuring that the cheese has fully melted into the rice

Serve immediately

CHEF SECRETS (CONTINUED)

"We often play the 'If you had only one meal to eat, what would it be' game with my chefs at my bistros. My answer is always the same… 'Black Current Duck'."

"No-one made it better than my good friend Chef Rene Verdon. I was fortunate enough to enjoy his version of this traditional French dish and I provide his recipe here for you to enjoy as well."

Chef J Stephen

URUGUAY

Lamb Chops & Saffron Pilaf

SERVES 4, PREP 35MIN, TOTAL 1HOUR 20MIN

Ingredients

2 tbsp unsalted butter
¼ cup orzo pasta
1 cup white rice
½ tsp saffron
1 ¾ cups chicken stock
1 cup pomegranate juice
½ cup red wine
2 tbsp Worcestershire sauce
6 peppercorns
3 whole cloves
1 fresh bay leaf
1 ½ tbsp corn starch
12 rib lamb chops
¼ tsp table salt
¼ tsp black pepper
2 tbsp virgin olive oil
2 large garlic cloves (chopped)
1 lb fresh spinach

Chef Secrets

"Of all the meats, lamb has the most unique taste. Some folks love it, others not so much. Whatever camp you fall into, this recipe proved to be a guest favorite at my New York bistro."

"Much like the classic Duck à l'Orange, this recipe compliments the deep lamb flavor with a sweet balancing pomegranate. In addition, your saffron pilaf base is the perfect accompaniment."

Chef J Stephen

Instructions

Preheat the broiler in your oven

Place a large pot over medium heat. Add your unsalted butter. When your butter has melted, add your orzo and stir. Cook until your orzo is light brown, approx. 4 minutes. Add your rice and combine. Add your saffron and chicken stock. Bring to a boil, then reduce to a simmer and cover. Cook until tender, approx. 16 minutes

1 cup of juice is produced. Stir in the wine, Worcestershire, peppercorns, cloves, and bay leaf. Bring to a boil, lower the heat to a simmer and reduce the liquid by half, about 6 minutes. Pour a little sauce into a small bowl, stir in the cornstarch, and then pour the mixture into the sauce. Cook until thickened, about 1 minute. Remove and discard the peppercorns, whole cloves, and the bay leaf

Arrange the chops on a broiler pan and season with salt and pepper, to taste. Broil for 3 to 4 minutes, or only 1 minute on each side for pink centers

When the chops go into the broiler, heat the extra-virgin olive oil in a medium skillet over medium heat. Add the garlic and stir for 2 minutes, then add the spinach and let it wilt. Season with salt, pepper, and nutmeg, to taste

Arrange 3 chops on each serving plate. Drizzle with pomegranate sauce, and serve the saffron pilaf and wilted spinach alongside

Peru

Papa Rellena

Serves 3, Prep 10min, Total 1 hour 20min

Instructions

Dough
Place your russet potatoes into a large pot of salted boiling water until fork tender (approx. 20 minutes). Peel and pass through a potato presser until all lumps are gone. Add your table salt. Separate into six portions and set aside to cool

Filling
Place 3 tbsp of avocado oil in a large sauce pan on medium heat. Add your onions and sauté until they are opaque approx. 8 minutes. Add your garlic, yellow pepper, and tomato. Sauté for approx. 2 more minutes. Add your ground beef and stir continually until cooked fully (beef no longer pink). Add your water, pepper, raisins, table salt, chopped egg, and olives, then cook for approx. 3 additional minutes

It's now time to assemble your potatoes. To do this lightly flour your hands (to prevent your dough from sticking). Place one of the six portions of your dough between your hands and flatten. Repeat for each portions of your dough

Place three tbsp of your filling in three of the portions of your flattened dough. Make sure there's an ample amount of filling and that your flattened dough is not too thin or too thick

Cover each of the three layers of filling topped dough with the remaining three portions of your flattened dough, stretch the ends of your dough with your fingers, to form into the traditional Papa Rellena oval shape, making sure to press the ends of the dough to seal your Rellena

Gently cover each potato with AP (all purpose) flour and chuño, let them sit for 10 minutes. Place 3 cups of avocado oil in a large pot. Heat to fry (350°). Fry your Rellenas until golden brown, approx. 3 minutes per Rellena

Garnish with chopped fresh parsley

Ingredients

- 3 tbsp avocado oil
- ⅓ cup raisins
- 2¼ lbs russet potatoes
- ½ cup water
- 1 peeled tomato
- 1 white onion
- 1¼ lb ground beef
- 1 tsp ground garlic
- 1 tsp yellow pepper (ground)
- 6 Botjia olives (seeded)
- 2 eggs (boiled)
- ¼ tsp table salt
- ¼ tsp black ground pepper
- ½ cup chuño flour
- 3 cups avocado oil (for frying)

Chef Secrets

"Although you can use an olive of your choice, I like to make my dishes as traditional as I found them. Botjia olives are the traditional olive used in Peru, they are sometimes hard to find. I purchase mine from Thrive Market online."

"Chuño is a dried potato flour used extensively in Peru. You can find it online at Zocalo Foods and in specialty grocery stores."

Chef J Stephen

ITALY

NERO DI SEPPIA PASTA

Serves 2, Prep 20min, Total 20min

INSTRUCTIONS

Pasta
Bring a large pot of salted water to a boil (see "Pasta Continued" at end of recipe)

Sauce
Heat your virgin olive oil in a large skillet over medium/high heat until lightly smoking. (DO NOT OVERHEAT

Add your shrimp and sauté until opaque, approx. 1 minute for each side

Remove shrimp from pan. Reheat the same virgin olive oil and cook your scallops until they are also opaque and lightly browned, approx. 2 minutes per side. DO NOT OVERCOOK

Remove your scallops and add your chopped garlic to your skillet. Cook, over medium heat while stirring often to prevent burning, until your garlic has turned a light brown, about 2 minutes

Add your basil, grape tomatoes, black pepper, salt, wine, chopped tomato, parsley, red pepper flakes, and cook over high heat until your sauce is reduced by half, approx.10 minutes

Add your lime juice and unsalted butter and add back in your shrimp and scallops. Mix well and set skillet on low to keep warm

Pasta Continued
Add your pasta to your pot of boiling water and cook al dente. When cooked, remove, plate, pour your cooked seafood sauce over your pasta top with your sprouts and serve immediately

INGREDIENTS

- ¾ lb squid ink pasta
- ¼ cup virgin olive oil
- ¾ cup dry white wine
- ½ tsp red pepper flakes
- ¼ tsp black pepper
- ¼ tsp sea salt
- ⅓ cup chopped tomato (seeded)
- 6 medium shrimp (shelled and deveined)
- 6 medium sea scallops
- 3 large garlic cloves (thinly sliced)
- ½ cup fresh parsley (chopped)
- ⅛ cup lime juice
- 1 tbsp unsalted butter
- ¼ cup fresh basil
- ⅛ cup sprouts
- ½ cup grape tomatoes

CHEF SECRETS

"Chef Maximillano Castillo at the Four Seasons Hotel in Buenos Aires treated me to this wonderful dish. You may think that black squid pasta (which is what this dish is) sounds terrible but it's actually quite delicious. The squid ink adds a rich seafood taste to your dish that is missing with traditional pasta. That's why squid ink pasta is always served with seafood."

"Because locating the specific ingredients for this pasta can be a challenge it's one of the few dishes where I suggest you buy your pasta. If you still want to make your own, check out my Squid Ink Pasta recipe. You'll be happy you did. If not, you'll note that most of the providers offer spaghetti, but I prefer the traditional macaroni. You can find an excellent Gemelli squid ink macaroni at nuts.com."

Chef J Stephen

ITALY

RAVIOLINI

Serves 6, Prep 30min, Total 40min

Instructions

Dough
Mound your AP flour and table salt together on a work surface. Form a well in the center

Beat your virgin olive oil, large eggs, water, and milk in a mixing bowl. Pour half of this egg mixture into your flour well

Combine your egg mixture with your flour. Use one hand to mix and the other hand to keep the flour mound steady. Add your remaining egg mixture and knead to form a dough

Knead your dough until it becomes smooth, approx. 8 to 10 minutes. If the dough becomes too sticky, simply add a bit more flour. Form your dough into a ball and wrap it in plastic wrap. Refrigerate for 1 hour

Filling
While the dough is resting it's a good time to create your filling

Combine your ricotta cheese, cream cheese, mozzarella cheese, provolone cheese, large egg, fresh parsley, and mix until fully incorporated. Set your filling aside

Sauce
Mix all your sauce ingredients **_Gently_** in a large mixing bowl. Use the oil that your sun-dried tomatoes were packed in. It adds excellent flavor to your dish

Continued on next page

Ingredients

Dough
¼ tsp table salt
2 large eggs
1 tsp virgin olive oil
3 cups AP (all purpose) flour
¼ cup water
¼ cup whole milk

Filling
1 large egg
8 ounces ricotta cheese
4 ounces cream cheese (softened)
½ cup mozzarella cheese (shredded)
½ cup provolone cheese (shredded)
1 ½ tsp fresh parsley

Sauce
½ lb roasted peppers
½ lb sun-dried tomatoes (in oil sliced ¼" wide)
2 ounces black olives (sliced)
¼ cup fresh flat leaf parsley (chopped)
¼ cup fresh basil (chopped)
2 tbsp kosher salt
½ tsp red pepper flakes
1 tsp mediterranean oregano
1 clove fresh garlic (chopped)
¼ cup red wine vinegar
¾ cup virgin olive oil (from sun-dried tomatoes)
¾ cup safflower oil

ITALY

RAVIOLINI

CONTINUED

Dough (finish)
Once your dough has cooled in the refrigerator for 1 hour, Sprinkle some flour LIGHTLY on your counter top

Place your dough on the floured surface and roll it out into thin sheets no thicker than ⅛"

Using an egg wash, brush your dough lightly. With a teaspoon, place your filling mixture on your dough. Space about 1" apart

Cover the filling with a top sheet of your dough pasta. Make sure you press out as much of the air as possible from around each portion of filling

Press firmly around the filling to assure a good seal. Cut into individual raviolis with a knife or pizza cutter. Reseal your edges after cutting

Place a large pot of water on high heat. Add 2 tbsp of table salt to the water. Bring to a boil

Gently, stir in your ravioli and return to a boil. Cook until your ravioli float to the surface, approx. 6 minutes. Drain and cool

Serving
Top your raviolis with your Raviolini sauce and serve

CHEF SECRETS (CONTINUED)

"Although there's nothing better than homemade pasta, you can substitute frozen ravioli's if you must. If you decide to use frozen ravioli's, you can skip the 'dough' and 'filling' steps and head right to the 'serving' step."

"For your dough, choose 'early harvest' olive oil in a dark bottle (a dark bottle preserves your oil longer). 'Early harvest' olive oil is oil squeezed from the olive before the olive is ripe. An unripe olive yields much less olive oil but much higher quality oil, so it will be expensive but well worth the price. You can find a great early harvest olive oil [Formaggio Kitchen](#)."

"For your sauce, make sure you use a sun dried tomato olive oil. Since this is a cold dish, you need an extra kick of flavor to provide that wow factor and sun dried tomato olive oil really makes the difference. You can find a good one at [Fratelli Carli](#)."

"Most dough recipe's call for water. You'll notice that I use ½ water and ½ whole milk. I find that the milk provides a bit smoother mouthfeel to my pasta dishes."

Chef J Stephen

Italy

Pesto Alfredo Tortellini

Serves 8, Prep 45min, Total 1Hour 10min

Ingredients

Dough
¼ tsp table salt
2 large eggs
1 tsp virgin olive oil
3 cups AP (all purpose) flour
¼ cup water
¼ cup whole milk

Filling
1 large egg
8 ounces ricotta cheese
4 ounces cream cheese (softened)
½ cup mozzarella cheese (shredded)
½ cup provolone cheese (shredded)
1 ½ tsp fresh parsley

Alfredo Sauce
8 ounces unsalted butter (melted)
1 tbsp AP (All Purpose) flour
1 ½ tbsp minced garlic
4 cups heavy cream
1 cup whole milk
1 ¼ cups shredded parmesan cheese
½ cup shredded gruyere cheese
5 tbsp fresh pesto
½ tsp kosher salt
1 tsp ground black pepper

Instructions

Dough
Mound your AP flour and table salt together on a work surface. Form a well in the center

Beat your virgin olive oil, large eggs, water, and milk in a mixing bowl. Pour half of this egg mixture into your flour well

Combine your egg mixture with your flour. Use one hand to mix and the other hand to keep the flour mound steady. Add your remaining egg mixture and knead to form a dough

Knead your dough until it becomes smooth, approx. 8 to 10 minutes. If the dough becomes too sticky, simply add a bit more flour. Form your dough into a ball and wrap it in plastic wrap. Refrigerate for 1 hour

Filling
While the dough is resting it's a good time to create your filling

Combine your ricotta cheese, cream cheese, mozzarella cheese, provolone cheese, large egg, fresh parsley and mix until fully incorporated. Set your filling aside

Alfredo Sauce
Melt your unsalted butter in a large pot over medium heat

Mince your fresh garlic. Add your AP flour, and minced garlic to your heated unsalted butter. Stir until fully incorporated. (Should be fragrant but not browned), approx. 2 minutes

Continued on next page

ITALY

PESTO ALFREDO TORTELLINI
CONTINUED

Alfredo Sauce
Whisking continually, add your heavy cream and whole milk. Mix for approx. 15 minutes (until slightly thickened)

Add your shredded parmesan cheese, shredded gruyere cheese, fresh pesto, kosher salt, and ground black pepper

Cook over medium heat until cheese has fully melted and incorporated, and your sauce has thickened. Stir often, approx. 13 minutes

Dough (finish)
Once your dough has cooled in the refrigerator for 1 hour. Sprinkle some flour **LIGHTLY** on your counter top

Place your dough on the floured surface and roll it out into thin sheets no thicker than 1/16"

Using an egg wash, brush your dough lightly

Using a 4" cookie cutter, cut out circles

Spoon ¼ teaspoon of your filling into the center. Fold the edge closest to you over the filling to meet the other side, press to seal the edge

Take the left and right corners and twist them around to meet each other, stick them together using a small dab of your egg wash

Place a large pot of water on high heat. Add 2 tbsp of table salt to the water. Bring to a boil

Gently, stir in your tortellini and return to a boil. Cook until your tortellini float to the surface, approx. 3-6 minutes. Drain

Serving
Top your tortellini with your Alfredo sauce and serve

CHEF SECRETS

"Although there's nothing better than homemade pasta, you can substitute frozen tortellini if you must. If you decide to use frozen tortellini, you can skip the 'dough' and 'filling' steps and head right to the 'Alfredo sauce' step."

"For your dough, choose 'early harvest' olive oil in a dark bottle (a dark bottle preserves your oil longer). Early harvest' olive oil is oil squeezed from the olive before the olive is ripe. An unripe olive yields much less olive oil but much higher quality oil, so it will be expensive but well worth the price. You can find a great early harvest olive oil Formaggio Kitchen"

"One of the cheese I use for my Alfredo sauce is gruyere. Through the years, I have had many discussions with my bistro guests about the difference between 'imported' gruyere and 'domestic' gruyere. Trust me, although it will be the most expensive ingredient in your dish, the difference is like night and day. I ALWAYS use an 'imported' gruyere from France or Switzerland and you should too. You can find an excellent gruyere cheese at the gourmet food store"

"Most dough recipe's call for water. You'll notice that I use ½ water and ½ whole milk. I find that the milk provides a bit smoother mouthfeel to my pasta dishes."

Chef J Stephen

United States

New Orleans Cajun Pasta

SERVES 4, PREP 45MIN, TOTAL 1HOUR 10MIN

Instructions

Dough

Mound your AP flour and table salt together on a work surface. Form a well in the center

Mix in a mixing bowl with a paddle, your virgin olive oil, large eggs, water, and milk. Pour half of this egg mixture into your flour well

Combine your egg mixture with your flour. Use one hand to mix and the other hand to keep the flour mound steady. Add your remaining egg mixture and knead to form a dough

Knead your dough until it becomes smooth, approx. 8 to 10 minutes. If the dough becomes too sticky, simply add a bit more flour. Form your dough into a ball and wrap it in plastic wrap. Refrigerate for 1 hour

Cajun Sauce

Place a large pot of water on high heat. Add 2 tbsp of table salt to the water. Bring to a boil

Gently, stir in your pasta and return to a boil. Cook approx. 3-6 minutes more al dente. Drain

In a large sauté pan heat 2 tbsp of virgin olive oil over medium heat. When hot, add your chopped onions, cherry tomatoes, and mushrooms. Cook for four minutes and then add your minced garlic, cook for an additional 25 seconds and then add your white wine. Reduce this mix to half, approx. 3 minutes and then add your paprika, cajun seasoning, kosher salt, white pepper, and tomato paste. Mix to fully incorporate

Once incorporated, add your heavy whipping cream. Just prior to boiling, turn heat to low and let the cream mix reduce to half about 2 minutes. Add your pasta to the cream sauce and cook additional two minutes. Top with your chopped parsley, gruyere and parmesan cheeses

Ingredients

Dough
- ¼ tsp table salt
- 2 large eggs
- 1 tsp virgin olive oil
- 3 cups AP (all purpose) flour
- ¼ cup water
- ¼ cup whole milk

Cajun Sauce
- ½ cup white onions (chopped)
- 2 tbsp virgin olive oil
- 2 tbsp fresh garlic (minced)
- 1 cup white wine
- 1 tbsp AP (All Purpose) flour
- 1 ½ tbsp minced garlic
- 2 cups heavy whipping cream
- 1 tbsp cajun seasoning
- ¼ cup shredded parmesan cheese
- 1 tbsp paprika
- ¼ cup shredded gruyere cheese
- 2 tbsp tomato paste
- 1 tsp kosher salt
- 1 tsp ground white pepper

Garnish
- ½ lb cremini mushrooms
- 1 tbsp fresh parsley (chopped)
- 24 cherry tomatoes

Chef Secrets

"If you have flour and eggs you can make most any pasta. It's much easier than most people think and the flavor and texture is far superior to store bought pasta and it's definitely healthier because it doesn't include any of the chemicals and preservatives they add to pre-made pasta."

Chef J Stephen

ITALY

SQUID INK PASTA

SERVES 5, PREP 20MIN, TOTAL 20MIN

INGREDIENTS

1 tbsp cuttlefish ink
2 ½ cups soft wheat TIPO "OO" flour
1 cup fine semolina flour
4 large eggs
1 tbsp virgin olive oil
1 tsp kosher salt

CHEF SECRETS

"If you have flour and eggs you can make most any pasta. It's much easier than most people think and the flavor and texture is far superior to store bought pasta and it's definitely healthier because it doesn't include any of the chemicals and preservatives they add to pre-made pasta."

"Locating the specific ingredients for squid ink pasta can be a challenge but the added taste is well worth the effort. I always use squid ink pasta for any seafood pasta dishes. It's the perfect compliment and because most people have never enjoyed it, adds a bit of intrigue to your dish."

"For those who are a bit squeamish about eating something with squid ink, simply use the name of my dish (which by the way is what it is called in Italy) 'Nero di Seppia Pasta.' This translates into Cuttlefish Ink Pasta but sounds much more palatable. And, don't worry because, once they've tasted it, they'll be hooked!"

Continued on next page

INSTRUCTIONS

If you are making your dough by hand

In a bowl, mix your eggs and cuttlefish ink, olive oil, and kosher salt until fully incorporated. Don't beat

Add your soft wheat TIPO "OO" flour and fine semolina flours into a mixing bowl with paddle and mix to incorporate

Mound your combined flour on a work surface. Form a well in the center

Pour your egg mixture into your flour well

Combine your egg mixture with your flour. Use one hand to mix and the other hand to keep the flour mound steady. Knead to form a dough

Knead your dough until it becomes smooth, approx. 8 to 10 minutes. If the dough becomes too sticky, simply add a bit more flour. Form your dough into a ball and wrap it in plastic wrap. Refrigerate for 1 hour

Cut each of your dough balls into quarters. Press and flatten one piece of dough to about 3/8-inch thick

Dust of excess flour and then fold the rolled dough into thirds, keeping the width of the piece approx. 5"

Lightly dust with more flour as needed. Repeat this rolling and folding until your dough is smooth

Once your dough is smooth, form it into the desired thickness for the type of macaroni/spaghetti you are creating

Continued on next page

ITALY

SQUID INK PASTA

CONTINUED

If you are using a tabletop mixer with a pasta attachment

Combine your two flours, virgin olive oil, and kosher salt in your mixer with a paddle and mix until a dough is formed. Replace your paddle with a dough hook and mix on slow speed until your dough is smooth and elastic, aprox 10 minutes

If your dough is still dry or crumbly, add 1 or 2 tsps of water. If your dough, is sticky, add in some flour until it is smooth

Press your dough into a ball. Split your ball in half and flatten your ball by hand. Wrap your dough in plastic wrap. Refrigerate for 1 hour

Attach your flat roller to your mixer and adjust your roller thickness to 1 (the thickest setting)

Remove your dough from the refrigerator and let warm to room temperature

Cut each of your dough balls into quarters. Flatten each piece of dough to about 3/8" thick. Turn on the mixer to low speed and feed your dough through the rollers

Dust of any excess flour and then fold your rolled dough into thirds. Make sure you keep the width of each piece approx. 5"

Lightly dust with a bit of flour and feed your dough through the rollers again. Repeat this rolling and folding process two more times (or until the dough is smooth. Once your dough is smooth, end your folding, and begin to increase your roller settings one notch at a time until you reach your desired thinness. Lightly flour your rolled dough

Continued on next page

CHEF SECRETS (CONTINUED)

"I've always found the making of pasta to be therapeutic. I put on Bocelli, slip on my AirPods and find a pace that suits me and knead away."

"If you have the time to make your own pasta, you need to venture on in. You'll find it not only an extremely rewarding experience but also healthier and most importantly delicious. One word of caution, be prepared, once you, your family or guests have enjoyed your homemade pasta, they'll NEVER want to go back!"

"As I mentioned, you may have a challenge locating the right ingredients for this recipe. You won't find cuttlefish ink in most grocery stores but will find it in any good Italian grocery store or online at [Marky's.](#) You should be able to find [semolina](#) flour locally. If you're having a problem finding it locally, you can find it and the soft wheat TIPO 'OO' flour online at the [Italian Food Online Store.](#)"

"One final note…. to make your pasta authentic, DON'T substitute the flours that are specified. If you're going to make a 'great' dish, it's always the little things that separate the 'good' dishes from the 'great' dishes. Make sure your dish is 'great' by always using the best!"

Continued on next page

ITALY

SQUID INK PASTA

CONTINUED

Replace your roller attachment your choice of cutting attachment. Feed each rolled piece of dough through your cutter

Dust your pasta liberally with a combined mix of your soft wheat TIPO "OO" flour and semolina flour and then spread your pasta out to dry

You can use your pasta immediately or freeze it for up to 30 days

Cooking instructions
Cautionary note: Fresh pasta cooks much faster than store purchased dried pastas. Cook in a pot of boiling salted water for only about 2-3 minutes or until al dente

CHEF SECRETS (CONTINUED)

"As with any dish where I use olive oil, for your dough, choose 'early harvest' olive oil in a dark bottle (a dark bottle preserves your oil longer). 'Early harvest' olive oil is oil squeezed from the olive before the olive is ripe. An unripe olive yields much less olive oil but much higher quality oil, so it will be expensive but well worth the price. You can find a great early harvest olive oil Formaggio Kitchen."

Chef J Stephen

Italy

Homemade Pasta

Serves 5, Prep 15min, Total 20min

Instructions

If you are making your dough by hand

In a bowl, mix your eggs, olive oil, and kosher salt until fully incorporated. Don't beat

In a mixing bowl with paddle, mix your soft wheat TIPO "OO" flour and fine semolina flours. Mix to fully incorporate

Mound your combined flour on a work surface. Form a well in the center

Pour your egg mix into your flour well

Combine your egg mix with your flour. Use one hand to mix and the other hand to keep the flour mound steady. Knead to form a dough

Knead your dough until it becomes smooth, approx. 8 to 10 minutes. If the dough becomes too sticky, simply add a bit more flour. Form your dough into a ball and wrap it in plastic wrap. Refrigerate for 1 hour

Cut each of your dough balls into quarters. Press and flatten one piece of dough to about 3/8-inch thick

Dust of excess flour and then fold the rolled dough into thirds, keeping the width of the piece approx. 5"

Lightly dust with more flour as needed. Repeat this rolling and folding until your dough is smooth

Once your dough is smooth, form it into the desired thickness for the type of macaroni/spaghetti you are creating

Ingredients

Dough
2 ½ cups soft wheat TIPO "OO" flour
1 cup fine semolina flour
4 large eggs
1 tbsp virgin olive oil
1 tsp kosher salt

Chef Secrets

"If you have flour and eggs you can make most any pasta. If you have a tabletop mixer with the pasta attachments, it's a breeze. Even with a manual mixer (as shown in my photo) it's not hard to make. And what you're making is something that is so far superior to pre-made store bought dried pasta that, once you make it, you'll never go back.

"An added benefit is that it's definitely healthier because it doesn't include any of the chemicals and preservatives they add to pre-made pasta and it is lower in carbs!"

"As with any dish where I use olive oil, for my dough, choose 'early harvest' olive oil in a dark bottle (a dark bottle preserves your oil longer). 'Early harvest' olive oil is oil squeezed from the olive before the olive is ripe. An unripe olive yields much less olive oil but much higher quality oil, so it will be expensive but well worth the price. You can find a great early harvest olive oil [Formaggio Kitchen](.)."

Chef J Stephen

Italy

Homemade Pasta

Instructions

If you are using a tabletop mixer with a pasta attachment

Combine your two flours, your virgin olive oil, and kosher salt in your mixer with a paddle and mix until a dough is formed. Replace your paddle with a dough hook and mix on slow speed until your dough is smooth and elastic, Aprox 10 minutes

If your dough is still dry or crumbly, add 1 or 2 tsps of water. If your dough, is overly sticky, add in some flour until it is smooth

Press your dough into a ball. Split your ball in half and flatten your ball by hand. Wrap your dough in plastic wrap. Refrigerate for 1 hour

Attach your flat roller to your mixer and adjust your roller thickness to 1 (the thickest setting)

Remove your dough from the refrigerator and let warm to room temperature

Cut each of your dough balls into quarters. Flatten each piece of dough to about 3/8" thick. Turn on the mixer to low speed and feed your dough through the rollers.

Chef Secrets (continued)

"If you have looked at a few of my recipes, you'll notice I use several different types of salt. I use different salt's for different purposes. I use a kosher salt if you're looking for robust flavor burst. It's also less likely to contain additives like anti-caking agents and iodine. I use a Fleur de Sel French Sea Salt because of its much higher amount of moisture than common salt (up to 10% as compared to 0.5% for common salt). This allows the crystals to stick together in snowflake-like forms which makes it taste even saltier than table salt. It's the perfect salt for a salty/sweet combination. Common table salt is fine for most other offerings. The bottom line… don't automatically grab the table salt. Instead, use the salt that fits the dish."

Chef J Stephen

ENGLAND

Braised Brisket & Wild Mushrooms

Serves 2, Prep 10min, Total 1hour 30min

Instructions

Brisket & Vegetables

Seam and de-fat your brisket, reserving half of the fat

Place your avocado oil in a large skillet on high heat. Once heated, sear your brisket on both sides

Peel your large carrot and onion and cut to large dice sizes

Tournée your red potatoes and slice your mushrooms

Remove your brisket and in the same pan, caramelize your onions and diced carrots to add color

Place your brisket in a pot, add your beef broth, bring to a boil and then reduce to a simmer. Cover and let cook for 1 ½ hours

Render your reserved fat and your AP flour to make a roux

Steam your red potatoes and baby carrots

Place your unsalted butter in a small skillet on medium heat. When the butter has melted, add your mushrooms. Cook until brown

Drain your mushrooms once cooked

Continued on next page

Ingredients

Brisket & Vegetables
12 ounces beef brisket
6 ounces beef broth
4 baby carrots
1 large fresh carrot (peeled)
¼ cup AP (all purpose) flour
1 lb cremini mushrooms
1 white onion
10 fresh red potatoes
¼ tsp black pepper
¼ tsp kosher salt
1 tbsp avocado oil
1 tbsp unsalted butter

White Rice
1 cup long-grain white rice
½ tsp kosher salt
1 ½ cups water

Chef Secrets

"Make sure you get a good piece of brisket from your local butcher. Quality cuts of brisket have not only a much improved flavor, but also is a more tender piece of meat than inferior cuts often found at your grocery store."

"You'll notice that I instruct you to 'sear' your meat. Searing is where you heat your pan to a high temperature and briefly 'sear' each sides of your meat. This browns the outsides, but leaves the insides rare."

Continued on next page

ENGLAND

BRAISED BRISKET & WILD MUSHROOMS

CONTINUED

CHEF SECRETS (CONTINUED)

"Tournée is French for the word 'turned.' The term refers to a method of cutting your potatoes into oblong, seven-sided football-like shapes. You Tournée to assure your potatoes cook more evenly."

"A roux is a mixture of fat and flour used in making a sauce."

"You'll notice that I 'NEVER' use vegetable oil. It's not made from vegetables and is not healthy. DON'T use it! Avocado oil is extremely high in oleic acid, which protects you against heart disease, diabetes, obesity, and high blood pressure. Although olive oil has the best flavor profile of all the oils, because avocado oil offers the same oleic acid benefits, robust anti-inflammatory qualities, AND has a relatively high 'smoke point', it should be your every day oil of choice."

Chef J Stephen

Remove your brisket from the pot. Remove half the remaining liquid and let cool

Puree the remaining liquid with your onions and carrots

With your roux, tighten your sauce

Add your puree and let simmer for 20 minutes

White Rice
In a medium saucepan, bring your water to a boil

Stir in your rice and salt, and return to a boil over medium-high heat

Reduce the heat to a simmer, cover, and cook until your rice is tender and has absorbed all the liquid, approx. 18 minutes

When your rice has cooked, remove it from the heat and let it steam, covered, for 8 minutes

Plating your dish
Slice your brisket to your desired thickness

Place your bed of rice on your plate

Remove and combine all your ingredients and place on your bed of rice

FRANCE

Veal Scaloppine a la Marsala

Serves 8, Prep 10min, Total 30min

Instructions

Pound your veal cutlets to the desired thickness

Place your AP flour in a large mixing bowl

Dredge your cutlets on both sides in the AP flour

Slice your mushrooms into quarters

Place your unsalted butter and virgin olive oil in a medium sized skillet on medium heat

When your butter is completely melted, add your sliced mushrooms

Sauté over medium heat until lightly brown

When your mushrooms have browned, add your veal and prosciutto

Sauté for 3 minutes

Turn your veal and prosciutto over and add your garlic, rosemary, kosher salt, and black pepper

Cook on medium heat for 2 more minutes

Add your Marsala wine and cover

Sauté on medium heat for 2 more minutes

Remove all your ingredients and add your peas and parsley

Sauté until your peas are cooked

Combine and serve

Ingredients

8 veal cutlets
1 cup AP (all purpose) flour
3 tbsp unsalted butter
1 tbsp virgin olive oil
4 slices prosciutto (thinly sliced)
½ fresh garlic clove (mashed)
½ tsp fresh rosemary (crumbled)
¼ tsp kosher salt
¼ tsp black pepper
3 tbsp Marsala wine
1 cup baby peas
4 sprigs fresh parsley (chopped)

Chef Secrets (continued)

"Always use 'early harvest' olive oil in a dark bottle (a dark bottle preserves your oil longer). 'Early harvest' olive oil is oil squeezed from the olive before the olive is ripe. An unripe olive yields much less olive oil but much higher quality oil, so it will be expensive but well worth the price. You can find a great early harvest olive oil Formaggio Kitchen."

"If you can find fresh peas at the farmers market, go for it. If not, frozen peas will work just fine."

"Make sure you get good pieces of veal and fresh prosciutto. Quality cuts of veal have a much improved mouth feel over inferior cuts. Fresh prosciutto adds a flavor to your dish that you won't find in deli packed prosciutto."

Chef J Stephen

HUNGARY

HUNGARIAN BEEF STROGANOFF

SERVES 4, PREP 20MIN, TOTAL 60MIN

INGREDIENTS

Gravy
2 tbsp beef drippings *(If you don't have beef drippings, you can substitute 1 beef bouillon cube (crushed)*
2 tbsp unsalted butter
2 tbsp AP (all purpose) flour
1 cup whole milk
1 cup water
½ tsp salt
½ tsp ground black pepper
¼ cup beef stock

Stroganoff
2 large white onions
1 lb fresh criminology mushrooms
2 ¼ lbs beef round
¼ tsp kosher salt
¼ tsp black pepper
3 tbsp unsalted butter
1 tbsp avocado oil
1 cup sour cream

OPTION
1 lb egg noodles

CHEF SECRETS

"Although it's not the traditional way to make Hungarian Beef Stroganoff, in the States, it's quite common to add noodles. Either way, it's a great traditional dish on a cold winter day."

Chef J Stephen

INSTRUCTIONS

Gravy
Drain off 2 tablespoons of the drippings from your fresh made beef dish. Place in a medium sauce pan over medium heat

Evenly sprinkle your flour over the drippings. Cook while continually stirring until brown

Slowly stir in your milk, whisking to assure all of the meaty drippings are fully incorporated. Once fully incorporated, slowly whisk in your water

Increase the heat to medium-high and cook, stirring continually, until your gravy thickens, approx. 10 minutes

Add your salt and black pepper

You can refrigerate your gravy for 6 days or freeze for 90 days

Stroganoff
Slice your white onions (Julianne style)

Slice your criminology mushrooms (quartered)

Place your unsalted butter in a medium sized skillet on medium heat

When your butter is completely melted, add your sliced mushrooms. Sauté over medium heat until mushrooms are lightly brown

Add your sliced onions. Sauté your onions until they are translucent (don't brown your onions)

Continued on next page

HUNGARY

HUNGARIAN BEEF STROGANOFF
CONTINUED

Remove your onions and mushrooms from the skillet. Add your avocado oil to the skillet. Put on high heat

When your oil is hot, cut bite sized strips of your beef in half. Place in skillet and sear briefly on both sides. DO NOT OVERCOOK

Remove your beef from the skillet. Add your beef droppings, sour cream, and beef stock. Bring to a simmer

Turn your heat to low and add your brown gravy, and beef. Simmer for approx. 20 minutes, or until your sauce has thickened and your steak is tender

Egg Noodles
If you're adding egg noodles to your dish, now is the time to do it

Bring a large pot of salted water to a boil and cook your egg noodles according to the package instructions

Once your sauce has thickened and your steak is cooked through, add your egg noodles in with the sauce until all is completely combined

Season to taste with your salt and black pepper

CHEF SECRETS (CONTINUED)

"Most people use canola or vegetable oil when they sauté. I always use avocado oil. Why? Simple, vegetable oil is not made from vegetables and is not healthy. DON'T use it! Canola Oil, because of its high 'smoke point' is a good oil to use when you're cooking especially when using high-temperatures but it has no nutritional value. Avocado oil, because it is extremely high in oleic acid, which protects you against heart disease, diabetes, obesity, and high blood pressure is the healthiest oil to use when 'cooking'."

"Although olive oil has the best flavor profile of all the oils, because avocado oil offers the same oleic acid benefits, robust anti-inflammatory qualities, AND has a relatively high 'smoke point', it should be your every day 'cooking' oil of choice. Save your olive oil for any fresh, uncooked dishes like salads and dump all your other oils."

Chef J Stephen

UNITED STATES

TURKEY TETRAZZINI

Serves 8, Prep 20min, Total 1hour 15min

INSTRUCTIONS

Pre-heat your oven to 350°

Slice your mushrooms into quarters

Place your unsalted butter and virgin olive oil in a large sized skillet on medium heat

When your butter is completely melted, add your sliced mushrooms. Cook until slightly brown

Bring a large pot of salted water to a boil and cook your linguine spaghetti according to the package instructions

When your mushrooms and linguine spaghetti are done, mix your chicken noodle soup and sour cream together in a large casserole dish

Add your linguine spaghetti and turkey to the mix

Bake until bubbly, approx. 1 hour

Top with fresh parmesan and fresh parsley

Season to taste with your salt and black pepper

You can refrigerate for 4 days or freeze up to 90 days

INGREDIENTS

2 tbsp unsalted butter
1 tbsp virgin olive oil
2 lbs linguine spaghetti
3 cans chicken noodle soup (family size 44.8 ounces)
40 ounces sour cream
2 lbs fresh mushrooms (diced)
6 cups cooked turkey (chopped)
1 cup fresh parmesan (grated)
¼ tsp table salt
¼ tsp white pepper
½ cup fresh parsley (chopped)

CHEF SECRETS

"What a great dish to make. It's not only great to use up all your leftover turkey but also is easy to make and freezes well for later use."

"You can make your own chicken soup and linguine spaghetti for this dish but that not only defeats the purpose of it being an easy dish to make but also doesn't really make that much a difference in the end result."

"Always use 'early harvest' olive oil in a dark bottle (a dark bottle preserves your oil longer). 'Early harvest' olive oil is oil squeezed from the olive before the olive is ripe. An unripe olive yields much less olive oil but much higher quality oil, so it will be expensive but well worth the price. You can find a great early harvest olive oil Formaggio Kitchen."

Chef J Stephen

POLAND

POLISH PIEROGIES

SERVES 4, PREP 45MIN, TOTAL 1HOUR 10MIN

INGREDIENTS

Dough
2 cups AP (all purpose) flour
½ tsp table salt
1 large egg
½ cup sour cream
4 tbsp unsalted butter (softened)

Potato Filling
½ cup mashed potatoes (warm)
½ cup sharp cheddar cheese (shredded)

Farmers Cheese Filling
5¼ ounces farmers cheese

Garnish/Topping
4 tbsp unsalted butter
2 medium shallots (diced)
2 tbsp sour cream
2 tbsp table salt

CHEF SECRETS

"I have fond memories of Polish pierogies. My grandmother hand-made them for Thanksgiving every year. Although in Poland, pierogies come in a myriad of fillings, my grandmother made the two most traditional fillings, farmers cheese and potato. To this day, that's what I have always offered at my bistros."

"It's not always easy to find real farmers cheese but you can find it at Central Market, HEB, and online at Russian Food States."

INSTRUCTIONS

Dough
Mound your AP flour and table salt together on a work surface. Form a well in the center

Add your large egg into your flour well

Combine your egg with your flour. Use one hand to mix and the other hand to keep the flour mound steady. Don't worry, your dough will be lumpy at this stage

Knead in your sour cream and soft butter until your dough is a sticky ball, approx. 6 minutes

Using just your hands, knead and fold your dough without adding additional flour until your dough becomes less sticky but is still moist

Wrap your dough in plastic wrap and refrigerate for 60 minutes. You can keep it refrigerated for up to 2 days if need be

Potato Filling
Combine your warm mashed potatoes (check out my home-made mashed potato recipe) and sharp cheddar cheese. Stir and mash until the cheese is melted and the filling is cool to the touch. Adjust your seasonings with salt and pepper

Pierogi Finish
With a 2" round cutter to cut circles of dough, roll half of your dough ⅛" thick. Repeat with the other half of the dough

Place 1 ½ tsp of filling on each round of dough. Gently fold the dough over, forming a pocket around the filling. Pinch the edges of each pierogi to seal, then seal again with the tines of a fork. Make sure your seals are tight

Continued on next page

Continued on next page

POLAND

POLISH PIEROGIES

CONTINUED

This is where you decide if you're going to eat all your pierogis or choose to freeze some. You can freeze your pierogies for 4 weeks, or refrigerate them uncooked for two days

To cook your pierogies, place a large sized pot filled with water and 2 tbsp of table salt on high flame. Bring to a boil

Carefully place a maximum of 12 pierogis at a time in the boiling water. (make sure you keep your cheese filled pierogis separate from your potato pierogis in order to plate them by choice or in an even distribution

When your pierogi's float, they're done. Carefully remove them from the boiling water with a slotted spoon and add the next batch into the water. Repeat until all your pierogis are cooked

Plate and top liberally with unsalted butter and a side of sour cream and sliced shallots

Save any cooked pierogies that are not eaten. You can pan fry them until golden brown in butter for a delicious side dish. My family always have any leftover pierogies pan fried, along with eggs and any leftover kielbasa for breakfast the next morning.

You can refrigerate your cooked pierogies for up to 3 days

CHEF SECRETS (CONTINUED)

"Of course I would recommend you make homemade mashed potatoes because you'll always have a need for mashed potatoes whether it be for pierogies or not."

"You may have noticed that I haven't recommended that you make your own farmers cheese. Although we always made our own farmers cheese at home when we made our pierogies, it's a time consuming process and it's one of the only recipes I have that specify its use and so, feel free to purchase your farmers cheese from a reputable cheesemaker like I mentioned in the previous page."

"If you would like to assure your dish is even more traditionally Polish, add a side of kielbasa sausage and a dab of spicy deli mustard and you'll be enjoying a traditional Polish dinner. Don't choose the kielbasa at the grocery store. It's not close to 'real' kielbasa. Instead, you can find an authentic Polish sausage at many (but not all) butchers or online at Piast Meats & Provisions."

Chef J Stephen

UNITED STATES

HJ (KINDA) FRIED CLAMS

SERVES 4, PREP 15MIN, TOTAL 30MIN

INGREDIENTS

1 cup evaporated milk
1 cup whole milk
1 large egg
¼ tsp Madagascar bourbon vanilla
¼ tsp table salt
¼ tsp black pepper
4 dozen freshly shucked clams*
1 cup cake flour
1 cup yellow cornmeal
Avocado oil (for frying)

CHEF SECRETS

"When I was growing up there were thousands of Howard Johnson's restaurants spread out across the country. They were famous for several things."

- *Their orange roofs*
- *Their 28 flavors of ice cream (yes you young-un's, believe it or not, back than, most places only served vanilla, chocolate and strawberry - Oh the horror!)*
- *All you can eat fish fry's on Fridays*
- *All you can eat fried clams on Wednesdays*

"NO ONE back then or to this day has made fried clams like Howard Johnson's! For years, I've played around trying to duplicate their recipe with varying levels of success."

"This recipe is as close as I can get. You oldsters will relish the days when the family hopped in your 57 chevy and hauled down to enjoy your HJ's feast! For everyone else, know that although it may not reach the perfection of a trip to HJ's, it's as close as you'll ever get to nirvana on a plate!"

Chef J Stephen

INSTRUCTIONS

Combine your
1 cup evaporated milk
1 cup whole milk
1 large egg
¼ tsp Madagascar bourbon vanilla
¼ tsp table salt
¼ tsp black pepper

Soak your 4 dozen freshly shucked clams in your combined mix

Combine your
1 cup cake flour
1 cup yellow cornmeal

Coat your clams in your flour mixture for a light but thorough coverage

Gently shake off any excess flour and fry in your avocado oil until golden brown

Serve with French-fried potatoes and tartar sauce

BTW: (you can find a great recipe for French-fries on my Paulina Potato French-fries recipe in this book)

* If you want to match the great Howard Johnson's clam dish you'll be in for a challenging journey. Howard Johnson's used fried clam strips made from the "foot" of hard-shelled sea clams. They are not easy to find and availability is usually limited if you're lucky enough to locate them at all. The closer you can get to this type of clam, the closer you'll get to the original offering..

Chef J Stephen

SPAIN

SPANISH PORK BITES

SERVES 4, PREP 25MIN, TOTAL 50MIN

INSTRUCTIONS

In a medium bowl, combine the coriander, cumin, paprika, salt, and pepper

Add the pork and toss to coat evenly, rub the spices into the meat until dry rub is completely absorbed. Rest at room temperature for 45 minutes

In a small skillet on medium heat, heat 2 tbsp of your olive oil and your finely grated garlic

In another bowl, combine your lemon juice and honey. Set aside

In a large skillet over high heat, heat 2 tbsp of avocado oil. Add your pork in a single layer. DO NOT MOVE until browned on one side, approx. 3 minutes. Flip your pork and continue to cook, turning occasionally, until cooked through and browned on all sides, approx. 3 minutes

Take off the heat, and pour your lemon juice, honey, and olive oil/garlic mixture over the meat

Toss to evenly coat, then transfer to your serving platter

Sprinkle your oregano over the pork and drizzle with the remaining 1 tbsp of olive oil

Top with your sesame seeds and sliced scallion

Serve with lemon wedges

INGREDIENTS

1½ tsp ground coriander
1½ tsp ground cumin
1½ tsp smoked paprika
¾ tsp kosher salt
¾ tsp black pepper
1 - lb pork tenderloin, trimmed and cut into 1½ inch pieces
1 tbsp lemon juice,
4 lemon wedges (for serving)
1 tbsp honey
1 large garlic clove (finely grated)
3 tbsp's extra virgin olive oil
2 tbsp's avocado oil
1 tbsp chopped fresh oregano
1 tbsp toasted sesame seeds
1 fresh scallion

CHEF SECRETS

The two keys to this dish is to make sure the dry rub has thoroughly penetrated the pork and make sure you deeply brown the pork on all sides.

Although any rice will do, this dish is traditionally served over basmati rice and green salad.

This dish also makes great shish kabobs.

Chef J Stephen

SIDE DISHES

"You can make a great main course, but if you saddle it with a canned, frozen or poorly made side, you can ruin the whole meal. Not only should your side be unique, it should also be presented well. You need to remember that it's part of the whole package."

"In this section, I've included several ways to make potatoes a great Risotto and one of the most popular side dishes in my Dallas bistro, my Baleada Jalapeño Grits. Although they are limited in quantity, they are truly special and will definitely compliment many of the main course dishes in my book. In addition, they are international in flavor, coming from not only the States but also Honduras, Italy, and Cuba."

Chef J Stephen

UNITED STATES

MASHED POTATOES

Serves 10, Prep 25min, Total 50min

INGREDIENTS

- 2 ½ lbs Russet potatoes
- 2 ½ lbs Yukon Gold potatoes
- 2 large clove fresh garlic (minced)
- 3 tsp sea salt
- 6 tbsp unsalted butter
- 1 cup whole milk
- 4 ounces cream cheese (room temperature)
- ¼ tsp white pepper
- 6 cups water

INSTRUCTIONS

Cut your potatoes into evenly-sized chunks, about an inch or so thick

Place your potatoes in a large pot. Fill with water. Your water should be 2" above your potatoes

While stirring, add your garlic and 1 tsp (only) of sea salt

Cook on high heat until the water comes to a boil. Reduce your heat to maintain a simmering boil. Cook for approx. 12 minutes (or until a knife can go through the center of your potatoes easily)

While your potatoes are boiling is the ideal time to make your butter mix. To do this, place your unsalted butter, whole milk, and remaining 2 tsp of sea salt in a small sauce pan on medium heat until the butter has melted. DO NOT BOIL THE MILK. Set aside

Drain your water keeping your potatoes in the pot. Set your heat on low for approx. 2 minutes while you shift your potatoes carefully (so that no single potato stays on the bottom of the pot too long) to steam dry your potatoes. Remove from flame

Mash your potatoes with a potato masher to your desired consistency (smooth or lumpy)

Once your potatoes have been mashed, pour in half your butter mix and fold in with a wooden spoon. Stir in until potatoes have soaked up most of the liquid. Repeat with the remaining half of your butter mix. DON'T OVER MIX

Season with your salt and pepper

You can refrigerate for up to 6 days

CHEF SECRETS

"There are so many ways of making mashed potatoes. Some folks like them lumpy, others creamy and still others, instant from the box. I always like to make my mashed potatoes from scratch because it's the only way to get that fresh potato flavor. I also prefer my mashed potatoes a bit lumpy, although some of my recipes call for 'creamy' mashed potatoes. Lumpy or creamy is more about how you mix your potatoes versus the specific recipe."

"Make sure you combine the two potato types. (As an alternative to mashed potatoes, check out my cauliflower mashed potatoes recipe in this book)."

"I prefer a 50/50 mix of Russet which are starchy and Yukon Golds which are buttery for my mashed potatoes. I think it makes a well-balanced mashed potato."

Chef J Stephen

UNITED STATES

CAULIFLOWER MASHED POTATOES

SERVES 10, PREP 55MIN, TOTAL 20MIN

INGREDIENTS

3 heads of fresh cauliflower
1 ½ ounces fresh chives
5 ounces sour cream
4 ounces sharp cheddar cheese (shredded)
½ tbsp white pepper
1 ½ ounces chopped chives
1 tbsp kosher salt
3 tbsp unsalted butter
3 ounces whole milk

Garnish
1 tbsp (per serving) unsalted butter (or gravy)
¼ tsp (per serving) kosher salt
¼ tsp (per serving) black pepper

CHEF SECRETS

"There's nothing healthier then cauliflower mashed potatoes and they're just as great tasting as mashed potatoes (see my mashed potatoes recipe in this book)."

*"There are two keys to great Cauliflower mashed potatoes.
(1) Make sure you squeeze all the water out after they have been microwaved.
(2) The more you mix them in the food processor the creamier they will be. In addition, you can add a bit more whole milk to add creaminess."*

"How good are they? Well, I teach healthy eating to elementary school children and I often give them cauliflower mashed potatoes and they NEVER can tell the difference. I also serve them at my bistro and they're always a big hit!"

Chef J Stephen

INSTRUCTIONS

Cut your heads of cauliflower into florets

Chop your fresh chives

Place your cauliflower florets into a large plastic or glass bowl and cover with clear wrap

Place your bowl into the microwave, steam until fork tender approx. 2 sets of 10 minutes

Cool your steamed cauliflower and squeeze out all water with a towel

Place your cauliflower in a food processor

Add your sour cream, sharp cheddar cheese, white pepper, chopped chives, kosher salt, unsalted butter, and whole milk

Mix until creamy smooth

Garnish with your choice of unsalted butter and parsley or gravy (see my gravy recipe)

Season with salt and pepper

You can refrigerate for up to 6 days

UNITED STATES

ROSEMARY FINGERLING POTATOES

Serves 6, Prep 55min, Total 20min

INGREDIENTS

2 lbs fingerling potatoes (assorted colors)
20 ounces water
4 tbsp virgin olive oil
¼ tsp black pepper
½ tsp kosher salt
2 tsp fresh minced garlic
2 tbsp fresh rosemary (chopped)

Garnish
1 sprig (per serving) fresh parsley

CHEF SECRETS

"Most people make boiled fingerling potatoes as a companion to seafood. To me they're good, but a bit too plain. I took a slightly different twist on the boil potato dish by adding a few additional seasonings to zip up the dish."

Chef J Stephen

INSTRUCTIONS

Preheat your oven to 400°

Scrub your fingerling potatoes under cool water to clean

Place cold water in a large pot (should be 2" over potatoes)

Place on high heat and bring to a boil

Add your washed fingerling potatoes to the pot

Cook for approx. 10 minutes (or until a knife can go through the center of your potatoes easily)

Drain thoroughly

While your potatoes are boiling, place your virgin olive oil, minced garlic, fresh rosemary, black pepper, and kosher salt mix, in a large mixing bowl

Coat your drained potatoes in the mix, making sure that all potatoes are evenly coated

Place your potatoes in a large casserole dish and place in your pre-heated oven for 10 minutes at 400°

You can refrigerate for up to 6 days

UNITED STATES

ROASTED QUARTERED POTATOES

Serves 10, Prep 55min, Total 20min

Ingredients

4 large russet potatoes
4 tbsp virgin olive oil
¼ tsp black pepper
½ tsp kosher salt
2 tsp fresh minced garlic

Garnish
1 sprig (per serving) fresh parsley

Instructions

Preheat your oven to 375°

Place your virgin olive oil, minced garlic, black pepper, and kosher salt mix, in a medium bowl. Mix thoroughly

Slice your russet potatoes into ⅛ size pieces (see photo)

Toss your sliced potatoes gently in the virgin olive oil mix making sure that all the potatoes are evenly coated

Place potatoes in a large glass casserole dish

Cook at 375° for approx. 45 minutes (or until crispy)

You can refrigerate for up to 6 days

Chef Secrets

"Every Christmas our family tradition is to enjoy prime ribs, roasted potatoes and Yorkshire pudding (the finest dish to ever come out of Great Britain). These are most assuredly my favorite way to enjoy potatoes. Interestingly, they are called quartered potatoes but are actually cut in eighths. I have no idea why but they're fantastic nonetheless."

"Always choose 'early harvest' olive oil in a dark bottle (a dark bottle preserves your oil longer). 'Early harvest' olive oil is oil squeezed from the olive before the olive is ripe. An unripe olive yields much less olive oil but much higher quality oil, so it will be expensive but well worth the price. You can find a great early harvest olive oil Formaggio Kitchen."

Chef J Stephen

ITALY

RISOTTO

SERVES 10, PREP 55MIN, TOTAL 20MIN

INSTRUCTIONS

In a medium saucepan over medium heat, bring your chicken stock to a simmer. Reduce the heat to low to keep warm

In a large skillet heat your unsalted butter and avocado oil. Once the butter has melted and the oil/butter combo is hot, add your arborio rice

Stir to assure an even coating of your rice, approx. 2 minutes

Add a ½ cup of your warm chicken broth while continuing to stir. Once it has thoroughly mixed, let it rest while the broth is mostly absorbed, approx. 3 minutes

Once absorbed, stir while adding another cup of your warmed chicken broth, while continually stirring

Cook (do not stir) until the chicken broth is entirely absorbed

Repeat this procedure until approx. ½ cup of your chicken broth remains (total cook time should be approx.15 minutes)

Turn off heat

Add your kosher salt, whatever remains of your chicken broth, your grated parmesan and gruyere cheese

Stir gently to fully incorporate the cheese assuring that the cheese has fully melted into the rice

Garnish with chopped chives

Serve immediately

INGREDIENTS

32 ounces unsalted chicken stock
1 tbsp unsalted butter
1 tbsp avocado oil
1 cup Arborio rice
¼ tsp kosher salt
¼ cup parmigiano-reggiano cheese (grated)
¼ cup gruyere cheese (shredded)

Garnish
1 fresh chive (chopped)

CHEF SECRETS

"This is a dish that your timing between stages has to be watched closely to assure a rich creamy texture. But, if you do it right, this creamy delight is well worth the trouble. And besides, no one else will be serving it so you'll definitely stand out from the crowd."

"I always use Parmigiano Reggiano Stravecchio cheese, that I grind myself. You can find a good one at igourmet. If you can't find that, most any Parmigiano Reggianos are not quite as good but will work fine. Get a quarter of a wheel and store it. It will keep well."

"Through the years, I have had many discussions with my bistro guests about the difference between 'imported' gruyere and 'domestic' gruyere. Trust me, although it will be the most expensive ingredient in your soup, the difference is like night and day. I ALWAYS use an 'imported' gruyere from France or Switzerland and you should too. You can find an excellent gruyere cheese at the gourmet food store."

Chef J Stephen

Cuba

Fried Plantains

SERVES 10, PREP 55MIN, TOTAL 20MIN

Ingredients

Santiago de Cuba Version
2 very ripe plantains
4 tbsp streusel
1 tbsp unsalted butter

Cinnamon Streusel
¼ lb unsalted butter
1 ounce cake flour (you can substitute A/P flour)
¼ lb dark brown Muscovado sugar
½ tbsp Saigon cinnamon

Habana Version
2 unripe plantains
4 tbsp avocado oil
1 tbsp sea salt

Chef Secrets

"Most people know of the Spanish influence in Cuba. Although the country is predominantly Spanish, what they don't know is that western Cuba has much more of a french influence in its dishes. This is most prominent in the way they prepare their fried plantains."

"In eastern Cuba's Habana, they are made as a savory dish, served alongside black beans and rice. In western Cuba's Santiago de Cuba, you'll find the sweet version where the plantains are served as a sweet dessert. I provide both versions for you to try. They both make excellent side dishes that are uniquely Caribbean."

Chef J Stephen

Instructions

Santiago de Cuba Version
Peel your very ripe plantains

Slice horizontally in half

Carefully spread a thick portion of your cinnamon streusel on both sides of your sliced plantain

Place your unsalted butter in a medium skillet on medium heat. When your butter has melted, place your plantains in the pan to fry. Turn to assure both sides are cooked

When golden brown remove and serve

Habana Version
Peel your unripe plantains

Slice your plantains vertically ¼" thick (will look like thick potato chips)

Place your avocado oil in a medium skillet on medium heat. When your oil begins to simmer, add your plantains. Turn to assure both sides are cooked

When golden brown remove, season with your sea salt, and serve

Streusel
Cut your unsalted butter into 4" squares and then place into a mixing bowl, combine your cake flour, dark brown Muscovado sugar, and Saigon cinnamon

Mix until all the lumps are gone and then add your unsalted butter to the mix. Mix until fully incorporated. (It will be course and granular)

Honduras

Baleada Jalapeño Grits

Serves 8, Prep 15min, Total 25min

Ingredients

10 ½ ounces pickled jalapeños
10 ½ ounces sour cream
10 ½ ounces mayonnaise
10 ½ ounces Tostito chips
1 tbsp kosher salt
¼ tsp black pepper
½ ounce Monterey Jack cheese

Garnish
1 sprig (per serving) fresh parsley or chives (chopped)

Chef Secrets

"Street vendors sell corn tortillas filled with this wonderfully, spicy filling. Not a true grits. This dish is more like a polenta. Since we added the cheese and serve it in a bowl, we decided to call it a grits. Whatever you call it, this has always been from the day of its introduction, by far the most popular side dish at my bistros.

My servers continually hear comments like 'I don't like grits, but these are the best grits I've ever had' or 'I've never had anything like this, they're great!' We even make a 'can't refuse' offer for those afraid to try. We'll pay for the dish if you don't like it. BTW: We have never had to make good on that offer!"

"One important note, you must use 'pickled' jalapeños (not fresh) to get the great taste."

Chef J Stephen

Instructions

Pre-heat your oven to 400°

Grits preparation
Place your tostito chips in your food blender and blend to a medium-fine grits texture

Place your chips in a large mixing bowl

Drain the juice from your pickled jalapeños

Place your drained jalapeños in your food blender and blend to a fine texture

In a large mixing bowl, combine your chopped jalapeños, sour cream, mayonnaise, kosher salt, black pepper, and your chopped Tostito chips

Blend thoroughly, until fully incorporated

Microwave Directions
Place each serving of your grits in small serving cup. Top with Monterey Jack cheese

Place in your microwave for 30 seconds. Torch your cheese topping and serve

Oven Directions
Place each serving of your grits in small oven safe ramekin cups. Top with Monterey Jack cheese

Bake until cheese topping has fully melted

Garnish with your choice of chopped parsley or chives

You can refrigerate for up to 6 days or freeze for 120 days

Switzerland

Baked Asparagus

Serves 4, Prep 15min, Total 25min

Instructions

Pre-heat your oven to 425°

*Zest your large lemon

Cut off the woody ends of your asparagus

Pour your virgin olive oil, black pepper, kosher salt, and your lemon zest into a medium bowl

Toss your asparagus in your virgin olive oil/lemon zest mix. Make sure you coat your asparagus thoroughly

Place your asparagus on your lined pan

Top with your shredded gruyere and parmesan cheeses

Place in your oven for 10-15 minutes (or until the largest asparagus stalk is fork tender)

Ingredients

1 bunch fresh asparagus
1 large lemon (zested)
¼ cup parmesan cheese (shredded)
¼ cup gruyere cheese (shredded)
¼ cup virgin olive oil
½ tsp black pepper
½ tsp kosher salt

Chef Secrets

"I always use Parmigiano Reggiano Stravecchio cheese, that I grind myself. You can find a good one at [igourmet](). If you can't find that, most any Parmigiano Reggianos are not quite as good but will work fine. Get a quarter of a wheel and store it. It will keep well."

"Through the years, I have had many discussions with my bistro guests about the difference between 'imported' gruyere and 'domestic' gruyere. Trust me, although it will be the most expensive ingredient in your soup, the difference is like night and day. I ALWAYS use an 'imported' gruyere from France or Switzerland and you should too. You can find an excellent gruyere cheese at the [gourmet food store]()."

"Choose 'early harvest' olive oil in a dark bottle (a dark bottle preserves your oil longer). 'Early harvest' olive oil is oil squeezed from the olive before the olive is ripe. An unripe olive yields much less olive oil but much higher quality oil, so it will be expensive but well worth the price. You can find a great early harvest olive oil [Formaggio Kitchen]()."

*"Zest - scrape off the outer colored part of the peel of (a piece of citrus fruit) for use as flavoring. Make sure you don't scrape too deep to prevent bitterness."

Chef J Stephen

SWITZERLAND

MACARONI & CHEESE

SERVES 4, PREP 15MIN, TOTAL 25MIN

INGREDIENTS

12 ounces elbow macaroni *(To really make it special, check out my macaroni recipe and make your own)*
1 cup gruyere cheese (shredded)
1 cup cheddar cheese (shredded)
1 cup Monterey Jack cheese (shredded)
12 ounces evaporated milk
1 ½ cups whole milk
6 ounces Taylor ham
½ tsp dry mustard
¼ tsp kosher salt
¼ tsp black pepper
⅛ tsp fresh nutmeg (ground)
1 tbsp unsalted butter
Garnish
¼ tsp paprika
3 sprigs fresh parsley

CHEF SECRETS

"I always use Parmigiano Reggiano Stravecchio cheese, that I grind myself. You can find a good one at igourmet. If you can't find that, most any Parmigiano Reggiano are not quite as good but will work fine. Get a quarter of a wheel and store it. It will keep well."

"I ALWAYS use an 'imported' gruyere cheese from France or Switzerland and you should too. You can find an excellent gruyere cheese at the gourmet food store."

"Although it's not very common outside the NYC area Taylor ham is unlike any ham you've ever had. In order to make this dish special you MStatesT use Taylor ham. It's not easy to find locally purchased, but believe me, it's well worth the effort to locate and it keeps well. You can find it online at Mercado."

Chef J Stephen

INSTRUCTIONS

In order to make this right, you'll need a crock pot

Place your unsalted butter in a medium skillet on medium/high heat

Slice your Taylor ham into small strips

Place your Taylor ham in your skillet

Cook for 3 minutes stirring to assure all side of your ham are cooked

Spray the inside of your crock pot with pan spray

If you're making your own pasta, make sure it is thoroughly dried before using

Add and combine in your crock pot your macaroni, three cheeses, evaporated milk, and whole milk. Stir to combine

Cover and cook on low for approx. 1½ hours (or until your cheese is melted and your pasta is nearly al dente

Fold and stir in the dry mustard, ground nutmeg, kosher salt, Taylor ham, and black pepper

Mix in thoroughly to assure all your cheeses, dry ingredients, and Taylor ham are added and evenly distributed

Cook on low heat for another 30 minutes. Continue to check. When your macaroni is al dente, you're good to go. DO NOT OVERCOOK

Garnish with your paprika and fresh parsley

SANDWICHES

"The beauty of a sandwich is that you can enjoy a great sandwich any time of the day. Using fresh ingredients and a really good bread can make the difference from a so-so sandwich to a masterpiece."

"You'll notice that most of my sandwiches are hot. This goes back to my childhood. Because my mom had rheumatic fever as a child, she was often in and out of hospitals. During those times, my dad took over making our meals. My dad was no cook and besides, he had little time working, making our meals and herding us all to the hospital for visiting hours."

"Although he was pretty good at making breakfast, his idea of lunch and dinner was limited to bean soup or pea soup, made in giant pots that would last us for weeks and cold cut sandwiches (usually olive loaf or bologna). Because of this, you'll never find a bean soup, pea soup or cold cut sandwich in any of my recipe's. If you're looking for those soups or sandwiches, you'll have to hunt elsewhere. However, the sandwiches I do include are my favorite go-to sandwiches, which I think you'll find quite satisfying.. And besides, you won't have to repeat eating them, day after day!"

Chef J Stephen

FRANCE

CROQUE-MONSIEUR PROVENÇAL SANDWICH

SERVES 1, PREP 10MIN, TOTAL 15MIN

INGREDIENTS

2 slices sour dough bread
2 ounces imported gruyere cheese (shredded)
2 ounces taylor ham
1 tsp dijon mustard
1 tbsp béchamel*
¾ ounce unsalted butter
2 slices heirloom tomato
⅛ tsp table salt
Garnish
Chips and a pickle
* See my French Béchamel Sauce recipe

CHEF SECRETS

"There's a few key ingredients here that separate this sandwich from all others. The first is Taylor ham. It's absolutely unlike any other ham you've ever had. I use it not only here but in several dishes most notably my Taylor ham and egg sandwich. It's not very common outside the NYC area, but it's well worth the effort to locate and it keeps well. You can find it online at [Mercado](.)."

"The second ingredient is imported gruyere cheese. Through the years, I have had many discussions with my bistro guests about the difference between 'imported' gruyere and 'domestic' gruyere. Trust me, although it will be the most expensive ingredient in your sandwich, the difference is like night and day. I ALWAYS use an 'imported' gruyere from France or Switzerland and you should too. You can find an excellent gruyere cheese at the [gourmet food store](.)."

"The last is béchamel. Used in soufflé's, you can buy it online, BUT it's so much better home-made and it's a must have difference-maker in this sandwich."

Chef J Stephen

INSTRUCTIONS

Cut two thick slices of sour dough bread

Slice your Taylor ham into 5 thin slices

Cut 2 slices of a fresh heirloom tomato - medium thickness

Pre-heat your oven to 350° and a small skillet on medium heat

Place your béchamel sauce and dijon mustard in small microwavable bowl in your microwave. Set it for 10 seconds

Spread your heated béchamel/mustard sauce on each slice of your sour dough bread. Top with ½ of your shredded gruyere cheese. Then top that with your Taylor ham. Finally top that with your slices of tomato and a pinch of table salt

Spread unsalted butter on both sides of your sandwich

Place your sandwich on your preheated skillet for approx. 1-2 minutes on each side (or until lightly browned)

Remove your sandwich and top with your remaining shredded gruyere cheese

Place on your lined sheet pan in your pre-heated oven for approx. 6-10 minutes (or until cheese is melted)

Remove from your oven and plate

Garnish with chips and pickle

UNITED STATES

Taylor Ham & Egg Sandwich

Serves 1, Prep 50min, Total 10min

Ingredients

1 Kaiser roll (any hard roll will work)
1 ounce Taylor Ham (sliced ⅛" thick)
3 tbsp unsalted butter
2 large eggs
½ ounce gruyere cheese (shredded)

Chef Secrets

"There's not much to this sandwich but my regular bistro guests would go crazy if I didn't include it in my recipe book. It is by far the most popular breakfast dish we offered and it's quite simple to make as long as you use two key ingredients. Although it's not very common outside the NYC area, Taylor ham is unlike any ham you've ever had. In order to make a sandwich that your guests and family members will ask for over and over again, you MStatesT use Taylor ham. It's not easy to find locally, but believe me, it's well worth the effort to locate and it keeps well. You can find it online at Mercado."

'The second ingredient is the imported gruyere cheese. Through the years, I have had many discussions with my bistro guests about the difference between 'imported' gruyere and 'domestic' gruyere. Trust me, although it will be the most expensive ingredient in your sandwich, the difference is like night and day. I ALWAYS use an 'imported' gruyere from France or Switzerland and you should too. You can find an excellent gruyere cheese at the gourmet food store."

Chef J Stephen

Instructions

Pre-heat your oven to 350°

Slice your roll horizontally in half and butter both sides

Sprinkle a pinch of your gruyere cheese on both sides

Place your roll (open faced) in your oven and heat until your cheese has melted and your roll is slightly crisp

Place unsalted butter in a small skillet pan on medium heat

Place 2 - ⅛" slices of Taylor ham in your small skillet

Cook, continually flipping on both sides, until well done. (Helpful hint; make a couple of small slices on the outer edges towards the middle, but not all the way, of each slice to prevent your ham from curling up)

In another small skillet pan, place unsalted butter and set on medium flame

Place your two large eggs in your skillet pan

Cook "over easy" (yolks runny, egg whites NOT runny)

Place your cooked Taylor ham on the bottom of your toasted roll. Top your Taylor ham with your "over easy" cooked eggs

Cover your sandwich with the top of your roll, slice and serve

Italy

Tuscany Garden Sandwich

Serves 1, Prep 5min, Total 10min

Instructions

Pesto Spread
Place your pesto in a small ramekin. Add your virgin olive oil and stir with a spoon until fully incorporated

Sandwich
Pre-heat your oven to 350°

Slice your roll horizontally in half and place your roll (open faced) in your oven. Heat until your roll is crispy

Once your roll has been toasted, remove from the oven and spread your pesto on the toasted roll

Slice your fresh mozzarella into two ¼" slices

Layer, as shown, with 2 slices heirloom tomato and 2 slices fresh mozzarella

Sprinkle your kosher salt and black pepper on top of mozzarella/tomato

Close your sandwich and slice in half

Garnish with a sliced fresh strawberry, a bunch of red grapes, and an orange slice

Ingredients

Sandwich
1 Panini roll (any hard roll will work)
½ ounce pesto spread
2 ounces fresh mozzarella
¼ tsp kosher salt
¼ tsp black pepper

Pesto Spred
3 tbsp Pesto*
1 tbsp virgin olive oil

*See my pesto recipe

Chef Secrets

"A great light lunch sandwich that has three key ingredients. (1) Heirloom tomatoes - There's nothing like a fresh tomato and an heirloom tomato is the best of the best. Heirloom tomatoes offer interesting colors and a great 'old world' tomato taste that can no longer be found with the tomatoes found in todays farmers market or grocery stores. (2) Although you can easily buy pre-made pesto, it tastes so much better when it's home-made, has no preservatives, it's quite easy to do and stores well in the freezer. (3) 'Fresh' Mozzarella is a must and the best in the States is from a little company in Dallas, TX called The [Mozzarella Company](.)."

Chef J Stephen

UNITED STATES

PORTOBELLO BURGER

SERVES 1, PREP 5MIN, TOTAL 10MIN

INGREDIENTS

Sandwich
1 Panini roll (any hard roll will work)
1 ½ ounces sun-dried tomato aioli*
1 large portobello mushroom
2 ounces Monterey Jack cheese
1 slice hierloom tomato
½ ounce fresh baby spinach
1 piece fresh romaine lettuce
1 tsp unsalted butter

Portobello Marinade
¾ tsp Greek seasoning
3 ounces virgin olive oil
1 medium fresh garlic clove

* See my Sun-Dried Tomato Aioli recipe

CHEF SECRETS

"If you're in the mood for a burger, why not try a grilled portobello burger? I know so many don't like the taste or mouth feel of a mushroom but portobello's are different from all other mushrooms. The most common reaction I get from first timers who enjoy this sandwich at my bistros is that it tastes just like a juicy burger! The benefit… you'll satisfy your burger craving AND eat a great tasting healthy sandwich!"

"The two keys here are the marinade and sun-dried tomato aioli, make sure you use both."

Chef J Stephen

INSTRUCTIONS

Portobello Marinade
Mince your fresh garlic clove

Place your greek seasoning, extra virgin olive oil and minced garlic clove into a small mixing bowl and mix all ingredients thoroughly

Sandwich
Pre-heat your oven to 375°

Slice your roll horizontally in half and place your roll in your oven. Keep roll closed to avoid toasting inside. Heat until your roll is crispy

Once your roll has been toasted, remove from the oven and spread your sun-dried tomato aioli on the toasted roll

Pull the stem off your portobello mushroom and wash thoroughly but gently

Brush your portobello mushroom marinade over both sides of mushroom

Fill the inside of your mushroom with your Monterey Jack cheese

Place your mushroom (cheese side up) in your pre-heated oven for approx. 7 minutes

Place your unsalted butter in a skillet on medium heat. Add your baby spinach. Cook until fully wilted

Place your cooked portabella mushroom on your toasted roll

Top with your cooked baby spinach

Garnish with a slice beefsteak tomato and a piece of romaine lettuce on the side

GERMANY

GRILLED CHEESE SANDWICH

SERVES 3, PREP 30MIN, TOTAL 55MIN

INGREDIENTS

Sandwich
6 slices multi-grain bread
9 ounces imported gruyere cheese (3 ounces per sandwich)
9 ounces fresh button mushrooms
9 ounces white onions (sliced)
5 ounces Grilled cheese spread
5 ounces unsalted butter

Grilled Cheese Spread
3 ounces mayonnaise
2 ¼ tsp spicy mustard

Caramelized Onions
1 large white onion
¼ ounce unsalted butter

Sautéed Mushrooms
4 ounces button mushrooms
1 ½ ounces unsalted butter

CHEF SECRETS

"There's nothing like a good grilled cheese, but to make it more than just a kids sandwich you need to make it GREAT and the way to do that is by using a great recipe that I found in Fribourg, Germany. It will make your grilled cheese sandwiches a favorite with adults as well as kids."

"The key here is the grilled cheese spread and the imported gruyere cheese. If you want it to stand out, don't substitute."

Continued on next page

INSTRUCTIONS

Grilled Cheese Spread
Place your mayonnaise and spicy mustard in a small mixing bowl and mix thoroughly

Caramelized Onions
Peel your white onion and slice Julianne style

Place your unsalted butter in a medium skillet on med/high

Add your onions

Cook, while stirring constantly, until caramelized (MStatesT BE BROWN - DO NOT BURN)

Sautéed Mushrooms
Slice your mushrooms thin

Place your unsalted butter in a medium skillet on med/high

Add your sliced mushrooms

Cook, while continually stirring, until your mushrooms are lightly brown on all sides. DO NOT BURN

Grilled Cheese Sandwich
Spread your grilled cheese spread on each of your slices of bread

Top half of your bread with your shredded gruyere cheese (cheese should be at least ¼" thick (the width of your index finger)

Continued on next page

GERMANY

GRILLED CHEESE SANDWICH

CONTINUED

Top your cheese with your sliced mushrooms and caramelized onions

Spread out all your ingredients evenly

Top your sandwich with your remaining bread

Stuff the edges of your cheese in so it's compacted into your bread

Spread unsalted butter on the outside of both sides of your sandwiches

Place your sandwiches on a large skillet on medium heat

Turn your sandwiches to brown evenly

Before you remove, check in the center of your sandwiches to assure the cheese has melted fully. If your cheese has not fully melted and your bread is fully toasted, use a torch to fully melt your cheese

Cut your sandwiches in half and plate

Garnish with baked potato chips on the side

CHEF SECRETS (CONTINUED)

"Always use <u>imported</u> gruyere cheese. Through the years, I have had many discussions with my bistro guests about the difference between 'imported' gruyere and 'domestic' gruyere. Trust me, although it will be the most expensive ingredient in your sandwich, the difference is like night and day. I ALWAYS use an 'imported' gruyere from France or Switzerland and you should too. You can find an excellent gruyere cheese at the gourmet food store."

Chef J Stephen

UNITED STATES

IMPOSSIBLE BURGER SLIDERS

Serves 1, Prep 33min, Total 45min

INGREDIENTS

Slider
6 ounces Impossible Burger meat
¼ ounce sharp cheddar cheese (shredded)
1 ounce
¼ tsp black pepper
¼ tsp kosher salt
3 small Paisano rolls (you can substitute and hard crust roll if you can't find Paisano rolls)
1 tbsp unsalted butter

Sun-Dried Tomato Aioli Dip (Serves 6)
1 ½ medium garlic cloves
3 large sun-dried tomatoes
1 cup mayonnaise
2 tbsp lemon juice
¼ tsp kosher salt
½ tsp black pepper

French Moutarde (Serves 7)
¾ cup Hellmans Mayonnaise
2 tbsp spicy deli mustard
1 tsp horseradish

Caramelized Onion/Garlic Topping (Serves 6)
1 small white onion (julienned)
1 tbsp unsalted butter
2 medium garlic cloves (minced)

Garnish
1 sprig fresh parsley

(see "Chef's Secrets" on next page)

INSTRUCTIONS

Pre-heat your oven to 350°

Sun-Dried Tomato Aioli Dip
Peel your garlic cloves by crushing them lightly with the flat side of a knife and the heel of your hand. Chop your garlic fine

Chop your sun dried tomatoes into small diced sizes

Place your mayonnaise, chopped sun-dried tomatoes, lemon juice, kosher salt, black pepper, and garlic into a blender and mix on high until puree'd

French Moutarde Dip
Place your mayonnaise, horseradish, and spicy mustard in a medium mixing bowl

Mix by hand, thoroughly

Caramelized Onion/Garlic Topping
Peel your small white onion julienne style

Mince your garlic cloves

Place your unsalted butter in large skillet

Set your flame on medium high. Add your sliced onions

Caramelize your onions (SHOULD BE BROWN - BUT NOT BURNED)

Add your minced garlic 5 minutes prior to completion of the caramelization of your onions

Continued on next page

UNITED STATES

IMPOSSIBLE BURGER SLIDERS

CONTINUED

Sliders
Form your (3) 2 ounce sliders using a 2¾" biscuit cutter

Spread your unsalted butter across both sides of each of your Paisano rolls and then place ⅓ of your sharp shredded cheddar cheese on the inside top of each roll.

Place your rolls in your pre-heated oven and heat until the cheese is melted and the rolls are toasted

Place your sliders on a grill or skillet (pan spray your skillet prior to placing your sliders)

Cook for approx. 4 minutes. Flip and cook for another 4 minutes. Make sure you add a pinch of black pepper and kosher salt on both sides of your sliders

Don't overcook your sliders. Don't worry about them being pink inside, remember, they're NOT meat so they're not really rare.

Place your sliders on your Paisano rolls and top with your garlic/caramelized onion topping

Garnish with your French Moutarde, Sun-Dried Tomato Aioli and 1 sprig of parsley

CHEF SECRETS

"Are you interested in eating healthy? Does eating foods that encourage sustainable farming, which leaves as small a carbon footprint as possible, appeal to you? Sounds great, but if it doesn't taste GREAT, does all that wonderfulness go out the door? If so, have I got a burger for you!"

"If you're like me, you want to eat healthy, but veggie burgers leave me cold. They may be healthy, but they're definitely NOT a juicy burger! To me, they're like cardboard in a roll."

"Well, a couple of years ago I finally found a burger that has it all!"

"How about a juicy burger cooked rare, medium-rare or any way you want. How about topping it with caramelized onions and gooey sharp cheddar cheese. Sounds great right?"

"What if that burger has no cholesterol, higher protein, less fat and fewer calories than the average burger? "

"Better still, because the Impossible Burger uses 0% cows, it uses a fraction of the earth's natural resources."

"Compared to cows, the Impossible Burger uses 95% less land, 74% less water, and creates 87% less greenhouse gas emissions."

"Now you know why they call it the Impossible Burger!"

Chef J Stephen

Gravies, Sauces, Dips & Spreads

"So many times I hear of home cooks who spend hours preparing the perfect meal only to take shortcuts on preparing, or worse, still use pre-mades on their sauces, gravies, or toppings. Don't make that mistake. Not only is each an integral part of the meal, they often can be the miracle cure that saves a poorly prepared dish."

"Everyone has heard of the poorly cut or prepared steak that was only made edible by the use of steak sauce, or the fish stick that would only be eaten by the kids if they had catsup. I don't recommend either of those toppings, but you get the idea. A better example would be pasta. Pasta is great, but it's just not the same without a home-made red Sunday sauce or a creamy Alfredo white sauce."

"Gravies, sauces, and toppings should be prepared with the same care you would use in preparing your main dish. In most cases, a great gravy, sauce, or topping is easy to create and well worth the small effort. I've also included in this section the multitude of butters that I use, as well as, an assortment of dips, spreads, and dressings."

Chef J Stephen

Gravies, Sauces & Spreads

Beurre Manié

Use this for thickening sauces & gravy's

Ingredients

2 ½ cups all purpose flour
12 ounces unsalted butter

Instructions

In a large bowl, place your unsalted butter and AP (all purpose) flour

Mix together until a paste is formed
Roll into 4 ounce balls and wrap in freezer baggies

Store in your freezer for future use

Jalapeño Sausage Gravy

A wonderful gravy for Sausage Gravy & Biscuits

Ingredients

1 pound jalapeño sausage*
1 slice thick cut butcher bacon
3 tbsp AP (all purpose) flour
1 tsp table salt
½ tsp black pepper
4 cups whole milk
3 tbsp unsalted butter

* *"Check out my jalapeño sausage recipe."*

Serves 6

Instructions

Slice your bacon into thirds. Place in bottom of a sauté pan Cook both sides on medium heat until cooked through (not crispy). Remove your bacon, but leave bacon fat

Add your jalapeño sausage, break up your sausage while cooking (on medium/high heat) into ½" pieces

Turn flame down to medium heat and add your unsalted butter. Do not brown butter

Whisk in your AP flour. Whisk until fully incorporated for approx. 2 minutes

Add your whole milk, ⅓ at a time, while continuously stirring

Cook for approx. 6 minutes until thickened to a gravy consistency

Remove from flame

Add your salt and black pepper. Stir in with a whisk until fully incorporated

GRAVIES, SAUCES & SPREADS

PELICAN BAY CRÊPE SAUCE

WONDERFUL SAUCE FOR ANY FISH DISH

INGREDIENTS

1 ½ cups coconut milk
¾ cup heavy cream
1 tbsp fresh lime juice
1 tsp Jamaican Jerk seasoning (dry)
1 tsp kosher salt
½ tsp black ground pepper
¼ cup pineapple diced cubes

INSTRUCTIONS

Cut your diced pineapple cubes in half

Place your coconut milk, heavy cream, fresh lime juice, Jamaican Jerk seasoning, kosher salt, black ground pepper, and pineapple diced cubes into a medium sauce pan

Set your flame on medium and bring to a soft boil, continuously stirring (to reduce) for 10-15 minutes

You can store any extra crêpe sauce in your refrigerator for 4-6 days

---

COUNTRY WHITE GRAVY

A EASY TO MAKE, TRADITIONAL COUNTRY GRAVY FOR FOR BISCUITS & GRAVY

INGREDIENTS

3 tbsp AP (all purpose) flour
1 tsp salt
½ tsp black pepper
2 cups whole milk
3 tbsp unsalted butter

Serves 6

INSTRUCTIONS

In a small sauté pan add your unsalted butter. Melt the butter over medium heat

Add your AP flour. Stir in with a whisk until fully incorporated approx. 2 minutes

Add your whole milk, ⅓ at a time, while continuously stirring

Cook for approx. 6 minutes until thickened to a gravy consistency

Remove from flame

Add your salt and black pepper. Stir in with a whisk until fully incorporated

Gravies, Sauces & Spreads

Pesto

The final touch for your Caprese salads, Tuscany sandwiches & pasta dishes

Ingredients

2 cups fresh basil leaves
2 tbsp pine nuts
2 large cloves of garlic
½ cup extra virgin olive oil
½ cup grated gruyere cheese
1 tbsp kosher salt
½ tsp black pepper

Makes 6 ounces of pesto

Instructions

Peel your garlic cloves by crushing them lightly with the flat side of a knife and the heel of your hand. Chop finely. Use the flat of the blade and a paddling motion to squash the chopped garlic, working your way across the pile

Combine your crushed garlic, fresh basil leaves, gruyere cheese, and pine nuts in a food processor

Slowly add your olive oil, kosher salt, and black pepper

You can refrigerate for 7 days or freeze for 90 days

Pesto Alfredo Sauce

A creamy sauce with a pesto kick for any Alfredo pasta dish

Ingredients

1 ½ tbsp fresh garlic
8 ounces unsalted butter
1 tbsp AP (all purpose) flour
4 cups heavy cream
½ cup whole milk
½ cup shredded gruyere cheese
2 cups shredded parmesan cheese
½ tsp kosher salt
1 tsp ground black pepper
6 tbsp pesto

Serves 8

Instructions

Melt your unsalted butter in a medium pot over medium heat

Mince your fresh garlic. Add your minced garlic and all AP flour into your pot. Stir until fully incorporated. (Should be fragrant but not browned) for approx. 2 minutes

Whisking continually, add your heavy cream and whole milk. Mix for approx. 15 minutes until slightly thickened

Add your shredded parmesan cheese, shredded gruyere cheese, fresh pesto, kosher salt, and ground black pepper

Cook over medium heat until your cheese has fully melted and incorporated and your sauce has thickened, stirring often approx. 30 minutes

You can refrigerate for 4 days or freeze for 90 days

Gravies, Sauces & Spreads

Classic Mornay Sauce

A great dipping sauce for steaks or as a Hollandaise replacement for eggs

Ingredients

1 ½ tbsp unsalted butter
1 ½ tbsp AP (all purpose) flour
1 cup whole milk
2 ounces grated gruyere cheese
½ tsp kosher salt
½ tsp ground black pepper

Makes 1 cut of Mornay sauce

Instructions

Melt your unsalted butter on medium heat in a small sauce pan

Add your AP flour and whisk for approx. 1 minute to form a paste

While continually whisking, slowly add your whole milk. Your sauce will thicken and then thin back out once all the milk has been added. Add your black pepper and salt. Continue to stir with your whisk until your sauce thickens. Make sure you have no lumps

You can refrigerate for 7 days or freeze for 90 days

Marinara (Sunday) Sauce

Traditional Italian classic red sauce for all your pasta dishes

Ingredients

3 tbsp of virgin olive oil
6 ounces tomato paste
112 ounces (4 cans 28 ounces each) peeled tomatoes
1 tbsp garlic powder
4 tbsp minced garlic
1 ½ tbsp dried oregano
1 tbsp fresh basil
½ tbsp kosher salt

IF A THINNER SAUCE IS DESIRED
Add 1 can of cold water

TO MAKE THIS A MEAT SAUCE
Add 1 ½ pounds of sautéed chopped meat

Serves 8

Instructions

Place your virgin olive oil in a large frying pan on medium heat. Add your tomato paste. Stir occasionally to keep from burning (approx. 15 min.)

Pour your tomato paste and virgin olive oil into a large stock pot. Cut your peeled tomatoes into quarters. Add to your stock pot. Set on medium flame

OPTION: (If a thinner sauce is desired) Add 1 can of cold water

Heat to a rolling boil, stirring occasionally to prevent your sauce from burning

Add your garlic powder, minced garlic, dried oregano, fresh basil, and kosher salt. Set your flame to low. Simmer for 5 hours

You can refrigerate for 7 days or freeze for 90 days

Gravies, Sauces & Spreads

French Béchamel Sauce

Your key ingredient in making a great soufflé

Ingredients

2 tbsp unsalted butter
2 tbsp AP (all purpose) flour
1¼ cups (heated) whole milk
½ tsp kosher salt
½ tsp ground black pepper

Makes 1 cup of Béchamel sauce

Instructions

Heat your whole milk

Melt your unsalted butter in a medium saucepan. Add your flour and cook on medium heat, stirring continually for approx. 2 minutes until your sauce starts to bubble. Do not let it brown. Add your heated milk, continuing to stir as your sauce thickens. Bring to a boil. Add your salt and pepper, lower the heat, and continue to cook, stirring for approx. 3 minutes. Remove from the heat

You can refrigerate for 7 days or freeze for 90 days

Southern Style Brown Gravy

A classic gravy for your mashed potatoes and meatloaf

Ingredients

2 tbsp beef drippings

If your'e not making a beef dish with your gravy, you can substitutes beef stock and 1 beef bouillon cube (crushed)

2 tbsp unsalted butter
2 tbsp AP (all purpose) flour
1 cup whole milk
1 cup water
½ tsp salt
½ tsp ground black pepper

Serves 4

Instructions

Drain off 2 tablespoons of the drippings from your fresh made beef dish. Place in a medium sauce pan over medium heat

Evenly sprinkle your flour over the drippings. Cook while continually stirring until brown

Slowly stir in your milk, whisking to assure all of the meaty drippings are fully incorporated. Once fully incorporated, slowly whisk in your water

Increase the heat to medium-high, and cook, stirring continually, until your gravy thickens, approx. 10 minutes

Add your salt and black pepper

You can refrigerate for 6 days or freeze for 90 days

Gravies, Sauces & Spreads

Hollandaise Sauce

A great topping sauce for your eggs Benedict or asparagus

Ingredients

3 large eggs
¼ tsp dijon mustard
1 tsp key lime juice
¼ tsp tabasco sauce
4 ounces unsalted butter
Makes 6 ounces 2 servings of pesto

"Don't use regular lime juice or God forbid lemon juice in this recipe. If you can't find 'real' Key Limes, you can purchase a pretty good 'natural' Key Lime juice locally or online from Nellie & Joe's."

Chef J Stephen

Instructions

Separate your eggs. Place the 3 egg yolks in a blender. Add your dijon mustard, key lime juice, and tabasco sauce. Do NOT turn on your blender just yet

Melt your unsalted butter in the microwave (or sauté pan) YOUR BUTTER MStatesT BE FULLY MELTED & HOT

Set your blender on high speed. Pour in your melted butter into the egg yolk mixture in a thin stream through open lid Your sauce should thicken in approx. 10 seconds

Serve immediately

Alfredo Sauce

The classic northern Italian cream sauce for any Alfredo pasta dish

Ingredients

1 ½ tbsp fresh garlic
8 ounces unsalted butter
1 tbsp AP (all purpose) flour
4 cups heavy cream
½ cup whole milk
½ cup shredded gruyere cheese
2 cups shredded parmesan cheese
½ tsp kosher salt
1 tsp ground black pepper

Serves 8

Instructions

Melt your unsalted butter in a medium pot over medium heat

Mince your fresh garlic. Add your minced garlic and all purpose flour into your pot. Stir until fully incorporated. (Should be fragrant but not browned) for approx. 2 minutes

Whisking continually, add your heavy cream and whole milk. Mix for approx. 15 minutes until slightly thickened

Add your shredded parmesan cheese, shredded gruyere cheese, kosher salt, and ground black pepper

Cook over medium heat until your cheese has fully melted and incorporated and your sauce has thickened, stirring often approx. 30 minutes

You can refrigerate for 4 days or freeze for 90 days

Gravies, Sauces & Spreads

Aioli

A LIGHT DIPPING SAUCE FOR MANY DISHES

Ingredients

8 garlic cloves
1 tsp sea salt
2 large egg yolks
1 ¼ tsp virgin olive oil
4 ½ tsp fresh squeezed lime juice
2 tbsp dijon mustard

Makes 6 servings

Instructions

Peel your garlic cloves by crushing them lightly with the flat side of a knife and the heel of your hand. Use a mortar and pestle to press your garlic into a paste. Add your sea salt

Place your garlic salt paste into a medium bowl. Whisk in your dijon mustard and egg yolks. While you continue to whisk slowly, add a ¼ cup (only) of your olive oil. Continue to whisk until your paste thickens. Add your lime juice and water. Add slowly, while containing to whisk, the rest of your olive oil. Consistency should be creamy

You can refrigerate for 6 days

Sun-dried Tomato Aioli

A TOPPING FOR MY GRILLED PORTOBELLO MUSHROOM BURGER & AS A DIP FOR MY SLIDER BURGERS

Ingredients

1 ½ medium garlic cloves
3 large sun dried tomatoes
1 cup mayonnaise
2 tbsp lemon juice
¼ tsp kosher salt
½ tsp black pepper

Serves 6

Instructions

Peel your garlic cloves by crushing them lightly with the flat side of a knife and the heel of your hand. Chop your garlic fine

Chop your sun-dried tomatoes into small diced sizes

Place your mayonnaise, chopped sun-dried tomatoes, lemon juice, kosher salt, black pepper, and garlic into a blender

Mix on high until puree'd

You can refrigerate for 8 days

GRAVIES, SAUCES & SPREADS

CAJUN CRAWFISH SAUCE

A SPICY CREAM SAUCE THAT I USE ON MY CRAWFISH BISCUITS

INGREDIENTS

4 tbsp virgin olive oil
12 tsp creole seasoning
4 tbsp shallots (minced)
4 tbsp garlic (minced)
4 pounds crawfish tails (drained)
4 tbsp hot sauce
1 tbsp Worcestershire sauce
4 tbsp unsalted butter
1 cup green onions (chopped)
½ tsp sea salt
½ tsp black pepper

Serves 5

INSTRUCTIONS

Heat your virgin olive oil in a sauce pan over medium heat

Add your minced garlic and minced shallots. While continually stirring, sauté for approx. 3 minutes. Do Not Burn

Add your crawfish tails and creole seasoning. Sauté for approx. 2 minutes

Add your Worcestershire and hot sauces

Bring to a boil. Reduce to simmer until thickened or "reduced" by approx. ½

You can refrigerate for 1 week

PEPPER JACK CRAWFISH CREAM SAUCE

A TASTY CREAM SAUCE FOR YOUR FISH DISHES

INGREDIENTS

1 pound crawfish tails (drained)
½ white onion (diced)
½ bell pepper (sliced)
1 tsp cajun seasoning
1 clove minced garlic
2 ounces unsalted butter
1 cup shredded pepper jack cheese
4 ounces cream cheese
2 cups heavy whipping cream

Serves 4

INSTRUCTIONS

Melt your unsalted butter in a microwave or sauce pan

Place your diced onion and sliced bell pepper in pan. Add your minced garlic and sauce for approx. ½ minute

Add your heavy whipping cream and cream cheese. Stir until smooth

Add your shredded pepper jack cheese. Stir until completely melted

Add your crawfish. Turn heat to low. Cook for 5 minutes

Serve immediately

Gravies, Sauces & Spreads

Avocado Dip

A WONDERFUL LIGHT DIPPING SAUCE FOR MY IMPOSSIBLE BURGER SLIDERS

Ingredients

1 fresh, ripe avocado
1 tbsp plain greek yogurt
1 tbsp Tahini sauce
1 tbsp fresh squeezed lime juice
¾ minced garlic
½ tsp sea salt
1 ⅓ tsp water

Makes 5 servings

Instructions

Remove the pit and scoop out your avocado. Discard the skin

Mince and mash your garlic into a paste

Combine your avocado, yogurt, Tahini sauce, lime juice, minced garlic paste, water, and sea salt into a food processor

Pulse until smooth. Scrape the sides as you pulse as necessary

You can refrigerate for 6 days

French Moutarde Dip

ANOTHER LIGHT DIPPING SAUCE USED FOR MY IMPOSSIBLE BURGER SLIDERS

Ingredients

¾ cup Hellmans Mayonnaise
2 tbsp spicy deli mustard
1 tsp horseradish

Serves 7

Instructions

Place your mayonnaise, horseradish, and spicy mustard in a medium mixing bowl

Mix by hand, thoroughly

You can refrigerate for 8 days

Banana Butter

ONE OF MY MANY CUSTOM BUTTERS USED AS TOPPING FOR MY JAMAICA BANANA RUM FRENCH TOAST

Ingredients

8 ounces unsalted butter
2 ounces Monin banana syrup
¼ tsp kosher salt

Serves 12

Instructions

Soften your unsalted butter to room temperature. Place in a mixing bowl and whisk on high speed until fluffy
Add your banana syrup and salt
Whisk on high speed for approx. 15 seconds or until fluffy

You can refrigerate for 2 weeks or freeze for 90 days

Gravies, Sauces & Spreads

Basil Butter

One of the bases for your tomato basil soup

Ingredients

1 cup fresh basil leaves
8 ounces unsalted butter

Makes 3-5 servings

Instructions

Melt your unsalted butter in a microwave or sauce pan. Pluck your fresh basil leaves off stems. Place your basil leaves in a blender. Chop for approx. 10 seconds, pause, add your melted butter. Blend for an additional 10 seconds

You can refrigerate for 9 days or freeze for 90 days

Bourguignon Garlic Butter

Ideal for making garlic bread

Ingredients

2 small garlic cloves
¾ tsp kosher salt
8 ounces unsalted butter, softened
3 teaspoons finely minced shallots
2 tbsp finely chopped fresh flat-leaf parsley
½ tsp black pepper
2 tbsp dry white wine

Serves 6

Instructions

Pre-heat your oven to 450°
Mince and mash your garlic into a paste. Add ⅛ tsp of your kosher salt into your paste

Beat together your unsalted butter, shallots, garlic paste, parsley, your remaining ¼ teaspoon kosher salt, and black pepper in a small mixing bowl with an electric mixer until it's combined well. Add your dry white wine and combine well

Place your escargot butter into the oven until your escargot butter is completely melted approx. 4 minutes. Remove your heated escargot butter from the oven

You can refrigerate for 4 days

Lemon Butter

My custom butter for my Gamberaia Blueberry Ricotta Pancakes

Ingredients

8 ounces unsalted butter
5 ounces homemade lemon curd

Serves 15

Instructions

Soften your unsalted butter to room temperature. Place in a mixing bowl and whisk on high speed until fluffy
Add your lemon curd
Whisk on high speed for approx. 15 seconds or until fluffy

You can refrigerate for 2 weeks or freeze for 90 days

GRAVIES, SAUCES & SPREADS

WAFFLE BUTTER

My custom butter used as topping for Gaufre Liège Waffles

INGREDIENTS

½ cup homemade streusel
8 ounces unsalted butter

Makes 11 servings

INSTRUCTIONS

Soften your unsalted butter to room temperature. Place in a mixing bowl and whisk on high speed until fluffy
Add your homemade streusel
Fold in with spatula

You can refrigerate for 2 weeks or freeze for 90 days

ORANGE BUTTER

My custom butter for my Grand Mariner French Toast

INGREDIENTS

2 medium orange
1 ounce fresh squeezed orange juice
3 ounces unsalted butter
2 tbsp Grand Mariner

*"Zest - scrape off the outer colored part of the peel of (a piece of citrus fruit) for use as flavoring. Make sure you don't scrape too deep to prevent bitterness."

Serves 5

INSTRUCTIONS

Soften your unsalted butter to room temperature.

*Zest your medium oranges and juice them to get your 1 ounce of orange juice
Place your butter, orange juice, Grand Mariner, and orange zest in mixing bowl. Whisk on high speed for approx. 25 seconds or until fluffy (if your butter separates, don't worry, it will still taste perfectly).

You can refrigerate for 2 weeks or freeze for 90 days.

CLOTTED CREAM

Traditional English butter commonly used on scones

INGREDIENTS

8 ounces unsalted butter
8 ounces heavy whipping cream

Serves 6

INSTRUCTIONS

Soften your unsalted butter to room temperature. Place in a mixing bowl and whisk on high speed until fluffy
In a separate mixing bowl, add your heavy whipping cream
Whisk on high speed for approx.15 seconds or until dry peaks are formed
Fold your whipped cream into your whipped butter. Drain any liquid that may form from the bottom of your bowl
You can refrigerate for 6 days

Gravies, Sauces & Spreads

Grilled Cheese Spread

The finishing touch for a great grilled cheese

Ingredients

¾ cup Hellmans Mayonnaise
2 tbsp spicy deli mustard

Serves 6

Instructions

Place your mayonnaise and spicy deli mustard in a small mixing bowl

Mix by hand, thoroughly

You can refrigerate for 1 week

Pesto Spread

A great topping for your Caprese salad

Ingredients

3 tbsp Pesto*
1 tbsp virgin olive oil

* See my pesto recipe

Serves 4

Instructions

Place your pesto in a small ramekin. Add your virgin olive oil

Stir with a spoon until fully incorporated. You can stir again to re-emulsify as needed

Serve at room temperature. You can refrigerate for 2 weeks

Passion Fruit Dip

A delightfully tropical Caribbean dip

Ingredients

5 ounces passion fruit puree
¾ cup dark brown Muscovado sugar
1 ¾ tsp chipotle powder
2 tbsp water
½ tbsp kosher salt

Serves 10

Instructions

Place your frozen passion fruit puree in a medium sauce pan

Add your dark brown Muscovado sugar, kosher salt, chipotle powder, and water

Cook to reduce on medium heat for approx. 15 minutes
Since this dip will thicken as it sets, (DO NOT MAKE TOO THICK)

You can refrigerate for 1 week or freeze for 90 days

Gravies, Sauces & Spreads

Cuban Sofrito

EXCELLENT ADDITION TO STEWS, BEANS AND SOUPS

INGREDIENTS

¼ cup extra-virgin olive oil
1 large green bell pepper (stemmed, seated and dried)
1 white onion (diced)
3 large garlic cloves (peeled and finally minced)
2 tsp kosher salt
1 tsp ground black pepper
½ tsp dried oregano
½ tsp dried cumin
½ cup dry white wine
¼ cup green olives (stuffed with pimentos-thinly sliced)
1 dried bay leaf
2 tbsp sherry vinegar
1 tsp white granulated sugar

Serves 5

INSTRUCTIONS

Chop your green pepper, white onion, and garlic to fit into a food processor or blender. Make sure you remove all seeds and stems

Add all your ingredients into your food processor or blender and blend well. Should be well processed similar to a pesto

You can refrigerate for 90 days or freeze for 1 year

Parmesan Croutons

A TASTY ADDITION TO ANY SALAD OR SOUP

INGREDIENTS

32 ounces (1 loaf) bread
4 ounces unsalted butter
⅔ cup parmesan cheese

Serves 20

INSTRUCTIONS

Cube 1 loaf of bread into ½" squares and store extra cube's in your freezer for future use. Any bread (including stale bread) will do

To prepare for your salads, melt 4 ounces unsalted butter

Place your cubed bread into a large mixing bowl. Add your melted butter and toss until coated

Add your freshly ground parmesan cheese and toss again

Place your croutons on a lined sheet pan and bake at 375° for 5-10 minutes (until brown)

You can store store in your freezer for 6 month's

Gravies, Sauces & Spreads

Toasted Walnuts

A GREAT ADDITION TO ANY SALAD

Ingredients

½ cup water
4 tbsp white sugar
1 tsp Saigon cinnamon
5 cups shelled walnuts
½ cup dark brown Muscovado sugar

Serves 20

Instructions

Combine in a medium sauce pan, on low-medium heat, your water, sugar, and Saigon cinnamon

Add your walnuts making sure to coat completely

Stir until mixture thickens

Spread your coated walnuts across a lined sheet pan and sprinkle evenly with dark brown Muscovado sugar over top

Bake for approx. 4 minutes @ 375°

Toss and bake for an additional 3 minutes

You can store store in your freezer for 1 year

Chicken Broth*

A SIMPLE BASE FOR SO MANY RECIPE'S

Ingredients

6 cups cold water
1 whole fresh chicken (organic preferably)
3 large fresh carrots (peeled and chopped)
3 stalks fresh celery (chopped)
1 white onion (quartered)
3 peeled fresh garlic cloves
1 sprig fresh thyme
1 bayleaf
1 bundle parsley
1 tbsp black pepper
1 tbsp kosher salt

*For beef broth simply substitute your chicken with 5 lbs. of pre-cooked beef knuckle bones (with marrow).

Serves - Varies with use

Instructions

Making ANY broth is a great way to use left over vegetables

Place a washed, whole, preferably organic chicken into a large 10 quart pot (remove the giblets). Add your chopped celery, chopped carrots, quartered onion, and your whole peeled garlic cloves. Add 1 sprig of thyme, 1 bayleaf, and 1 sprig of parsley, wrapped in a tied [Bouquet Garni](). Add your black pepper and table salt

Cover with your cold water. On high heat partially cover your pot to allow some steam to be released. Once your water reaches boiling, reduce to low heat and simmer for 4 hours

Carefully remove your chicken and vegetables. Strain with cheese cloth or strainer to arrive at a clear broth

You can refrigerate for 3 days or freeze for 120 days

Gravies, Sauces & Spreads

How To Fix Store Bought Tomato Sauce
When you just don't have time to cook from scratch

Instructions

I understand with the tight schedules that families have to deal with today, especially when both parents are working long hours, making a great sauce from scratch may be impractical. But, there are ways to liven up even the worst bottled pre-made tomato sauce. My fix may not taste exactly like home-made, but it will be pretty darn close.

Chef J Stephen

Place 3 tbsp of virgin olive oil in a pot

Mince a medium onion and sauté it over medium heat

Add 2–3 cloves of finely minced garlic (or more if you love garlic like I do)

Cook over medium heat for one minute

Add your jar of pre-made tomato sauce

Stir

Add ½ tsp of crushed, dried basil (fresh basil is better but I know your in a time crunch so, dried will work), ½ tsp of oregano, and ¼ tsp of dried red pepper flakes

Stir

Simmer with a lid on the pot over low heat for 20 to 30 minutes

If you would like to give your sauce extra flavor or make a meat sauce, add in some pan seared chopped meat when you're ready to serve

That's all there is to it. AND, if you discard the jar before anyone shows, they'll never know the difference!!

"Creating a dish is like art. Where else can you craft something that people will remember for years."

Rene Verdon

Fillings, Frostings & Toppings

"There's a real art to crafting the right topping to match a cake. Too many so called 'pastry chefs' spend hours perfecting their cakes only to go to the standard fare of buttercream, ganache, marzipan, or fondant toppings. To make matters worse, they choose standard out of the jar jams and chocolates as their fillings. Most wedding cakes are works of art, but... have you ever had a wedding cake that everyone talked. Not about howe it looked, but how it tasted? Probably not, because the 'baker' spent all their time concentrating on the design at the expense of the cake."

"There's nothing fancy about my family's 400-year-old artisan crumb cake. Why? Simple. Back then, they concentrated on what it tasted like NOT what it looked like! You won't find any buttercream, ganache, marzipan, or fondant recipes in my book. For that you'll have to look elsewhere. What you will find is great, natural, flavor-packed toppings and fillings that will not only compliment your cake but also, in some cases, make your cake great!"

Chef J Stephen

Fillings, Frostings & Toppings

Crème Anglaise

A WONDERFUL TOPPING USED AS A COMPLIMENTARY TOPPING FOR JAPANESE PANCAKES

Ingredients

½ cup heavy whipping cream
½ cup whole milk
½ tsp Madagascar bourbon vanilla
3 tbsp white granulated sugar
3 large egg yolks

Makes 4 servings

Instructions

Combine your milk and heavy whipping cream in a medium saucepan

Add your Madagascar bourbon vanilla. Bring to a simmer and then remove from heat

Whisk your egg yolks and sugar in a medium mixing bowl to blend

Slowly whisk in your heated milk/cream/Madagascar bourbon vanilla mixture into your yolk/sugar mixture. Return this combined mix to your saucepan. Stir over low heat until your Crème Anglaise thickens (should hold to the back of a spoon) approx. 5 minutes (do not boil)

Transfer to a bowl. Cover with plastic wrap and chill in the refrigerator

You can refrigerate for 4 days

Lemon Curd

USED TO MAKE MY LEMON BUTTER AND IN MY VILLAFRANCA LEMON CRUMB CAKES

Ingredients

The zest of 1 lemon
⅔ cup fresh lemon juice
1 cup white granulated sugar
2 large egg yolks
2 large eggs
3 ounces unsalted butter
⅛ tbsp sea salt

Serves 9

Instructions

In a large mixing bowl, add your butter and sugar and whisk for approx. 2 minutes.

Slowly add your eggs and yolks. Whisk for 1 minute. Add your lemon juice. Don't worry about curdled look, it will smooth into a curd as it cooks

In a medium saucepan, cook your curd over low heat until it becomes smooth. Raise the heat to medium and cook, stirring continually, until the curd thickens, approx. 15 minutes (should hold to the back of a spoon). Do not boil!

Remove your curd from the heat. Sir in your lemon zest. Transfer your curd to a bowl. Cover with plastic wrap on the surface of the curd and chill in the refrigerator. The curd will thicken further as it cools

You can refrigerate for 1 week or freeze for 90 days

FILLINGS, FROSTINGS & TOPPINGS

KEY LIME CURD

A TANGY TOPPING USED IN MY KEY LIME CRUMB CAKES

INGREDIENTS

The zest of 2 Key Limes
⅔ cup fresh Key Lime juice*
1 cup white granulated sugar
2 large egg yolks
2 large eggs
3 ounces unsalted butter
⅛ tbsp sea salt

"Don't substitute with regular lime juice. If you can't find real Key Limes, you can find Key Lime juice at (Nellie & Joe's) on [Amazon](#)."

Serves 9

INSTRUCTIONS

In a large mixing bowl, add your butter and sugar and whisk for approx. 2 minutes.

Slowly add your eggs and yolks. Whisk for 1 minute. Add your Key Lime juice. Don't worry about curdled look, it will smooth into a curd as it cooks

In a medium saucepan, cook your curd over low heat until it becomes smooth. Raise the heat to medium and cook, stirring continually, until the curd thickens, approx. 15 minutes (should hold to the back of a spoon). Do not boil

Remove your curd from the heat. Stir in your Key Lime zest. Transfer your curd to a bowl. Cover with plastic wrap on the surface of the curd and chill in the refrigerator. The curd will thicken further as it cools

You can refrigerate for 1 week or freeze for 90 days

FRUIT MACERATE

THIS MAKES A GREAT TOPPING FOR MANY DESSERTS. I USE IT ON MY GRAND MARINER FRENCH TOAST

INGREDIENTS

¼ cup fresh strawberries
¼ cup fresh blueberries
¼ cup fresh blackberries
¼ cup fresh raspberries
2 ounces white granulated sugar
2 ounces of fresh squeezed lemon juice

Serves 7

INSTRUCTIONS

Wash your fresh fruit thoroughly and pat to dry
Slice off the tops of your strawberries and slice in half and place in a medium in a bowl
Sprinkle your sugar over top of your fruit and add your lemon juice
Mix your fruit to assure equal coverage. Keep at room temperature for 1 hour or warm in microwave if needed immediately
Refrigerate overnight for use the following day

You can refrigerate for 1 week (if you refrigerate for longer than 1-day, leave out the raspberries and blackberries until the day before serving). Can also freeze for 90 days

Fillings, Frostings & Toppings

Cinnamon Streusel Ice Cream Topping

Combine with Cinnamon Crumb Ice Cream Topping to make my Crumbler ice cream

Ingredients

½ cup water
½ cup cinnamon streusel*
½ cup white granulated sugar

* See my cinnamon streusel recipe

Serves 10

Instructions

Place your water and white granulated sugar in a medium pot

Whisk until incorporated then add your cinnamon streusel

Place over high heat, stirring continually to prevent burning

"Reduce" by ⅓ (will take approx. 30 minutes)

Cool to room temperature. Pour over Madagascar bourbon vanilla bean ice cream

You can refrigerate for 30 days or freeze for 120 days

Cinnamon Crumb Ice Cream Topping

A delicious way to finish off an ice cream

Ingredients

5 ounces crumb mix

Serves 4

Instructions

Pre-heat your oven to 375°

Place your crumb mix in a food processor

Set your processor on pulse until crumbs are ½ pea size

Place your crumbs on a lined sheet pan

Bake at 375° until toasted DON'T OVER BAKE

Hand spread on top of your cinnamon streusel ice cream topping

You can refrigerate for 90 days or freeze for 6 month's

Fillings, Frostings & Toppings

Apple Strudel Filling/Topping

Used on and in my Apple Strudel crumb cake recipe

Ingredients

4 large Granny Smith apples
1 cup dark brown Muscovado sugar
2 tbsp unsalted butter
2 tbsp corn starch
1 tsp Saigon cinnamon
¼ tsp nutmeg
½ tsp kosher salt
¼ cup water

1 large egg - beaten

Makes enough for 1 cake

Instructions

Core, peel and quarter your Granny Smith apples

In a medium saucepan, combine your apples, dark brown Muscovado sugar, unsalted butter, corn starch, Saigon cinnamon, nutmeg, kosher salt, and water.

Stir to incorporate.

Cook on medium heat for approx. 10 minutes or until your sauce starts to thicken (should stick to the back of a spoon).

You can refrigerate for 60 days and freeze for 120 days

Cinnamon Streusel

An integral part of my family's 400-year-old family artisan crumb cake recipe

Ingredients

1 lb unsalted butter
½ cup cake flour (you can substitute A/P flour)
1 lb dark brown Muscovado sugar
2 tbsp Saigon cinnamon

Serves 20

Instructions

Cut your unsalted butter into 4" squares

Into a large mixing bowl, combine your cake flour, dark brown Muscovado sugar, and Saigon cinnamon

Mix until all the lumps are gone

Add your unsalted butter to the mix. Mix until fully incorporated (It will be course and granular)

You'll have extra streusel, but never fear, you can freeze your extra streusel for up to 6 month's future use

Fillings, Frostings & Toppings

Crumb Cake Crumb Mix

THE MOST IMPORTANT PART OF MY FAMILY'S 400-YEAR-OLD FAMILY ARTISAN CRUMB CAKE RECIPE

Ingredients

- 1 cup unsalted butter
- ½ cup white granulated sugar
- ½ cup dark brown Muscovado sugar
- 1 ½ tbsp Saigon cinnamon
- ½ tsp kosher salt
- 1 ½ tbsp Madagascar bourbon vanilla
- 1 ⅓ cups <u>cake</u> flour (no substitute)

"When finished, your crumbs won't look like crumbs. Don't worry, you will pull them apart and form your crumbs when you make your cake."

Makes enough crumbs for 1 cake

Instructions

Melt your unsalted butter in a microwave or sauce pan on low heat. DO NOT BOIL

Combine your granulated white sugar, dark brown Muscovado sugar, kosher salt, and Saigon cinnamon into a mixing bowl

Mix with a paddle, on slow speed until ALL lumps have been removed

Add your melted butter and Madagascar bourbon vanilla

Mix with a paddle on slow speed until fully incorporated

Add your cake flour into the mix, then mix on slow speed until fully incorporated

You can refrigerate for 60 days and freeze for 1 year

Toasted Coconut Topping

USED IN MY COCONUT CUSTARD CRUMB CAKE

Ingredients

1 ounce unsweetened coconut flakes

Makes enough for 1 cake

Instructions

Pre-heat your oven to 375°
Spread your unsweetened coconut flakes across a lined sheet pan or cookie sheet
Bake for approx. 3 minutes (or until lightly brown)
Toss your coconut and bake for an additional 3 minutes

You can refrigerate for 4 weeks or freeze for 120 days

Fillings, Frostings & Toppings

Cream Cheese Cake Frosting

The most important ingredient of a red velvet cake

Ingredients

4 ounces unsalted butter
8 ounces cream cheese
1 cup confectioners sugar
1 tsp Madagascar bourbon vanilla

Makes 2 cups

Instructions

Bring your butter and cream cheese to room temperature (Don't cheat, it must be at room temperature)

Place your butter in a mixing bowl with a paddle

Beat on medium-high speed until fluffy, approx. 2 minutes.

Add your cream cheese, and beat about 2 minutes more.

Add your confectioners sugar and Madagascar bourbon vanilla, and beat until combined, another 2 minutes.

Use immediately

Carrot Cake Topping

A bit of a twist on cream cheese topping

Ingredients

4 ounces unsalted butter
8 ounces cream cheese
1 cup confectioners sugar
1 tsp Madagascar bourbon vanilla
1 tsp all spice

Makes 2 cups

Instructions

Bring your butter and cream cheese to room temperature (Don't cheat, it must be at room temperature)

Place your butter in a mixing bowl with a paddle

Beat on medium-high speed until fluffy, approx. 2 minutes

Add your cream cheese, and beat about 2 minutes more

Add your confectioners sugar, all spice, and Madagascar bourbon vanilla, then beat until combined (another 2 minutes)

Use immediately

Fillings, Frostings & Toppings

Carrot Cake Filling

The filling for one of the most moist cakes you'll ever enjoy

Ingredients

2 large eggs
5 ounces unsalted butter
½ cup cake flour (do not substitute)
1 tsp baking powder
1 cup white granulated sugar
1 tsp baking soda
¼ tsp salt
1 tsp Saigon cinnamon
1 tsp all spice
1 tsp Madagascar bourbon vanilla
1 cup fresh grated carrots

Makes 3 ½ cups

Instructions

Bring your unsalted butter to room temperature
Grate your medium carrots
Place your cake flour, baking powder, white granulated sugar, baking soda, salt, Saigon cinnamon, and all spice together in a mixing bowl
Mix with paddle on slow setting to fully incorporate
Add your large eggs, unsalted butter, Madagascar bourbon vanilla, and grated carrots to your dry mix
Mix with a paddle on medium speed for 1 ½ minutes

You can refrigerate for 30 days

Cheesecake Filling/Topping

The cheesecake filling/topping I use in my artisan cheesecake crumb cake recipe

Ingredients

12 ounces unsalted butter
¾ cup white granulated sugar
16 ounces cream cheese
½ cup sour cream
3 ounces whole milk
2 large eggs
½ tbsp Madagascar bourbon vanilla
1 ounce AP (all purpose) flour

Makes 4 cups

Instructions

Bring your cream cheese to room temperature *(Must be room temperature, don't cheat)*

Combine in a mixer bowl, with paddle, your cream cheese and granulated sugar for approx. 30 seconds on medium speed

Add your whole milk and large eggs
Mix for 1 minute
Add your sour cream, Madagascar bourbon vanilla, and AP flour
Mix on medium speed for 15 seconds

You can refrigerate for 6 days or freeze for 30 days

Fillings, Frostings & Toppings

Chocolate Filling

The chocolate filling/topping I use in my artisan chocolate crumb cake recipe

Ingredients

2 cups semi-sweet chocolate nubs *(I use Callebaut Tanzanian chocolates)*
1 cup water

Makes 2 cups

Instructions

Place your water in the bottom of a double broiler
Set the flame on high

Place your chocolate nubs in top of a double broiler
Cover your broiler

Mix continually (to prevent burning) until melted
Cool until pourable but not runny

You can refrigerate for 30 days and freeze for 120 days

Coconut Custard Filling

The Coconut Custard filling I use in my artisan Coconut Custard crumb cake recipe

Ingredients

1 tsp Madagascar bourbon vanilla
1 large eggs whole (room temp)
1 large egg yolks (room temp)
2 cups whole milk
¾ cup white granulated sugar
1 tsp salt
2 ounces unsweetened coconut flakes (shredded)
¾ tsp nutmeg
1 ½ ounces unsalted butter (melted)
½ tbsp AP (all purpose) flour
1 ½ tbsp coconut syrup (Monin)
½ tsp coconut extract

Instructions

Separate your egg yolks
Melt your unsalted butter in microwave or sauce pan
Place all your ingredients (coconut syrup, egg yolks, whole eggs, white granulated sugar, salt, Madagascar bourbon vanilla, whole milk, nutmeg, your melted unsalted butter, AP flour, coconut extract, and shredded unsweetened coconut) into a medium sauce pan
Whisk all ingredients together
Place your sauce pan over medium heat
Stir continually for 10 minutes until nape is formed (liquid should coat the back of a spoon) **DO NOT BOIL** (*A nap is when your liquid thickens but still slowly slides off your ladle.*)

You can refrigerate for 7 days or freeze for 60 days

Makes 3 ¾ cups

Fillings, Frostings & Toppings
Coconut Custard Topping

This is the Coconut Custard topping I use in my artisan Coconut Custard crumb cake recipe

Ingredients

12 large egg yolks (room temp)
2 cups whole milk
2¼ cups white granulated sugar
¼ tsp salt
1½ ounces unsweetened coconut flakes (shredded)
6 ounces unsalted butter (melted)
1 cup coconut syrup (Monin)
½ tsp coconut extract

Makes 4 ½ cups

Instructions

Separate your egg yolks
Melt your unsalted butter in microwave or sauce pan
Place all your ingredients (coconut syrup, egg yolks, white granulated sugar, salt, your melted unsalted butter, coconut extract, and shredded unsweetened coconut) into a medium sauce pan
Whisk all ingredients together
Place your sauce pan over medium heat
Stir continually for 10 minutes until nape is formed (liquid should coat the back of a spoon) **DO NOT BOIL** (*A nap is when your liquid thickens but still slowly slides off your ladle.*)

You can refrigerate for 7 days or freeze for 60 days

Egg Nog Cheesecake Filling/Topping

Used as a filling and topping for my Egg Nog Cheesecake crumb cake recipe

Ingredients

16 ounces cream cheese
¾ cup white granulated sugar
½ cup sour cream
½ tsp Saigon cinnamon
2 large eggs
½ tbsp Madagascar bourbon vanilla
½ cup AP (all purpose) flour
¾ cup egg nog
¼ tsp ground nutmeg
1 ½ tsp Tuaca liqueur

Makes enough for 1 cake

Instructions

Place your cream cheese in a plastic bowl and place in your microwave for 30 second intervals, stirring in between until smooth
Combine in a mixer bowl, with a paddle, your cream cheese and white granulated sugar for approx. 30 seconds on medium speed
Add your egg nog, Tuaca and large eggs
Mix for approx. 1 minute on medium speed
Add your sour cream, Madagascar bourbon vanilla, ground nutmeg, Saigon cinnamon, and AP flour
Mix for approx. 15 seconds on medium speed

You can refrigerate for 30 days and freeze for 90 days

Fillings, Frostings & Toppings

Caramel

THERE IS NOTHING LIKE HOME-MADE CARAMEL… NEVER SUBSTITUTE

Ingredients

¼ cup heavy whipping cream
1 ounce unsalted butter
1 ounce clear Kari syrup
¼ cup water
1 cup white granulated sugar

IMPORTANT
To create a decent caramel, timing is of utmost importance. Have a timer at the ready and pre-measure all your ingredients. Place each ingredient (in order of use) by the pot. Don't vary your time from the directions.

Makes 1 ½ cups

Instructions

Pour your water into a medium pot
Add your white granulated sugar. Dissolve the sugar by whisking in the water (NO FLAME)

Cook on medium high flame, continue to dissolve
DO NOT STIR. Bring to a boil

Boil for approx. 20 minutes. Boil until the mix <u>starts</u> to turn golden brown
Remove from flame immediately

Add your clear Karo syrup and mix with a whisk for 30 seconds
Set your flame to low

Return your mix to the flame, while continually mixing
Cook for 1 minute

Add your unsalted butter
Mix for 30 seconds

Add your heavy cream
CAREFUL OF STEAM
Turn off flame

Stir until caramel stops boiling
Cool in pot

Pour when cool but still pourable, into a storage container

You can refrigerate for 90 days

Fillings, Frostings & Toppings

Graham Cracker Filling

Used in all my Cheesecake, Key Lime & Peaches & Cream Crumb Cakes

Ingredients

1 package (5 ounces) graham crackers

Makes enough for 2 cakes

Instructions

Place your graham crackers in a food processor on high until uniformly fine

You can refrigerate for 4 weeks or freeze for 120 days

Marshmallow Filling/Topping

A fun light filling for cakes, hot chocolate and of course S'mores

Ingredients

1 ½ cups white cane sugar
1 cup Karo light corn syrup
½ cup cold water
¼ tsp kosher salt
3 tsp Madagascar bourbon vanilla
4 tbsp egg whites

Serves 7

Instructions

Place your egg whites in mixing bowl and beat on high speed with a whisk until stiff

Place your white granulated sugar, Karo corn syrup, cold water and kosher salt into a medium sauce pan

Place your saucepan over high heat
Heat to 240° *(This is an important step that requires a digital thermometer)*

Pour your saucepan mix slowly into your whipped egg whites
Mix slowly to incorporate

Add your Madagascar bourbon vanilla and mix to incorporate for approx. 10 seconds

Use immediately

Fillings, Frostings & Toppings
Hot Toffee Butter Rum Filling & Topping

Used to make our filling & topping in my Hot Toffee Butter Rum crumb cake

INGREDIENTS

2 cups heavy whipping cream
½ cup white granulated sugar
2 ½ ounces dark Kari syrup
¾ cup water
2 ounces unsalted butter
½ cup Jamaican dark rum
1 ½ tbsp Tuaca liqueur
½ cup milk chocolate toffee bits
½ tsp corn starch

Makes enough for 2 cakes

INSTRUCTIONS

Pour your water into large sauce pan. Add your white sugar. Dissolve your sugar in the water stirring for approx. 30 seconds (NO FLAME). Cook on high flame to continue to dissolve. Bring to a low boil. Boil for approx. 5 minutes

Add your milk chocolate toffee bits. Stir until fully incorporated (melted). Add your unsalted butter stir until fully incorporated (melted). Add your dark Karo syrup. Incorporate. Add your Jamaican spiced rum and Tuaca liqueur. Reduce your flame to a simmer. Add your heavy cream

FILLING
Stir your mixture until reduced to a thin nape (approx. 15 min.) (*A nape is when your liquid thickens but still slowly slides off your ladle.*)

Pour ½ (only) of the mixture into a holding container. When cool, but still pourable, place your filling into a plastic pour container

TOPPING
Add your corn starch into the remaining half of your mix Place over medium/high flame to reduce (approx. 25 min.) Stir occasionally

Pour your topping when cool, but still pourable, place into a separate plastic pour container. Store in your refrigerator for future use

You can refrigerate both mixes for 3 weeks

Fillings, Frostings & Toppings

Peaches & Cream Filling

Used to make peaches & cream filling in my Peaches & Cream crumb cake

Ingredients

3 ounces whole milk
2 cups cream cheese
¾ cup white granulated sugar
½ cup sour cream
2 large eggs
½ tsp Madagascar bourbon vanilla
1 ounce AP (all purpose) flour
1 tsp natural peach extract

Makes enough for 1 cake

Instructions

Place your cream cheese in a plastic bowl in your microwave for 30 second intervals, stirring in between until smooth

Combine in a mixer bowl, with a paddle, your cream cheese and white granulated sugar for approx. 30 seconds on medium speed

Add your whole milk and large eggs. Mix for approx. 1 minute

Add your sour cream, Madagascar bourbon vanilla, natural peach extract, and AP flour. Mix for approx. 15 seconds on medium speed

You can refrigerate for 1 week

Pecan Pie Filling

Used to make pecan pie filling in my Pecan Pie crumb cake

Ingredients

½ cup fresh pecans (shelled)
2 ounces unsalted butter
1 cup dark corn syrup
2 large eggs
1 cup white granulated sugar
1 tbsp Madagascar bourbon vanilla
1 tbsp Tuaca liqueur

Makes enough for 1 cake

Instructions

Place your unsalted butter in your microwave for 20 seconds (or until melted)

Place your melted butter, dark corn syrup, white granulated sugar, large eggs, Madagascar bourbon vanilla, and Tuaca into a mixing bowl

Mix on slow speed until thoroughly incorporated
Fold in your pecan halves

You can refrigerate for 1 week

"If you really want to make a friend, go to someone's house and eat with him...the people who give you their food give you their heart."

Cesar Chavez

DESSERTS

"In my bakery and bistro in New York, we offered a multitude of desserts. Although it was impossible to include all of the desserts we offered, I have included our most popular offerings for you to try your hand at. Although we had a full offering of desserts, my family's crumb cakes were always the main attraction with lines of 'Cakers' (as they were called) waiting patiently for our doors to open to grab a slice of their favorite flavor."

"Because my bistro in Dallas was focused almost entirely on breakfast, lunch and brunch, my family's 400-year-old artisan crumb cakes were our main focus for dessert. We ship our crumb cakes worldwide and have a following of enthusiasts who anxiously await the announcements of not only our standard offerings but also our limited edition 'Cake's of the Month' offerings on our Facebook page and enthusiast emails. The recipe book you are holding in your hands is the first and only time my family's crumb cake recipe has been shown to anyone outside of my family."

Chef J Stephen

UNITED STATES

CHOCOLATE CHIP COOKIES

SERVES 4, PREP 20MIN, TOTAL 45MIN

INSTRUCTIONS

Preheat your oven to 325°

Soften 1 lb unsalted butter

Place your butter in a mixing bowl. Set your mixer with a paddle, on medium speed. Beat until smooth approx. 30 seconds. Add your dark brown Muscovado sugar, and white granulated sugar

In a separate bowl, place your large eggs and Madagascar bourbon vanilla. Mix by hand

Set your mixing bowl with paddle on low. Add your egg/Madagascar bourbon vanilla mix

Set your mixer to medium. Add your cake flour, baking soda, AP flour, and chocolate chips. Mix on high speed for approx. 10 seconds (until smooth)

Place 12 heaping serving spoons (approx. 7 ounces each) of mix on a lined sheet pan or cookie sheet. Your mix should make 13 cookies

Bake for approx. 25 minutes. Cookies should spring back to light touch and have lightly browned edges. Use your nose. That delicious cookie smell signifies cookie completion as effectively as a timer

Continued on next page

INGREDIENTS

1 lb unsalted butter
2 cups dark brown Muscovado sugar
1 cup white granulated sugar
4 large eggs
¼ cup Madagascar bourbon vanilla
3 cups cake flour
2 cups AP (all purpose) flour
2 cups chocolate chips (or nibs if you prefer larger pieces of chocolate)
1 tsp baking soda

CHEF SECRETS

"If you don't have the time to make home-made chocolate chip cookies, check out my Nestle Toll House® 'Make Em' Like Home Cooked' Tips on the next page."

Chef J Stephen

UNITED STATES
Nestle Toll House®
Chocolate Chip Cookies

Make Em' Like Home Cooked
-Tips-

"If you don't want to go to the effort of making your own chocolate chip cookies and choose to make the Nestle Toll House® chocolate chip cookie recipe, you can still make them taste like home-made with a few tips."

Tips

Ooey-Gooey - *Add 2 cups more flour*

Crispy with a Soft Center - *Use ¼ teaspoon baking powder and ¼ teaspoon baking soda*

A nice Tan - *Set the oven higher than 350° (maybe 360°). Caramelization, which gives cookies their nice brown tops, occurs above 356°*

Chewy - *Substitute bread flour for all-purpose flour*

Uniformity - *If looks count, add one ounce corn syrup and one ounce granulated sugar*

More. Just, more - *Chilling the dough for at least 24 hours before baking deepens all the flavors*

Tips

Just like Store-Bought - *Trade the butter for shortening. This ups the texture but reduces some flavor. Suggestion to help retain flavor; use half butter and half shortening*

Thick and Less Crispy - *Freeze the batter for 30 to 60 minutes before baking. This solidifies the butter, which will spread less while baking*

Cakey - *Use more baking soda because it releases carbon dioxide when heated, which makes cookies puff up*

Butterscotch flavored- *Use ¾ cup packed light brown sugar (instead of the same amount of combined granulated sugar and light brown sugar)*

You can refrigerate for 7 days or freeze for 90 days

Chef Secrets

Although I much prefer dark semi-sweet chocolate, I know most people prefer milk chocolate in their chocolate chip cookies. Either way, don't buy the chocolate chips you find in the grocery store. Stick to a high quality chocolate chip. My favorite quality chocolate provider is [Barry Callebaut](#)."

Chef J Stephen

Italy

Almond Biscotti

Serves 36, Prep 20min, Total 1hour 50min

Instructions

Preheat your oven to 325°. Position your rack in the center

Place your extra large eggs in a medium bowl. Add your extra large egg white, almond extract, virgin olive oil, and Madagascar bourbon vanilla. Whisk together

In a separate mixing bowl, add your pastry flour, granulated sugar, dark brown Muscovado sugar, baking soda, baking powder, kosher salt, and slivered almonds. Whisk until fully incorporated

Add your egg mixture to your dry mixture and mix together until fully incorporated

Line a sheet pan or cookie sheet

Use a large serving spoon to scoop out your dough and place it on the lined cookie sheet. Add another scoop adjacent to the batter on the cookie sheet and keep going until you have formed two logs with your hands

Place in your pre-heated oven for approx. 30 minutes or until lightly brown. Remove from your oven and place on a cutting board. Slice your cookies with a knife at an angle about ¾ inches thick. Place your sliced cookies back on your cookie sheet, return to your oven, and bake for 10 minutes, flip your cookies over. Bake for an additional 10 minutes

Remove and cool. Wrap with clear wrap

You can keep your biscotti cookies indefinitely in a cool dry place

Ingredients

- ½ cup white granulated sugar
- ¾ cup dark brown Muscovado sugar
- ¾ tsp baking powder
- 2¼ cups pastry flour
- ¾ tsp baking soda
- ½ cup virgin olive oil
- ½ tsp kosher salt
- 2 extra large eggs
- 1 extra large egg white (only)
- 1 cup slivered almonds
- ¾ tbsp natural almond extract
- ½ tsp Madagascar bourbon vanilla

Chef Secrets

"From the Tuscan region of Italy, these cookies are DEFINITELY not the typical prepackaged biscotti's that you'll find at Starbucks.® These cookies are meant to be hard. Ideal for dunking in coffee or tea. The word biscotti means twice baked. Twice baking removes all the moisture and without the moisture, your cookies will last you indefinitely!"

"Make sure you use 'Pastry' flour, NOT AP (all purpose) flour for your biscotti's. Pastry flour strikes the ideal balance between flakiness and tenderness, making it perfect for pies, tarts and most cookies. You can find a great pastry flour at King Arthur Flour."

Chef J Stephen

DENMARK

DANISH PANCAKE PUFFS

SERVES 8, PREP 25MIN, TOTAL 35MIN

INSTRUCTIONS

Pre-heat your pancake puff pan

Place your unsalted butter in microwave to melt

Separate your large eggs. Place your egg <u>yolks</u> in a mixing bowl
Place your large egg <u>whites</u> and granulated white sugar in another mixing bowl

Mix your egg <u>whites</u> with a whisk on high until the peaks are high and firm, approx. 1-2 minutes

Add to your <u>whipped egg whites</u>, your egg yolks, AP flour, baking soda, kosher salt, and vanilla

Mix with a whisk on low while gradually adding your buttermilk and melted butter. Mix until fully incorporated

Fold your egg whites into the batter

Spray with pan spray your pre-heated pancake puff pan

Fill each compartment ¾ full with batter

Turn 90° when edges begin to get firm

Let your batter flow into the pan

Note the hole. Fill it with a small amount of batter and turn 90° to allow the hole to close

Continue to turn regularly to assure even baking
When done, fill with 1 ounce of jam of choice

Top with Crème Anglaise (see my recipe) or confectioners sugar

INGREDIENTS

3 ½ ounces unsalted butter
3 large eggs
1 tbsp granulated white sugar
1 cup AP (all purpose) flour
½ tsp baking soda
¼ tsp kosher salt
1 tbsp Madagascar bourbon vanilla
½ cup buttermilk

CHEF SECRETS

"If you're looking for something unique to serve your guests Danish Pancake Puffs will absolutely fit the bill. If you don't have a puff pan, they're available for under $50 locally at most stores (they are often called Ebleskiver Pans) or online at [Bed Bath & Beyond](#)."

"NEVER use imitation vanilla. The chemical composition of imitation vanilla is different than 'real' vanilla and interacts differently with creations. The finest vanilla is Madagascar bourbon vanilla, pure vanilla extract. I use Nielson-Massey because of their cold extraction process, which draws out over 300 flavor compounds from the vanilla bean. You can find it online at [My Spice Sage.](#)"

"It's hard to find 'regular' buttermilk in the grocery stores. Their offerings are usually limited to non-fat. Go the extra mile and find 'regular' buttermilk. you need the fat in the buttermilk to provide the smooth mouthfeel that is such a vital part of this dish."

Chef J Stephen

AUSTRIA

Linzer Torte Cookie

Serves 14, Prep 60min, Total 1 hour 45min

Instructions

Preheat your oven to 325°

Soften your butter in a microwave

Place your softened butter in a mixing bowl with a whip attachment. Set on medium. Beat until smooth approx. 30 seconds

Set your mixer to slow and add your white granulated sugar, cake flour, and Madagascar bourbon vanilla. Gradually increase your mixer speed to medium until completely mixed

Wrap your dough in half and refrigerate until cool approx. ½ hour

Cut cooled dough in half and place half on clear wrap. Cover top with equal sized clear wrap. Clear wrap should be wider and longer than dough to accommodate rolling

With wrap remaining on top and bottom, roll out dough to ¼" thickness

Cut out 1" round holes in top piece of dough (you can save the cute outs for mini-liner torte cookies)

Line two sheet pans or cookie sheets

Place tops, bottoms and cut-outs separately on the pan's leaving at least ¼" space between each tart

Place in your pre-heated oven at 325° for approx. 40-45 minutes or until lightly brown

Remove and cool

Continued on next page

Ingredients

24 ounces unsalted butter
2 cups white granulated sugar
¼ cup Madagascar bourbon vanilla
8 cups pastry flour
½ cup confectionary sugar

Chef Secrets

"These are my favorite cookies. My Aunt Phyllis used to make these just like they were made in the old country. Although you can fill them with whatever filling you choose, the traditional fillings are raspberry, apricot or prune. My favorite is raspberry."

"Make sure you use 'Pastry' flour, NOT AP (all purpose) flour for your cookies. pastry flour strikes the ideal balance between flakiness and tenderness, making it perfect for pies, tarts and most cookies. You can find a great pastry flour at [King Arthur Flour.](#)"

"Also make sure you use Hungarian Lekvar for your raspberry and prune fillings and Blenheim apricot, for your apricot filling.. Prune Hungarian Lekvar is pretty easy to find. Raspberry is not. If you can't find raspberry make sure your filling is sugar free and made from natural fruit. You can find a great apricot filling at [B&R Farms](#)."

Chef J Stephen

AUSTRIA

LINZER TORTE COOKIE
CONTINUED

Transfer the bottoms of your cookies (those without the 1" cut-out holes) and half of the mini tops (the 1" center cuts) to lined sheet pan or cookie sheet. Top each cookie with your choice of filling ¼" thick (approx. 2 ½ to 3 ounces for the large cookies and a 1 tbsp of filling for the mini cookie)

With your confectionery sugar, sprinkle to cover each of the cookie tops (those with 1 inch holes in them) and mini cookie tops

Place your cookie tops on top of the filling covered cookie bottoms and push down firmly to raise filling through holes

You can refrigerate for 7 days or freeze for 90 days

ENGLAND

Cranberry Orange Scones

SERVES 12, PREP 30MIN, TOTAL 1 HOUR 5MIN

Ingredients

12 ounces unsalted butter
1 ½ cups white granulated sugar
5 cups cake flour
2 tbsp baking powder
½ tbsp baking soda
2 cups sour cream
2 tsp fresh squeezed orange juice
1 cup dried cranberries
1 tbsp orange zest

Instructions

Preheat your oven to 325°

Soften your butter in a microwave

Place your softened butter in a mixing bowl with a whip attachment. Set on medium. Beat until smooth approx. 30 seconds

Zest your large orange

Set your mixer to slow and add your white granulated sugar, cake flour, baking soda, baking powder, orange zest, dried cranberries, and sour cream. Gradually increase your mixer speed to medium until thoroughly incorporated

Line a sheet pan or cookie sheet

Place 1 large heaping scoop per scone on lined sheet pan. Scone should be about 1 ½" high. Scones should have a mounded, uneven texture when finished

Place in pre-heated oven for 25-30 minutes

Remove and cool

You can refrigerate for 7 days or freeze for 90 days

Chef Secrets

"I don't make my scones dry like the traditionally British scone. You'll find these scones deliciously moist."

"Make sure you use 'Cake' flour, NOT AP (all purpose) flour for your scones. Cake flour is the perfect flour for scones. You can find a great cake flour at [King Arthur Flour](). In addition, make sure your baking powder is fresh (no older than 6-month's old.)"

"If you'd like to eat your scones the traditional British way, check out my Clotted Cream recipe."

**"Zest* - scrape off the outer colored part of the peel of (a piece of citrus fruit) for use as flavoring. Make sure you don't scrape too deep to prevent bitterness."*

Chef J Stephen

Italy

Cannoli's

Serves 24, Prep 45min, Total 2 hours 25min

Instructions

Shells*
In a large bowl, whisk together your pastry flour, white granulated sugar, Saigon cinnamon, and kosher salt

Add your unsalted butter and rub it into flour with your hands until your dough looks like bread crumbs

Add your Marsala wine and 2 lightly beaten eggs. Mix by hand until a dough forms. Transfer your dough to a floured work surface and knead with your hands until smooth, approx. 6-8 minutes. Wrap in plastic wrap and refrigerate for 1 hour

Divide your dough into quarters. Working with one quarter at a time, pass your dough through widest setting on a pasta roller. Decrease the setting by one notch and pass your dough through roller again. Repeat, decreasing the width by one level each time, until you reach 1/16" thick

Using a 4" round biscuit cutter, cut out your dough and transfer to parchment paper. repeat with all your remaining dough

Working with one dough circle at a time, wrap your dough around a cannoli core, and brush the edges with your lightly beaten egg white to seal. Repeat with remaining dough. Set aside

Ingredients

Filling
1 lb. ricotta impastata cheese
¾ cup confectioners sugar (sifted)
2 tsp Madagascar bourbon vanilla
1 tsp ground Saigon cinnamon
1 tsp orange zest

Shells
2 ½ cups pastry flour
¼ cup white granulated sugar
1 tsp ground Saigon cinnamon
1 tsp kosher salt
4 tbsp unsalted butter (cubed and chilled)
5 tbsp Marsala wine
2 eggs (lightly beaten)
1 egg white (lightly beaten)
4 cups Avocado oil (for frying)
¼ cup confectioners sugar (for topping)

Chef Secrets

"You can't go very far in Italy without seeing a bakery offering cannoli's. They are as quintessentially Italian as pasta. In the States, they use ricotta cheese for their filling. I make my cannoli's like they do in Italy with impastata cheese. Impastata cheese is a smoother, dryer version of ricotta. It makes a creamier filling that doesn't make the shell soggy. It's not easy to find in the States but it's one of the key ingredients that will make your cannoli's stand out from all others. You can find Impastata online at Pasta Cheese."

Continued on next page

Continued on next page

Italy

Cannoli's

Continued

Shells

Pour your avocado oil into a large pot to a depth of approx. 2″ and heat over medium-high heat until your thermometer reads 350°

Working in batches, fry your cannoli shells until they are light brown and crisp, approx. 1-2 minutes

Using tongs, transfer your cannoli shells to paper towels to drain all oils while hot, carefully remove cannoli shells from the core's and set aside on a wire rack to cool

* If you find the making of cannoli shells too much of a chore, you can buy the shells online. They won't be as good, but it will make your task easier

Filling

*Zest your orange

Combine your impastata, white granulated sugar, Madagascar bourbon vanilla, Saigon cinnamon, and orange zest in a large bowl and whisk until smooth, approx. 2-3 minutes

Transfer to a piping bag fitted with a 3/4″ wide plain tip. Pipe your impastata mixture into your cannoli shells to fill

Garnish with confectioners sugar

You can refrigerate for 7 days or freeze for 90 days

Chef Secrets

"Most people don't have cannoli cores in their kitchen tool kits. They're not expensive (around $15 for a set) and can be found online or at their stores at [Sur la Table](#)."

"It may seem like a lot of work to make your own shells but you really can taste the difference. If you choose to go the easy way (which is unfortunately what most places that sell cannoli's do), you can buy your shells online at [Yummy Bazaar](#)."

"You don't need a piping bag to fill your cannoli. You can fill them by hand or even cut a hole in a baggie, but it's much easier to fill your cannoli's if you have one. You can find sets at [Sur le Table](#)."

"Although I'm a traditionalist and like my cannoli's like you find them in Italy, as an added treat, you can add chocolate chips to your filling and dip your cannoli shells in dark chocolate."

*"Zest - scrape off the outer colored part of the peel of (a piece of citrus fruit) for use as flavoring. Make sure you don't scrape too deep to prevent bitterness."

Chef J Stephen

Italy

Tiramisu

SERVES 12, PREP 35MIN, TOTAL 35MIN

Instructions

Combine your espresso and Kahlúa in a medium mixing bowl and refrigerate for 15 minutes

Separate your eggs and grate your chocolate

Place your egg yolks and castor sugar into a large mixing bowl with a whisk and beat at medium speed until fully incorporated, (will have a yellow color)

Put your egg whites in another mixing bowl with a whisk and beat on high speed until your egg whites form stiff peaks

In the bowl that has your egg and sugar mixture, add your mascarpone cheese and mix on slow speed until fully incorporated

Gently fold your egg whites into this mixture until thoroughly blended

Assembly
Dip your ladyfingers into your espresso mixture (to prevent them from getting soggy, do not soak)

Place one layer of dipped ladyfingers on the bottom of a serving dish

Top that layer with ½ of your whipped cream mixture spread evenly over your ladyfingers layer

Add another layer of dipped ladyfingers on top of that layer

Top this layer with your remaining whipped cream mixture

Sprinkle your whipped cream layer with cocoa and powder and your grated chocolate

Refrigerate a minimum of 6 hours prior to serving

Ingredients

2 cups coffee
4 ounces kailua
6 large eggs
⅔ cups castor sugar
⅓ cup spiced rum
17½ pounces mascarpone cheese
48 ladyfinger cookies
3 tbsp unsweetened cocoa powder
2 ounces unsweetened dark chocolate

Chef Secrets

"Interestingly, Tiramisu is not an age-old Italian dish having been created at Le Beccherie restaurant in Treviso Italy in the 1960's. Although it is relatively new to a civilization that is world renowned for its historic dishes, it has become THE classic Italian dessert. Growing up as a child, I can't remember any special dinner that had guests that was not accompanied by Tiramisu."

"Requiring no cooking whatsoever, this is a pretty easy dish to prepare. The key here is to make sure you use a good cocoa powder and dark chocolate. You can use white granulated sugar but the caster sugar will assure a creamier finish."

Chef J Stephen

Bavaria Eclairs

SERVES 6, PREP 50MIN, TOTAL 1HR 10MIN

Ingredients

Eclair Shell
1 cup whole milk
4 ounces unsalted butter
1 cup pastry flour
4 jumbo eggs

Bavarian Cream
1 ½ cups heavy cream
¼ ounce unflavored gelatin
⅔ cup of cold water
6 large eggs (separated)
⅔ cup castor sugar
2 ¼ cups whole milk
1 tbsp Madagascar bourbon vanilla
3 cups ice water

Topping
2 ounces unsweetened dark chocolate

Chef Secrets

"It takes a bit of work to craft a good eclair, but once you get it down, you'll find that they are absolutely nothing like store bought eclairs and are well worth the effort."

"Because they are a French staple and are served alongside 'other' French desserts, most people are surprised to learn that eclairs actually come from Bavaria. The misconception is due to the fact that Isabeau de Bavière, the daughter of a Bavarian duke brought them to France in the 14th century when she married French King Charles VI. Once there, the French, understanding like no other country what goes into a great dessert, assimilated it into their offerings."

Continued on next page

Instructions

Eclair Shells
Pre-heat your oven to 350°

Place your butter in a medium pot over high flame

Add your whole milk, stirring continually, bring to a boil

Add your pastry flour and stir continually until dry (comes away from the sides of your pot)

Once you can form it into a ball, place into a mixer bowl with a paddle

Set the speed to slow and mix for approx. 1 minute (this is to release the hot air from your mix)

Gradually add your jumbo eggs until a crumbly dough is formed (CAUTION: Make sure your dough is not too hot before adding your eggs. if your mix is too hot and your eggs are added too quickly, your eggs will cook)

Once your dough is fully incorporated, raise the speed to high. Mix until your dough is wet and doughy

Place your dough in a large pastry bag (without a tip)

Pipe (squeeze out of pastry bag) into 3" long eclairs (tubular shape) on a lined sheet pan

Bake at 350° for approx. 30 minutes (or until you have a firm crust but puffy)

Cool for 30 minutes

Continued on next page

BAVARIA

CHEF SECRETS (CONTINUED)

"NEVER use imitation vanilla. The chemical composition of imitation vanilla is different than 'real' vanilla and interacts differently with creations. The finest vanilla is Madagascar bourbon vanilla, pure vanilla extract. I use Nielson-Massey because of their cold extraction process, which draws out over 300 flavor compounds from the vanilla bean. You can find it online at [My Spice Sage](.)."

"Two other key ingredients are the castor sugar and the pastry flour. Eclairs are finicky, don't substitute. Your gelatin does not provide any flavor but instead, is used to thicken up your cream."

"A few of tips on assuring your eclairs stay fluffy and crisp; (1) To prevent your dough from sinking in the middle, make sure your dough is not runny and make sure you place even amounts of dough from end to end; (2) When piping, use a star tip (this will help prevent cracking of your crust); (3) Don't open your oven too soon (this lets out the steam and makes your shells collapse); and (4) Instead of pouring the chocolate topping over your eclairs, dip your eclair tops into the chocolate. This provides a much more even coating."

Chef J Stephen

ECLAIRS
CONTINUED

Bavarian Cream
Place your heavy cream into a mixer bowl with a whip and whip on high speed until soft peaks form. Refrigerate

Place your cold water into a small bowl and add your unflavored gelatin. Stir and let it thicken up for approx.12 minutes

In a large bowl, fill with ice water (make sure this bowl is big enough to fit your custard bowl inside). Pour 2 cups of your whole milk into a saucepan and bring to a boil. Remove from the heat and add your vanilla

In a mixing bowl, mix your egg <u>yolks</u> and castor sugar until your sugar is fully dissolved in the egg yolks. Whisk in your remaining $\frac{1}{4}$ cup of whole milk, then pour this egg mixture into your hot milk vanilla mix. Cook over low heat, while continually stirring. Cook until your mix thickens, approx. 10 minutes or until the mixture coats the back of your spoon without falling off and then whisk in the dissolved gelatin until dissolved

Place your bowl with the custard into your ice water bowl (to stop cooking) and stir your custard until it has cooled and thickened and then fold in your whipped cream, and refrigerate until your custard sets. Usually within 5 hours

Create Your Eclairs
Melt your unsweetened chocolate in a double broiler (or microwave) being careful not to burn. Remove from range and let cool to a thick but pourable consistency

Cut each eclair in half horizontally & remove tops. Place your custard into a pastry bag and squeeze out your custard into the bottom of your 3" long eclairs

Dip the tops into your melted chocolate & cover

Serve at room temperature or slightly chilled within 12 hours

ENGLAND

NEW ORLEANS BREAD PUDDING

SERVES 6, PREP 50MIN, TOTAL 1HR 10MIN

INGREDIENTS

1 loaf french bread
32 ounces whole milk
3 extra large eggs
2 cups white granulated sugar
2 tbsp Madagascar bourbon vanilla
3 tbsp unsalted butter (melted)
1 cup raisins
¼ tsp table salt

Whisky Sauce
4 ounces unsalted butter (melted)
1 cup white granulated sugar
1 extra large egg
¼ cup whiskey

INSTRUCTIONS

Bread
Pre-heat your oven to 375°

Place your butter in a small skillet over medium flame to melt. Set to the side

Soak your french bread in your milk. Crush it into the milk with your hands until thoroughly soaked

Add your eggs, white granulated sugar, Madagascar bourbon vanilla, raisins, and mix until fully incorporated

Pour your melted butter into the bottom of a large pan 9x13 is the ideal size

Bake until firm, approx. 40-45 minutes. Let cool

Whiskey Sauce
Mix your white granulated sugar and egg until your sugar is fully dissolved in with the egg

Place your butter in a small skillet over medium flame to melt. Set to the side

Add your melted butter as you continue to melt sugar. When fully incorporated, add your whiskey and fully incorporate

Prepare your bread pudding
Slice your bread pudding into individual servings

When ready to serve, add your whisky sauce and heat under your broiler until slightly browned or in your microwave until hot

CHEF SECRETS

"Bread pudding can trace its history to the early 11th century, as frugal cooks looked for ways to use their stale, leftover bread instead of letting it go to waste. In England, bread pudding was known as 'poor mans pudding,' because it was a popular dish with the lower classes. Today, it's become a popular dish that's offered at many restaurants."

"There are many variations but the two most popular versions is the brandy based and creamy New Orleans whisky styles. At my bistro's we offered a New Orleans style bread pudding that I learned while staying at my favorite landing spot when visiting the bourbon street area, the Saint Charles Hotel."

Chef J Stephen

UNITED STATES

BANANA CREAM PIE

SERVES 6, PREP 50MIN, TOTAL 1HR 10MIN

INGREDIENTS

2 cups whole milk (room temp)
3 large eggs (separated)
½ cup white granulated sugar
3 tsp Madagascar bourbon vanilla
2 tbsp unsalted butter (melted)
3 tbsp cornstarch
¼ tsp table salt
2 tsp vanilla extract
4 fresh bananas (sliced)

Whipped Cream
2 cups heavy whipping cream
2 tbsp confectioners sugar

Vanilla Wafer Pie Crust
3 ounces unsalted butter (melted)
60 vanilla wafers

Graham Cracker Pie Crust
3 ounces unsalted butter (melted)
1 ½ cups graham crackers (crumbled)
⅓ cup white granulated sugar

CHEF SECRETS

"Banana Cream pies are pretty easy to make. You're actually making two different dishes, pudding and pie. In addition, there are two different types of crust. I've given you the recipe for both. Pick the type that you prefer."

Continued on next page

INSTRUCTIONS

Banana Pudding
Pre-heat your oven to 350°. Bake your pie crust and remove to cool

Separate your eggs and slice your bananas

Add your whole milk, white granulated sugar, cornstarch, and table salt to a medium saucepan over medium heat, stirring continually, until the mixture is bubbling slowly. Once you reach this stage, cook for an additional 5 minutes while continually stirring to prevent burning. Remove from the heat

Once your mix has cooked you need to temper in your egg yolks. You can do this by placing your hot mix into a blender, setting it on slow speed and then adding your egg yolks

Pour you tempered mix back into your saucepan place on medium heat and whisk for approx. 3 minutes (or until thickened to a pudding consistency)

Remove from the heat and add in your melted butter and Madagascar bourbon vanilla while continuing to whisk

Place your banana slices on the bottom of your pie shell, cover the slices with your pudding and lay clear wrap onto the pie gently touching the pudding, to prevent a skin from forming on the surface

Continued on next page

UNITED STATES

BANANA CREAM PIE

SERVES 6, PREP 50MIN, TOTAL 1HR 10MIN

CONTINUED

Cool your pie in the fridge for four hours

Just prior to serving, add banana slices to the top and top with your whipped cream

Whipped Cream
In a mixing bowl, with a whip, add your confectioners sugar and your heavy cream

Beat on high speed until it forms medium peaks, approx. 2 minutes

Pie Crust
Vanilla Wafer Crust - Mix your vanilla wafers and melted butter together. Press into a pie dish and bake at 350° for 11 minutes

Graham Cracker Crust - Mix your graham cracker crumbs, white granulated sugar and melted butter together by hand. Press into a pie dish and baked at 350° for 11 minutes

CHEF SECRETS (CONTINUED

"I know it's so easy to simply buy whipped cream, BUT it's almost as easy to make it and it tastes so much better, has no preservatives, artificial flavorings or chemicals. Two minutes of your time is all it takes to (excuse the pun) 'whip' it up."

"You'll notice I mention 'tempering' your eggs. Tempering eggs is a process of slowly warming the eggs before introducing them to your recipe. If you put your eggs into a hot pot of milk, you'll end up with little scrambled egg bits in the milk instead of a smooth mixture. Tempering your eggs assures a smooth mix with no egg lumps."

"To prevent your bananas from turning brown, wait until just before serving to slice and add your banana's on the top of your whipped cream."

Chef J Stephen

UNITED STATES

CHOCOLATE CREAM PIE

Serves 6, Prep 50min, Total 1hr 10min

INGREDIENTS

2 cups whole milk (room temp)
4 large eggs (separated)
½ cup white granulated sugar
3 tsp Madagascar bourbon vanilla
2 tbsp unsalted butter (melted)
¼ cup cornstarch
¼ tsp table salt
½ tsp espresso powder
¾ cup dark brown Muscovado sugar
6 ounces semisweet dark chocolate (chopped)

Whipped Cream
2 cups heavy whipping cream
2 tbsp confectioners sugar

Vanilla Wafer Pie Crust
3 ounces unsalted butter (melted)
60 vanilla wafers

Graham Cracker Pie Crust
3 ounces unsalted butter (melted)
1 ½ cups graham crackers (crumbled)
⅓ cup white granulated sugar

CHEF SECRETS

"Chocolate Cream pies are pretty easy to make. You're actually making two different dishes, pudding and pie. In addition, there are two different types of crust. I've given you the recipe for both. Pick the type that you prefer."

Continued on next page

INSTRUCTIONS

Chocolate Pudding
Pre-heat your oven to 350°. Bake your pie crust and remove to cool

Add your whole milk and chocolate to a medium saucepan over low heat, stirring continually with a whisk, until your chocolate has completely melted

Separate your eggs. In a large bowl, place your egg yolks (save your egg whites for later) and dark brown Muscovado sugar until you start to see the formation of ribbons as you mix, approx. 3 minutes. Add your cornstarch, table salt, and espresso powder. Mix until fully incorporated

Slowly whisk your heated milk mixture into the bowl with your egg mix, make sure you whisk continually while adding to keep your eggs from cooking. Whisk until smooth

Return your combined mix to your saucepan and cook over medium heat, whisking occasionally, until your mixture thickens and bubbles begin to form around the edges of the pan, approx. 6 minutes

Remove from heat and whisk until smooth

When smooth, transfer your chocolate pudding filling into your pie crust

Lay clear wrap onto the pie gently touching the pudding, to prevent a skin from forming on the surface

Continued on next page

UNITED STATES

Chocolate Cream Pie

Serves 6, Prep 50min, Total 1hr 10min

Continued

Cool your pie in the fridge for four hours

Slice semi-sweet dark chocolate swirls (see photo)

Top your chocolate pudding filling with your whipped cream and garnish with your dark chocolate swirls

Whipped Cream
In a mixing bowl, with a whip, add your confectioners sugar and your heavy cream. Beat on high speed until it forms medium peaks, approx. 2 minutes

Pie Crust
Vanilla Wafer Crust - Mix your vanilla wafers and melted butter together. Press into a pie dish and bake at 350° for 11 minutes

Graham Cracker Crust - Mix your graham cracker crumbs, white granulated sugar and melted butter together by hand. Press into a pie dish and baked at 350° for 11 minutes

Chef Secrets (continued)

"I know it's so easy to simply buy whipped cream, BUT, it's almost as easy to make it and it tastes so much better, has no preservatives, artificial flavorings or chemicals. Two minutes of your time is all it takes to (excuse the pun) 'whip' it up."

"NEVER use that store bought cooking chocolate for your pudding filling OR your chocolate swirls. Wait until just before serving to slice and add your chocolate shavings on the top of your whipped cream."

Chef J Stephen

AUSTRIA

APPLE STRUDEL CRUMB CAKE

SERVES 12, PREP 45MIN, TOTAL 1HR 45MIN

INGREDIENTS

Cake
¾ cup sour cream (room temperature)
4 large eggs (separated; room temperature)
1 ½ tsp Madagascar bourbon vanilla
6 ounces unsalted butter (room temperature)
¾ cup cake flour (sifted)
¾ cup castor sugar
¼ tsp kosher salt
½ tsp baking powder
½ tsp baking soda

Crumb Topping (serves 1 cake)
1 cup unsalted butter
½ cup white granulated sugar
½ cup dark brown Muscovado sugar
1 ½ tbsp Saigon cinnamon
½ tsp kosher salt
1 ½ tbsp Madagascar bourbon vanilla
1 ⅓ cups cake flour (no substitute)

Apple Strudel Filling/Topping (makes 3 cups)
2 cups Granny Smith apples (peeled, cored, and diced)
1 tbsp fresh lemon juice
1 ½ cups water
½ cup white granulated sugar
1 ½ ounces cornstarch
½ tsp Saigon cinnamon
⅛ tsp kosher salt
⅛ teaspoon fresh nutmeg (ground)

(see "Chef's Secrets" on next page)

INSTRUCTIONS

Apple Strudel Filling
Place your Granny Smith apples in a large bowl and toss with your lemon juice

Place your water, white granulated sugar, cornstarch, Saigon cinnamon, kosher salt, and fresh ground nutmeg in a medium saucepan

Mix to combine thoroughly

Place on range over medium heat and while stirring often, bring to a boil. Continue to boil for 2 minutes and then add your Granny Smith apples

Turn to a simmer and cover

Cook, stirring often, until your apples soften, approx. 7 minutes

Cool at room temperature then cover and refrigerate for a minimum of three hours. The cooling process will cause your filling to thicken to the proper thickness

Crumbs Topping
Melt your unsalted butter in a microwave or sauce pan on low heat. DO NOT BOIL

Combine your granulated white sugar, dark brown Muscovado sugar, kosher salt, and Saigon cinnamon into a mixing bowl

Mix with a paddle, on slow speed until ALL lumps have been removed

Continued on next page

AUSTRIA

APPLE STRUDEL CRUMB CAKE

CONTINUED

Crumbs Topping (continued)
Add your melted butter and Madagascar bourbon vanilla

Mix with a paddle on slow speed until fully incorporated

Add your cake flour into the mix and mix on slow speed until fully incorporated

"When finished, your crumbs won't look like crumbs. Don't worry, you will pull them apart and form your crumbs when you make your cake."

Cake Preparation
Preheat your oven to 300°

Take out your apple strudel filling from the refrigerator

CREATE YOUR DRY MIX
Sift your cake flour into a mixing bowl and add your castor sugar, kosher salt, baking powder, and baking soda. Combine to create your dry mix

CREATE YOUR WET MIX
Separate your large eggs, placing the yolks in a bowl. (You will not be using your egg whites). Add your Madagascar bourbon vanilla to your egg yolks

Place your sour cream in a medium deli container

COMBINE MIXES
Cut your unsalted butter into ⅛" thick pieces

Add your cut unsalted butter to your dry mix

Add ¾ (only) of the sour cream to your dry mix

Continued on next page

CHEF SECRETS

"My crumb cake recipe is an updated version of my family's 400-year-old recipe from Austria (to bake my family's original recipe, see my Old World Style Crumb Cake recipe). The crumbs and streusel used in all my crumb cake recipe's are exactly as they were from the original recipe. The only change to the original recipe is the use of a golden cake versus a yeast dough cake base. The reason for this change is due to spoilage. I ship my cakes worldwide and because yeast cakes only retain their freshness for 3-4 days (without preservatives), I was faced with a dilemma. I NEVER use any artificial flavors, chemicals, colorants or preservatives in any of my cakes. The average time a client would receive my shipped cakes in the States is 2-4 days, just as they were started to reach their freshness limits. Properly wrapped, a golden cake will retain its freshness for 7-10 days. The choice was simple and that is why, all of my crumb cakes (except for my Old World Style Crumb Cake recipe) feature a golden cake recipe."

"My family's double bake process is unique to baking a crumb cake. It assures that the fillings and crumbs topping will remain on the top of the cake and not drift into the cake mix."

"It's important that you use they type of ingredients specified without substitution. Cinnamon - Most cinnamon sold in the States is an inferior Cassia cinnamon that provides overpowering spikes in taste. The subtle complexity of flavor and texture of Ceylon cinnamon from Vietnam, is far superior. It builds gradually into a complex symphony of rich floral flavors and aromas that compliment rather than overwhelm as Cassia does. Although expensive and often hard to find, Ceylon cinnamon also known as Saigon cinnamon should be a vital part of your basic ingredient set.."

Continued on next page

AUSTRIA

APPLE STRUDEL CRUMB CAKE
CONTINUED

Cake Preparation (continued)
Mix with a paddle for 1 minute 30 seconds (start slow, progress to med/high speed)

Add your remaining ¼ of your sour cream and the your egg yolk, vanilla wet mix to the dry mix

Mix for 1 minute (start slow, progress to med/high speed)

Create Cake
With pan spray, spray a 10" cake pan (include sides) and pour cake mix into your sprayed cake pan

Bake at 300° for approx. 30 minutes (your cake should be partially cooked but firm enough to hold your topping and crumbs)

Remove your cake from oven and using a spatula, top your cake with a thin layer (approx. 6 ounces) of your apple strudel filling

Make sure your cake is completely covered with your layer of apple strudel

Break up, with your hands, your crumb topping to form crumbs. Top your apple strudel filling layer with your crumbs

Top your crumbs with your remaining apple strudel filling (approx. 6 ounces) in an irregular pattern (see photo)

Place your cake back in your oven at 300° for an additional 30 minutes

Check your cake with a toothpick in the center. When your cake is done, remove from oven. Place your cake on a cooling rack to cool

You can refrigerate for 10 days or freeze for 120 days

CHEF SECRETS (CONTINUED)

"Vanilla - NEVER use imitation vanilla. The chemical composition of imitation vanilla is different than 'real' vanilla and interacts differently with creations. The finest vanilla is Madagascar bourbon vanilla, pure vanilla extract. I use Nielson-Massey because of their cold extraction process, which draws out over 300 flavor compounds from the vanilla bean. You can find it online at [My Spice Sage](#)."

"Castor Sugar - Also known as superfine sugar produces a finer, lighter, more delicate cake which is what you're looking for here. You can find castor sugar at some grocers and online at [India Tree](#)."

"Cake Flour - Although you can use AP (all purpose) flour for most of your baking needs, it's always better to use the specific flour designed for the task. Cake Flour is a low protein, low gluten flour that is perfect for cakes, muffins, biscuits, and most other baked goods. That's why you'll always see it specified in my cake recipe's. You can find cake flour at most of your grocery stores. I believe that Swans Down is the best and you can find it at [Walmart](#)."

Chef J Stephen

AUSTRIA

BLENHEIM APRICOT CRUMB CAKE

Serves 12, Prep 45min, Total 1hr 45min

Ingredients

Cake
¾ cup sour cream (room temperature)
4 large eggs (separated; room temperature)
1 ½ tsp Madagascar bourbon vanilla
6 ounces unsalted butter (room temperature)
¾ cup cake flour (sifted)
¾ cup castor sugar
¼ tsp kosher salt
½ tsp baking powder
½ tsp baking soda

Crumb Topping (serves 1 cake)
1 cup unsalted butter
½ cup white granulated sugar
½ cup dark brown Muscovado sugar
1 ½ tbsp Saigon cinnamon
½ tsp kosher salt
1 ½ tbsp Madagascar bourbon vanilla
1 ⅓ cups cake flour (no substitute)

Blenheim Apricot Filling/Topping
12 ounces Blenheim apricot topping

Chef Secrets

"When it comes to your apricot filling, you can use apricot jam, BUT it won't taste near as good as apricot filling. What you traditionally find in the grocery store are Turkish apricots and they don't come close to the robust flavor of Blenheim apricots. Blenheim apricots come from California and I use Blenheim apricot topping on all my apricot cakes and you can find it at the same place we buy ours online at: B&R Farms. Their topping beat all others."

Continued on next page

Instructions

Crumbs Topping
Melt your unsalted butter in a microwave or sauce pan on low heat. DO NOT BOIL

Combine your granulated white sugar, dark brown Muscovado sugar, kosher salt, and Saigon cinnamon into a mixing bowl

Mix with a paddle, on slow speed until ALL lumps have been removed

Add your melted butter and Madagascar bourbon vanilla

Mix with a paddle on slow speed until fully incorporated

Add your cake flour into the mix and mix on slow speed until fully incorporated

"When finished, your crumbs won't look like crumbs. Don't worry, you will pull them apart and form your crumbs when you make your cake."

Cake Preparation
Preheat your oven to 300°

CREATE YOUR DRY MIX
Sift your cake flour into a mixing bowl and add your castor sugar, kosher salt, baking powder, and baking soda. Combine to create your dry mix

Continued on next page

199

AUSTRIA

BLENHEIM APRICOT CRUMB CAKE

CONTINUED

CHEF SECRETS (CONTINUED)

"My crumb cake recipe is an updated version of my family's 400-year-old recipe from Austria (to bake my family's original recipe, see my Old World Style Crumb Cake recipe). The crumbs and streusel used in all my crumb cake recipe's are exactly as they were from the original recipe. The only change to the original recipe is the use of a golden cake versus a yeast dough cake base. The reason for this change is due to spoilage. I ship my cakes worldwide and because yeast cakes only retain their freshness for 3-4 days (without preservatives), I was faced with a dilemma. I NEVER use any artificial flavors, chemicals, colorants or preservatives in any of my cakes. The average time a client would receive my shipped cakes in the States is 2-4 days, just as they were started to reach their freshness limits. Properly wrapped, a golden cake will retain its freshness for 7-10 days. The choice was simple and that is why, all of my crumb cakes (except for my Old World Style Crumb Cake recipe) feature a golden cake recipe."

"My family's double bake process is unique to baking a crumb cake. It assures that the fillings and crumbs topping will remain on the top of the cake and not drift into the cake mix."

"It's important that you use they type of ingredients specified without substitution. Cinnamon - Most cinnamon sold in the States is an inferior Cassia cinnamon that provides overpowering spikes in taste. The subtle complexity of flavor and texture of Ceylon cinnamon from Vietnam, is far superior. It builds gradually into a complex symphony of rich floral flavors and aromas that compliment rather than overwhelm as Cassia does. Although expensive and often hard to find, Ceylon cinnamon also known as Saigon cinnamon should be a vital part of your basic ingredient set.."

Continued on next page

Cake Preparation (continued)

CREATE YOUR WET MIX

Separate your large eggs, placing the yolks in a bowl. (You will not be using your egg whites)

Add your Madagascar bourbon vanilla to your egg yolks

Place your sour cream in a medium deli container

COMBINE YOUR MIXES

Cut your unsalted butter into ⅛" thick pieces

Add your cut unsalted butter to your dry mix

Add ¾ (only) of the sour cream to your dry mix

Mix with a paddle for 1 minute 30 seconds (start slow, progress to med/high speed)

Add your remaining ¼ of your sour cream, your egg yolk, and vanilla wet mix to the dry mix

Mix for 1 minute (start slow, progress to med/high speed)

Continued on next page

AUSTRIA

BLENHEIM APRICOT CRUMB CAKE

CONTINUED

CHEF SECRETS (CONTINUED)

"Vanilla - NEVER use imitation vanilla. The chemical composition of imitation vanilla is different than 'real' vanilla and interacts differently with creations. The finest vanilla is Madagascar bourbon vanilla, pure vanilla extract. I use Nielson-Massey because of their cold extraction process, which draws out over 300 flavor compounds from the vanilla bean. You can find it online at [My Spice Sage](#)."

"Castor Sugar - Also known as superfine sugar produces a finer, lighter, more delicate cake which is what you're looking for here. You can find castor sugar at some grocers and online at [India Tree](#)."

"Cake Flour - Although you can use AP (all purpose) flour for most of your baking needs, it's always better to use the specific flour designed for the task. Cake Flour is a low protein, low gluten flour that is perfect for cakes, muffins, biscuits, and most other baked goods. That's why you'll always see it specified in my cake recipe's. You can find cake flour at most of your grocery stores. I believe that Swans Down is the best and you can find it at [Walmart](#)."

Chef J Stephen

Create Cake
With pan spray, spray a 10" cake pan (include sides)

Pour your cake mix into your sprayed cake pan

Bake at 300° for approx. 30 minutes (your cake should be partially cooked but firm enough to hold your topping and crumbs)

Remove your cake from oven and using a spatula, top your cake with a thin layer (approx. 6 ounces) of your Blenheim apricot topping. Make sure your cake is completely covered with your layer of Blenheim apricot topping

Break up, with your hands, your crumb topping to form crumbs. Top your Blenheim apricot topping layer with your crumbs

Using a squeeze bottle or pastry bag, top your crumbs with an additional layer of Blenheim apricot topping (approx. 6 ounces) in an irregular pattern (see photo)

Place your cake back in your oven at 300° for an additional 30 minutes

Check your cake with a toothpick in the center. When your cake is done, remove from oven. Place your cake on a cooling rack to cool

You can refrigerate for 10 days or freeze for 120 days

AUSTRIA

BANANA'S FOSTER CRUMB CAKE

Serves 12, Prep 45min, Total 1hr 45min

INGREDIENTS

Cake
¾ cup sour cream (room temperature)
4 large eggs separated; (room temperature)
1 ½ tsp Madagascar bourbon vanilla
6 ounces unsalted butter (room temperature)
¾ cup cake flour (sifted)
¾ cup castor sugar
¼ tsp kosher salt
½ tsp baking powder
½ tsp baking soda

Crumb Topping (serves 1 cake)
1 cup unsalted butter
½ cup white granulated sugar
½ cup dark brown Muscovado sugar
1 ½ tbsp Saigon cinnamon
½ tsp kosher salt
1 ½ tbsp Madagascar bourbon vanilla
1 ⅓ cups cake flour (no substitute)

Banana's Foster Filling/Topping (makes 3 cups)
½ cup pecan halves
12 ounces unsalted butter
1 ½ cups dark brown Muscovado sugar
½ cup white granulated sugar
4 tsp dark spiced rum
¼ cup water
½ tbsp kosher salt
1 large fresh banana

(see "Chef's Secrets" on next page)

INSTRUCTIONS

Banana's Foster Filling
Place your pecan halves on a lined sheet pan or cookie sheet

Bake your pecans for 5 minutes (or until lightly toasted)

Melt your unsalted butter in a medium sauce pan on medium heat

Add your toasted pecans, dark brown Muscovado sugar, rum, water, and kosher salt to mix

Stir occasionally over high heat until it reaches the consistency of syrup (approx. 25 minutes)

Remove from heat and let cool

Crumbs Topping
Melt your unsalted butter in a microwave or sauce pan on low heat. DO NOT BOIL

Combine your granulated white sugar, dark brown Muscovado sugar, kosher salt, and Saigon cinnamon into a mixing bowl

Mix with a paddle, on slow speed until ALL lumps have been removed

Crumbs Topping (continued)
Add your melted butter and Madagascar bourbon vanilla

Mix with a paddle on slow speed until fully incorporated

Continued on next page

AUSTRIA

BANANA'S FOSTER CRUMB CAKE

CHEF SECRETS

"My crumb cake recipe is an updated version of my family's 400-year-old recipe from Austria (to bake my family's original recipe, see my Old World Style Crumb Cake recipe). The crumbs and streusel used in all my crumb cake recipe's are exactly as they were from the original recipe. The only change to the original recipe is the use of a golden cake versus a yeast dough cake base. The reason for this change is due to spoilage. I ship my cakes worldwide and because yeast cakes only retain their freshness for 3-4 days (without preservatives), I was faced with a dilemma. I NEVER use any artificial flavors, chemicals, colorants or preservatives in any of my cakes. The average time a client would receive my shipped cakes in the States is 2-4 days, just as they were started to reach their freshness limits. Properly wrapped, a golden cake will retain its freshness for 7-10 days. The choice was simple and that is why, all of my crumb cakes (except for my Old World Style Crumb Cake recipe) feature a golden cake recipe."

"My family's double bake process is unique to baking a crumb cake. It assures that the fillings and crumbs topping will remain on the top of the cake and not drift into the cake mix."

"It's important that you use they type of ingredients specified without substitution. Cinnamon - Most cinnamon sold in the States is an inferior Cassia cinnamon that provides overpowering spikes in taste. The subtle complexity of flavor and texture of Ceylon cinnamon from Vietnam, is far superior."

Continued on next page

CONTINUED

Add your cake flour into the mix and mix on slow speed until fully incorporated

"When finished, your crumbs won't look like crumbs. Don't worry, you will pull them apart and form your crumbs when you make your cake."

Cake Preparation
Preheat your oven to 300°

Take out your apple strudel filling from the refrigerator

CREATE YOUR DRY MIX
Sift your cake flour into a mixing bowl and add your castor sugar, kosher salt, baking powder, and baking soda. Combine to create your dry mix

CREATE YOUR WET MIX
Separate your large eggs, placing the yolks in a bowl. (You will not be using your egg whites). Add your Madagascar bourbon vanilla to your egg yolks

Place your sour cream in a medium deli container

COMBINE MIXES
Cut your unsalted butter into ⅛" thick pieces

Add your cut unsalted butter to your dry mix

Add ¾ (only) of the sour cream to your dry mix

Mix with a paddle for 1 minute 30 seconds (start slow, progress to med/high speed)

Add your remaining ¼ of your sour cream and the your egg yolk, vanilla wet mix to the dry mix

Continued on next page

AUSTRIA

BANANA'S FOSTER CRUMB CAKE
CONTINUED

CHEF SECRETS (CONTINUED)

"It builds gradually into a complex symphony of rich floral flavors and aromas that compliment rather than overwhelm as Cassia does. Although expensive and often hard to find, Ceylon cinnamon also known as Saigon cinnamon should be a vital part of your basic ingredient set."

"Vanilla - NEVER use imitation vanilla. The chemical composition of imitation vanilla is different than 'real' vanilla and interacts differently with creations. The finest vanilla is Madagascar bourbon vanilla, pure vanilla extract. I use Nielson-Massey because of their cold extraction process, which draws out over 300 flavor compounds from the vanilla bean. You can find it online at My Spice Sage."

"Castor Sugar - Also known as superfine sugar produces a finer, lighter, more delicate cake which is what you're looking for here. You can find castor sugar at some grocers and online at India Tree."

"Cake Flour - Although you can use AP (all purpose) flour for most of your baking needs, it's always better to use the specific flour designed for the task. Cake Flour is a low protein, low gluten flour that is perfect for cakes, muffins, biscuits and most other baked goods. That's why you'll always see it specified in my cake recipe's. You can find cake flour at most of your grocery stores. I believe that Swans Down is the best and you can find it at Walmart."

Chef J Stephen

Cake Preparation (continued)
Mix for 1 minute (start slow, progress to med/high speed)

Create Cake
With pan spray, spray a 10" cake pan (include sides) and pour cake mix into your sprayed cake pan

Bake at 300° for approx. 30 minutes (your cake should be partially cooked but firm enough to hold your topping and crumbs)

Remove your cake from oven and using a spatula, top your cake with a thin layer (approx. 6 ounces) of your banana's foster filling

Make sure your cake is completely covered with a layer of your banana's foster filling. Add ½ of your fresh banana

Break up, with your hands, your crumb topping to form crumbs. Top your banana's foster filling layer with your crumbs

Top your crumbs with the other ½ of your fresh banana and top with your remaining banana's foster filling (approx. 6 ounces) in an irregular pattern (see photo). Make sure your fresh bananas are covered by the filling

Place your cake back in your oven at 300° for an additional 30 minutes

Check your cake with a toothpick in the center. When your cake is done, remove from oven. Place your cake on a cooling rack to cool

You can refrigerate for 10 days or freeze for 120 days

AUSTRIA

Caramel Sea Salt Crumb Cake

Serves 12, Prep 45min, Total 1hr 45min

Ingredients

Cake
¾ cup sour cream (room temperature)
4 large eggs separated; (room temperature)
1 ½ tsp Madagascar bourbon vanilla
6 ounces unsalted butter (room temperature)
¾ cup cake flour (sifted)
¾ cup castor sugar
¼ tsp kosher salt
½ tsp baking powder
½ tsp baking soda

Crumb Topping (serves 1 cake)
1 cup unsalted butter
½ cup white granulated sugar
½ cup dark brown Muscovado sugar
1 ½ tbsp Saigon cinnamon
½ tsp kosher salt
1 ½ tbsp Madagascar bourbon vanilla
1 ⅓ cups cake flour (no substitute)

Caramel Filling/Topping (makes 1 ½ cups)
¼ cup heavy whipping cream
1 ounce unsalted butter
1 ounce clear Kari syrup
¼ cup water
1 cup white granulated sugar

Garnish
1 tbsp sea salt

IMPORTANT
To create a decent caramel, timing is of utmost importance. Have a timer at the ready and pre-measure all your ingredients. Place each ingredient (in order of use) by the pot. Don't vary your time from the directions.

(see "Chef's Secrets" on next page)

Instructions

Caramel Filling & Topping
Pour your water into a medium pot. Add your white granulated sugar. Dissolve the sugar by whisking in the water (**NO FLAME**)

Cook on medium high flame, continue to dissolve. **DO NOT STIR**. Bring to a boil. Boil for approx. 20 minutes. Boil until the mix starts to turn golden brown. Remove from flame immediately

Add your clear Karo syrup and mix with a whisk for 30 seconds. Set your flame to low

Return your mix to the flame, while continually mixing. Cook for 1 minute. Add your unsalted butter. Mix for 30 seconds

Add your heavy cream. (**CAREFUL OF STEAM**) Turn off flame. Stir until caramel stops boiling Cool in pot

Pour when cool but still pourable, pour into a squeeze bottle

Crumbs Topping
Melt your unsalted butter in a microwave or sauce pan on low heat. **DO NOT BOIL**

Combine your granulated white sugar, dark brown Muscovado sugar, kosher salt, and Saigon cinnamon into a mixing bowl. Mix with a paddle, on slow speed until ALL lumps have been removed. Add your melted butter and Madagascar bourbon vanilla. Mix with a paddle on slow speed until fully incorporated

Continued on next page

AUSTRIA

CARAMEL SEA SALT CRUMB CAKE

CHEF SECRETS

"My crumb cake recipe is an updated version of my family's 400-year-old recipe from Austria (to bake my family's original recipe, see my Old World Style Crumb Cake recipe). The crumbs and streusel used in all my crumb cake recipe's are exactly as they were from the original recipe. The only change to the original recipe is the use of a golden cake versus a yeast dough cake base. The reason for this change is due to spoilage. I ship my cakes worldwide and because yeast cakes only retain their freshness for 3-4 days (without preservatives), I was faced with a dilemma. I NEVER use any artificial flavors, chemicals, colorants or preservatives in any of my cakes. The average time a client would receive my shipped cakes in the States is 2-4 days, just as they were started to reach their freshness limits. Properly wrapped, a golden cake will retain its freshness for 7-10 days. The choice was simple and that is why, all of my crumb cakes (except for my Old World Style Crumb Cake recipe) feature a golden cake recipe."

"My family's double bake process is unique to baking a crumb cake. It assures that the fillings and crumbs topping will remain on the top of the cake and not drift into the cake mix."

"It's important that you use they type of ingredients specified without substitution. Cinnamon - Most cinnamon sold in the States is an inferior Cassia cinnamon that provides overpowering spikes in taste. The subtle complexity of flavor and texture of Ceylon cinnamon from Vietnam, is far superior."

Continued on next page

CONTINUED

Add your cake flour into the mix and mix on slow speed until fully incorporated

"When finished, your crumbs won't look like crumbs. Don't worry, you will pull them apart and form your crumbs when you make your cake."

Cake Preparation
Preheat your oven to 300°

CREATE YOUR DRY MIX
Sift your cake flour into a mixing bowl and add your castor sugar, kosher salt, baking powder, and baking soda. Combine to create your dry mix

CREATE YOUR WET MIX
Separate your large eggs, placing the yolks in a bowl. (You will not be using your egg whites). Add your Madagascar bourbon vanilla to your egg yolks

Place your sour cream in a medium deli container

COMBINE MIXES
Cut your unsalted butter into ⅛" thick pieces

Add your cut unsalted butter to your dry mix

Add ¾ (only) of the sour cream to your dry mix

Mix with a paddle for 1 minute 30 seconds (start slow, progress to med/high speed)

Add your remaining ¼ of your sour cream and the your egg yolk, vanilla wet mix to the dry mix

Mix for 1 minute (start slow, progress to med/high speed)

Continued on next page

AUSTRIA

CARAMEL SEA SALT CRUMB CAKE

CONTINUED

CHEF SECRETS (CONTINUED)

"It builds gradually into a complex symphony of rich floral flavors and aromas that compliment rather than overwhelm as Cassia does. Although expensive and often hard to find, Ceylon cinnamon also known as Saigon cinnamon should be a vital part of your basic ingredient set."

"Vanilla - NEVER use imitation vanilla. The chemical composition of imitation vanilla is different than 'real' vanilla and interacts differently with creations. The finest vanilla is Madagascar bourbon vanilla, pure vanilla extract. I use Nielson-Massey because of their cold extraction process, which draws out over 300 flavor compounds from the vanilla bean. You can find it online at [My Spice Sage](#)."

"Castor Sugar - Also known as superfine sugar produces a finer, lighter, more delicate cake which is what you're looking for here. You can find castor sugar at some grocers and online at [India Tree](#)."

"Cake Flour - Although you can use AP (all purpose) flour for most of your baking needs, it's always better to use the specific flour designed for the task. Cake Flour is a low protein, low gluten flour that is perfect for cakes, muffins, biscuits and most other baked goods. That's why you'll always see it specified in my cake recipe's. You can find cake flour at most of your grocery stores. I believe that Swans Down is the best and you can find it at [Walmart](#)."

"Make sure you only use 'sea salt' on your cake. I use Baleine French sea salt, which you can find locally at your grocer and online at [Instacart.](#)"

Chef J Stephen

Create Cake
With pan spray, spray a 10" cake pan (include sides) and pour cake mix into your sprayed cake pan

Bake at 300° for approx. 30 minutes (your cake should be partially cooked but firm enough to hold your topping and crumbs)

Remove your cake from oven and using a spatula, top your cake with a thin layer (approx. 6 ounces) of your caramel (if your caramel is too thick to pour, microwave briefly)

Make sure your cake is completely covered with a layer of your caramel

Break up, with your hands, your crumb topping to form crumbs. Top your banana's foster filling layer with your crumbs

Place your cake back in your oven at 300° for an additional 30 minutes

Check your cake with a toothpick in the center. When your cake is done, remove from oven. Place your cake on a cooling rack to cool

Once your cake is completely cooled, top it with your caramel (approx. 6 ounces) in an irregular pattern (see photo)

Evenly sprinkle your sea salt on top of your cake

You can refrigerate for 10 days or freeze for 120 days

AUSTRIA

CARROT CAKE CRUMB CAKE

SERVES 12, PREP 45MIN, TOTAL 1HR 45MIN

INSTRUCTIONS

Carrot Cake Topping

Place your cream cheese in plastic bowl in your microwave for approx. 30 second, (or until smooth)

Place your unsalted butter in your microwave for 10 seconds

Place your softened cream cheese, softened unsalted butter, all spice and Madagascar bourbon vanilla (All ingredients except confectioners sugar) into a mixing bowl. Mix using a whisk until creamed and then add your confectioners sugar slowly while continuing to mix until fully incorporated. Pour into a squeeze bottle

Carrot Cake Filling

Place your unsalted butter into your microwave for 10 seconds to soften
Grate your carrots

Place your cake flour, baking powder, white sugar, baking soda, salt, cinnamon, all spice together in a mixing bowl and then mix with a paddle on slow. When it's fully mixed, add your large egg, softened unsalted butter, vanilla, and grated carrots to dry mix. Mix on medium for 1½ minutes

Lemon Curd

In a large mixing bowl, add your butter and sugar and whisk for approx. 2 minutes

Slowly add your eggs and yolks. Whisk for 1 minute. Add your lemon juice. Don't worry about curdled look, it will smooth into a curd as it cooks

Continued on next page

INGREDIENTS

Cake
¾ cup sour cream (room temperature)
4 large eggs separated; (room temperature)
1 ½ tsp Madagascar bourbon vanilla
6 ounces unsalted butter (room temperature)
¾ cup cake flour (sifted)
¾ cup castor sugar
¼ tsp kosher salt
½ tsp baking powder
½ tsp baking soda

Crumb Topping (serves 1 cake)
1 cup unsalted butter
½ cup white granulated sugar
½ cup dark brown Muscovado sugar
1 ½ tbsp Saigon cinnamon
½ tsp kosher salt
1 ½ tbsp Madagascar bourbon vanilla
1 ⅓ cups cake flour (no substitute)

Carrot Cake Topping (serves 1 cake)
½ ounce cream cheese
1 ounce confectioners sugar
¼ ounce unsalted butter (room temperature)
¼ tsp all spice
¼ tsp Madagascar bourbon vanilla

Carrot Cake Filling (serves 1 cake)
1 Large egg
2 ½ ounces unsalted butter
¼ cup cake flour
½ tsp baking powder
½ tsp baking soda
½ cup white granulated sugar
⅛ tsp kosher salt

Continued on next page

AUSTRIA

CARROT CAKE CRUMB CAKE
CONTINUED

Lemon Curd (continued)
In a medium saucepan, cook your curd over low heat until it becomes smooth. Raise the heat to medium and cook, stirring continually, until the curd thickens, approx. 15 minutes (should hold to the back of a spoon). DO NOT BOIL. Remove your curd from the heat; stir in your lemon zest. Transfer your curd to a bowl. Cover with plastic wrap on the surface of the curd and chill in the refrigerator. The curd will thicken further as it cools

Cheesecake Filling
Place your cream cheese in plastic bowl and place in your microwave for approx. 30 second intervals (or until smooth)

In a mixer bowl, with paddle, combine your cream cheese and granulated sugar for approx. 30 seconds on medium speed. Add your whole milk and large egg and mix for approx. 1 minute. Add your sour cream, Madagascar bourbon vanilla and AP flour and mix for approx. 15 seconds on medium speed

Crumbs Topping
Melt your unsalted butter in a microwave or sauce pan on low heat. DO NOT BOIL

Combine your granulated white sugar, dark brown Muscovado sugar, kosher salt, and Saigon cinnamon into a mixing bowl and then mix with a paddle, on slow speed speed until ALL lumps have been removed. Add your melted butter and Madagascar bourbon vanilla and then mix with a paddle on slow speed speed until fully incorporated. Add your cake flour into the mix and mix on slow speed until fully incorporated

Continued on next page

INGREDIENTS (CONTINUED)

½ tsp Saigon cinnamon
½ tsp all spice
½ tsp Madagascar bourbon vanilla
4 fresh carrots (shredded)
¼ cup pecans (chopped)
2 ounces lemon curd

Lemon Curd
The zest of 1 lemon
⅔ cup fresh lemon juice
1 cup white granulated sugar
2 large egg yolks
2 large eggs
3 ounces unsalted butter
⅛ tbsp sea salt

Cheesecake Filling
3 ounces white granulated sugar
8 ounces cream cheese
2 ounces sour cream
1 ½ ounces whole milk
1 Large egg
¾ tsp Madagascar bourbon vanilla
¾ tbsp AP (all purpose) flour

AUSTRIA

CARROT CAKE CRUMB CAKE
CONTINUED

CHEF SECRETS

"My crumb cake recipe is an updated version of my family's 400-year-old recipe from Austria (to bake my family's original recipe, see my Old World Style Crumb Cake recipe). The crumbs and streusel used in all my crumb cake recipe's are exactly as they were from the original recipe. The only change to the original recipe is the use of a golden cake versus a yeast dough cake base. The reason for this change is due to spoilage. I ship my cakes worldwide and because yeast cakes only retain their freshness for 3-4 days (without preservatives), I was faced with a dilemma. I NEVER use any artificial flavors, chemicals, colorants or preservatives in any of my cakes. The average time a client would receive my shipped cakes in the States is 2-4 days, just as they were started to reach their freshness limits. Properly wrapped, a golden cake will retain its freshness for 7-10 days. The choice was simple and that is why, all of my crumb cakes (except for my Old World Style Crumb Cake recipe) feature a golden cake recipe."

"My family's double bake process is unique to baking a crumb cake. It assures that the fillings and crumbs topping will remain on the top of the cake and not drift into the cake mix."

"It's important that you use they type of ingredients specified without substitution. Cinnamon - Most cinnamon sold in the States is an inferior Cassia cinnamon that provides overpowering spikes in taste. The subtle complexity of flavor and texture of Ceylon cinnamon from Vietnam, is far superior."

Continued on next page

"When finished, your crumbs won't look like crumbs. Don't worry, you will pull them apart and form your crumbs when you make your cake"

Cake Preparation
Preheat your oven to 300°

CREATE YOUR DRY MIX
Sift your cake flour into a mixing bowl and add your castor sugar, kosher salt, baking powder, and baking soda. Combine to create your dry mix

CREATE YOUR WET MIX
Separate your large eggs, placing the yolks in a bowl. (You will not be using your egg whites). Add your Madagascar bourbon vanilla to your egg yolks

COMBINE MIXES
Cut your unsalted butter into ⅛" thick pieces

Add your cut unsalted butter to your dry mix

Add ¾ (only) of the sour cream to your dry mix

Mix with a paddle for 1 minute 30 seconds (start slow, progress to med/high speed)

Add your remaining ¼ of your sour cream and the your egg yolk, vanilla wet mix to the dry mix

Mix for 1 minute (start slow, progress to med/high speed)

Continued on next page

AUSTRIA

CARROT CAKE CRUMB CAKE
CONTINUED

Create Cake
With pan spray, spray a 10" cake pan (include sides) and pour your combined cake mix into your sprayed cake pan

In a medium bowl, combine half of your cheesecake mix and half of your carrot cake filling. Add your chopped pecans to the mix

Top your cake with this mix

Bake at 300° for approx. 30 minutes (your cake should be partially cooked but firm enough to hold your topping and crumbs)

Remove your cake from oven and using a spatula, top your cake with a layer of your lemon curd

Break up, with your hands, your crumb topping to form crumbs. Top your filling layer with your crumbs

Place your cake back in your oven at 300° for an additional 30 minutes

Check your cake with a toothpick in the center. When your cake is done, remove from oven. Place your cake on a cooling rack to cool

Combine the remaining half of your cheesecake mix and all of your carrot cake topping. Mix thoroughly. Pour into a squeeze bottle

Using your squeeze bottle, top your cake in a zig-zag pattern (see photo)

You can refrigerate for 10 days or freeze for 120 days

CHEF SECRETS (CONTINUED)

"It builds gradually into a complex symphony of rich floral flavors and aromas that compliment rather than overwhelm as Cassia does. Although expensive and often hard to find, Ceylon cinnamon also known as Saigon cinnamon should be a vital part of your basic ingredient set."

"Vanilla - NEVER use imitation vanilla. The chemical composition of imitation vanilla is different than 'real' vanilla and interacts differently with creations. The finest vanilla is Madagascar bourbon vanilla, pure vanilla extract. I use Nielson-Massey because of their cold extraction process, which draws out over 300 flavor compounds from the vanilla bean. You can find it online at My Spice Sage."

"Castor Sugar - Also known as superfine sugar produces a finer, lighter, more delicate cake which is what you're looking for here. You can find castor sugar at some grocers and online at India Tree."

"Cake Flour - Although you can use AP (all purpose) flour for most of your baking needs, it's always better to use the specific flour designed for the task. Cake Flour is a low protein, low gluten flour that is perfect for cakes, muffins, biscuits and most other baked goods. That's why you'll always see it specified in my cake recipe's. You can find cake flour at most of your grocery stores. I believe that Swans Down is the best and you can find it at Walmart."

Chef J Stephen

AUSTRIA

Chocolate de la Terre Crumb Cake

Serves 12, Prep 45min, Total 1hr 45min

Ingredients

Cake
¾ cup sour cream (room temperature)
4 large eggs separated; (room temperature)
1 ½ tsp Madagascar bourbon vanilla
6 ounces unsalted butter (room temperature)
¾ cup cake flour (sifted)
¾ cup castor sugar
¼ tsp kosher salt
½ tsp baking powder
½ tsp baking soda

Crumb Topping (serves 1 cake)
1 cup unsalted butter
½ cup white granulated sugar
½ cup dark brown Muscovado sugar
1 ½ tbsp Saigon cinnamon
½ tsp kosher salt
1 ½ tbsp Madagascar bourbon vanilla
1 ⅓ cups cake flour (no substitute)

Chocolate Filling/Topping
12 Callebaut semi-sweet chocolate nibs

Chef Secrets

"When it comes to your chocolate, you can use a lot of different chocolates, BUT although it may be a challenge to find, try to find Callebaut Chocolates. They are the worlds finest chocolates and it's the only chocolates I will use in my cakes. The specific chocolate I use is their [Ecuadorian Single Origin Chocolate](.) because it brings intense cocoa flavours with deep roasted hints and lots of fruity undertones. Hints of rum and whisky give this chocolate a very indulgent, round and balanced character, which is exactly what I'm looking for in my cake."

Continued on next page

Instructions

Crumbs Topping
Melt your unsalted butter in a microwave or sauce pan on low heat. DO NOT BOIL

Combine your granulated white sugar, dark brown Muscovado sugar, kosher salt, and Saigon cinnamon into a mixing bowl

Mix with a paddle, on slow speed until ALL lumps have been removed

Add your melted butter and Madagascar bourbon vanilla

Mix with a paddle on slow speed until fully incorporated

Add your cake flour into the mix and mix on slow speed until fully incorporated

"When finished, your crumbs won't look like crumbs. Don't worry, you will pull them apart and form your crumbs when you make your cake"

Cake Preparation
Preheat your oven to 300°

CREATE YOUR DRY MIX
Sift your cake flour into a mixing bowl and add your castor sugar, kosher salt, baking powder, and baking soda. Combine to create your dry mix

Continued on next page

AUSTRIA

CHOCOLATE DE LA TERRE CRUMB CAKE

CONTINUED

CHEF SECRETS (CONTINUED)

"My crumb cake recipe is an updated version of my family's 400-year-old recipe from Austria (to bake my family's original recipe, see my Old World Style Crumb Cake recipe). The crumbs and streusel used in all my crumb cake recipe's are exactly as they were from the original recipe. The only change to the original recipe is the use of a golden cake versus a yeast dough cake base. The reason for this change is due to spoilage. I ship my cakes worldwide and because yeast cakes only retain their freshness for 3-4 days (without preservatives), I was faced with a dilemma. I NEVER use any artificial flavors, chemicals, colorants or preservatives in any of my cakes. The average time a client would receive my shipped cakes in the States is 2-4 days, just as they were started to reach their freshness limits. Properly wrapped, a golden cake will retain its freshness for 7-10 days. The choice was simple and that is why, all of my crumb cakes (except for my Old World Style Crumb Cake recipe) feature a golden cake recipe."

"My family's double bake process is unique to baking a crumb cake. It assures that the fillings and crumbs topping will remain on the top of the cake and not drift into the cake mix."

"It's important that you use they type of ingredients specified without substitution. Cinnamon - Most cinnamon sold in the States is an inferior Cassia cinnamon that provides overpowering spikes in taste. The subtle complexity of flavor and texture of Ceylon cinnamon from Vietnam, is far superior. It builds gradually into a complex symphony of rich floral flavors and aromas that compliment rather than overwhelm as Cassia does. Although expensive and often hard to find, Ceylon cinnamon also known as Saigon cinnamon should be a vital part of your basic ingredient set."

Continued on next page

Cake Preparation (continued)

CREATE YOUR WET MIX
Separate your large eggs, placing the yolks in a bowl. (You will not be using your egg whites)

Add your Madagascar bourbon vanilla to your egg yolks

Place your sour cream in a medium deli container

Melt your chocolate nibs over a double boiler or in the microwave. BE CAREFUL NOT TO BURN

When it cools but is still pourable, pour into a squeeze bottle

COMBINE YOUR MIXES
Cut your unsalted butter into ⅛" thick pieces

Add your cut unsalted butter to your dry mix

Add ¾ (only) of the sour cream to your dry mix

Mix with a paddle for 1 minute 30 seconds (start slow, progress to med/high speed)

Add your remaining ¼ of your sour cream and the your egg yolk, vanilla wet mix to the dry mix.

Mix for 1 minute (start slow, progress to med/high speed)

Continued on next page

AUSTRIA

Chocolate de la Terre Crumb Cake

CONTINUED

Chef Secrets (continued)

"Vanilla - NEVER use imitation vanilla. The chemical composition of imitation vanilla is different than 'real' vanilla and interacts differently with creations. The finest vanilla is Madagascar bourbon vanilla, pure vanilla extract. I use Nielson-Massey because of their cold extraction process, which draws out over 300 flavor compounds from the vanilla bean. You can find it online at [My Spice Sage](#)."

"Castor Sugar - Also known as superfine sugar produces a finer, lighter, more delicate cake which is what you're looking for here. You can find castor sugar at some grocers and online at [India Tree](#)."

"Cake Flour - Although you can use AP (all purpose) flour for most of your baking needs, it's always better to use the specific flour designed for the task. Cake Flour is a low protein, low gluten flour that is perfect for cakes, muffins, biscuits and most other baked goods. That's why you'll always see it specified in my cake recipe's. You can find cake flour at most of your grocery stores. I believe that Swans Down is the best and you can find it at [Walmart](#)."

Chef J Stephen

Create Cake
Preheat your oven to 300°

With pan spray, spray a 10" cake pan (include sides)

Pour your cake mix into your sprayed cake pan

Bake at 300° for approx. 30 minutes (your cake should be partially cooked but firm enough to hold your topping and crumbs)

Remove your cake from oven and using a spatula, top your cake with a thin layer (approx. 6 ounces) of your melted chocolate. Make sure your cake is completely covered with your layer of chocolate

Break up, with your hands, your crumb topping to form crumbs. Top your chocolate layer with your crumbs

Using your squeeze bottle, top your crumbs with your remaining melted chocolate (approx. 6 ounces) in an irregular pattern (see photo)

Place your cake back in your oven at 300° for an additional 30 minutes

Check your cake with a toothpick in the center. When your cake is done, remove from oven. Place your cake on a cooling rack to cool

You can refrigerate for 10 days or freeze for 120 days

Austria

Cinnamon Streusel Crumb Cake

Serves 12, Prep 45min, Total 1hr 45min

Ingredients

Cake
¾ cup sour cream (room temperature)
4 large eggs separated; (room temperature)
1 ½ tsp Madagascar bourbon vanilla
6 ounces unsalted butter (room temperature)
¾ cup cake flour (sifted)
¾ cup castor sugar
¼ tsp kosher salt
½ tsp baking powder
½ tsp baking soda

Crumb Topping (serves 1 cake)
1 cup unsalted butter
½ cup white granulated sugar
½ cup dark brown Muscovado sugar
1 ½ tbsp Saigon cinnamon
½ tsp kosher salt
1 ½ tbsp Madagascar bourbon vanilla
1 ⅓ cups cake flour (no substitute)

Cinnamon Streusel Filling/Topping
2 ½ ounces unsalted butter
¾ cup cake flour (you can substitute AP flour)
½ cup dark brown Muscovado sugar
2 tbsp Saigon cinnamon

Chef Secrets

"I use dark Muscovado Sugar because of its fine, moist texture, high molasses content, and a strong lingering flavor that blends well and adds to the depth and richness of my cakes. There is no other dark brown Muscovado sugar that comes close to the rich, full-bodied taste. You can find it at India Tree."

Continued on next page

Instructions

Crumbs Topping
Melt your unsalted butter in a microwave or sauce pan on low heat. DO NOT BOIL

Combine your granulated white sugar, dark brown Muscovado sugar, kosher salt, and Saigon cinnamon into a mixing bowl

Mix with a paddle, on slow speed until ALL lumps have been removed

Add your melted butter and Madagascar bourbon vanilla

Mix with a paddle on slow speed until fully incorporated

Add your cake flour into the mix and mix on slow speed until fully incorporated

"When finished, your crumbs won't look like crumbs. Don't worry, you will pull them apart and form your crumbs when you make your cake."

Cake Preparation
Preheat your oven to 300°

CREATE YOUR DRY MIX
Sift your cake flour into a mixing bowl and add your castor sugar, kosher salt, baking powder, and baking soda. Combine to create your dry mix

Continued on next page

AUSTRIA

Cinnamon Streusel Crumb Cake

CONTINUED

CHEF SECRETS (CONTINUED)

"My crumb cake recipe is an updated version of my family's 400-year-old recipe from Austria (to bake my family's original recipe, see my Old World Style Crumb Cake recipe). The crumbs and streusel used in all my crumb cake recipe's are exactly as they were from the original recipe. The only change to the original recipe is the use of a golden cake versus a yeast dough cake base. The reason for this change is due to spoilage. I ship my cakes worldwide and because yeast cakes only retain their freshness for 3-4 days (without preservatives), I was faced with a dilemma. I NEVER use any artificial flavors, chemicals, colorants or preservatives in any of my cakes. The average time a client would receive my shipped cakes in the States is 2-4 days, just as they were started to reach their freshness limits. Properly wrapped, a golden cake will retain its freshness for 7-10 days. The choice was simple and that is why, all of my crumb cakes (except for my Old World Style Crumb Cake recipe) feature a golden cake recipe."

"My family's double bake process is unique to baking a crumb cake. It assures that the fillings and crumbs topping will remain on the top of the cake and not drift into the cake mix."

"It's important that you use they type of ingredients specified without substitution. Cinnamon - Most cinnamon sold in the States is an inferior Cassia cinnamon that provides overpowering spikes in taste. The subtle complexity of flavor and texture of Ceylon cinnamon from Vietnam, is far superior. It builds gradually into a complex symphony of rich floral flavors and aromas that compliment rather than overwhelm as Cassia does. Although expensive and often hard to find, Ceylon cinnamon also known as Saigon cinnamon should be a vital part of your basic ingredient set."

Continued on next page

Cake Preparation (continued)

CREATE YOUR WET MIX
Separate your large eggs, placing the yolks in a bowl. (You will not be using your egg whites). Add your Madagascar bourbon vanilla to your egg yolks

Streusel Filling/Topping
Cut your unsalted butter into 4" squares

Into a large mixing bowl, combine your cake flour, dark brown Muscovado sugar, and Saigon cinnamon. Mix until all the lumps are gone and then add your unsalted butter to the mix. Mix until fully incorporated (It will be course and granular)

COMBINE YOUR MIXES
Cut your unsalted butter into ⅛" thick pieces

Add your cut unsalted butter to your dry mix

Add ¾ (only) of the sour cream to your dry mix

Mix with a paddle for 1 minute 30 seconds (start slow, progress to med/high speed)

Add your remaining ¼ of your sour cream and the your egg yolk, vanilla wet mix to the dry mix.

Mix for 1 minute (start slow, progress to med/high speed)

Continued on next page

AUSTRIA

CINNAMON STREUSEL CRUMB CAKE

CONTINUED

CHEF SECRETS (CONTINUED)

"Vanilla - NEVER use imitation vanilla. The chemical composition of imitation vanilla is different than 'real' vanilla and interacts differently with creations. The finest vanilla is Madagascar bourbon vanilla, pure vanilla extract. I use Nielson-Massey because of their cold extraction process, which draws out over 300 flavor compounds from the vanilla bean. You can find it online at [My Spice Sage](.)."

"Castor Sugar - Also known as superfine sugar produces a finer, lighter, more delicate cake which is what you're looking for here. You can find castor sugar at some grocers and online at [India Tree](.)."

"Cake Flour - Although you can use AP (all purpose) flour for most of your baking needs, it's always better to use the specific flour designed for the task. Cake Flour is a low protein, low gluten flour that is perfect for cakes, muffins, biscuits and most other baked goods. That's why you'll always see it specified in my cake recipe's. You can find cake flour at most of your grocery stores. I believe that Swans Down is the best and you can find it at [Walmart](.)."

Chef J Stephen

Create Cake
With pan spray, spray a 10" cake pan (include sides)

Pour your cake mix into your sprayed cake pan

Bake at 300° for approx. 30 minutes (your cake should be partially cooked but firm enough to hold your topping and crumbs)

Place half of your streusel in the microwave to heat it to a spreadable texture

Remove your cake from oven and using a spatula, top your cake with a thin layer (approx. 6 ounces) of your heated streusel. Make sure your cake is completely covered with your layer of streusel

Break up, with your hands, your crumb topping to form crumbs. Top your layer of streusel with your crumbs

Top your crumbs with your remaining streusel (approx. 6 ounces) by placing four mounds evenly spaced around the perimeter of your cake and one mound in the center (see photo)

Place your cake back in your oven at 300° for an additional 30 minutes

Check your cake with a toothpick in the center. When your cake is done, remove from oven. Place your cake on a cooling rack to cool

You can refrigerate for 10 days or freeze for 120 days

AUSTRIA

COCONUT CUSTARD CRUMB CAKE

SERVES 12, PREP 45MIN, TOTAL 1HR 45MIN

INGREDIENTS

Cake
¾ cup sour cream (room temperature)
4 large eggs separated; (room temperature)
1 ½ tsp Madagascar bourbon vanilla
6 ounces unsalted butter (room temperature)
¾ cup cake flour (sifted)
¾ cup castor sugar
¼ tsp kosher salt
½ tsp baking powder
½ tsp baking soda

Crumb Topping (serves 1 cake)
1 cup unsalted butter
½ cup white granulated sugar
½ cup dark brown Muscovado sugar
1 ½ tbsp Saigon cinnamon
½ tsp kosher salt
1 ½ tbsp Madagascar bourbon vanilla
1 ⅓ cups cake flour (no substitute)

Coconut Custard Topping
3 ½ ounces Monin coconut syrup
6 large eggs
3 ounces unsalted butter (room temperature)
8 ½ ounces white granulated sugar
¼ tsp kosher salt
¾ ounces unsweetened coconut flakes
¼ tsp natural coconut extract

Coconut Custard Filling
¾ tbsp Monin coconut syrup
¼ tsp natural coconut extract
½ Madagascar bourbon vanilla
1 medium egg (whole)
1 medium egg (yolk)

Continued on next page

INSTRUCTIONS

Coconut Custard Topping
Separate your large egg yolks

Place your coconut syrup, egg yolks, white granulated sugar, coconut extract, kosher salt, and shredded unsweetened coconut into a sauce pan

Melt your unsalted butter in your microwave for approx. 30 seconds. Place your melted butter in with your other ingredients. Whisk until fully incorporated

Place your mix into a medium sauce pan over medium heat. Stir continually for 12-15 minutes until a nape is formed (liquid should coat the back of a spoon). DO NOT BOIL. (*A nap is when your liquid thickens but still slowly slides off your ladle.*)

Coconut Custard Filling
Separate 1 medium egg yolk

Melt your unsalted butter in your microwave for approx. 30 seconds

Place your coconut syrup, egg yolk, 1 whole egg, white granulated sugar, kosher salt, Madagascar bourbon vanilla, whole milk, nutmeg, unsalted butter (melted), AP flour, coconut extract, and shredded unsweetened coconut into a medium sauce pan. Whisk all your ingredients together

Place your sauce pan over medium heat Stir continually for approx. 10 minutes until a nape is formed (liquid should coat the back of a spoon). DO NOT BOIL

Continued on next page

AUSTRIA

COCONUT CUSTARD CRUMB CAKE

CONTINUED

INGREDIENTS (CONTINUED)

Coconut Custard Filling (continued)
8 ounces whole milk
6 tbsp white granulated sugar
½ tsp kosher salt
2 tbsp unsweetened coconut flakes
½ tsp fresh ground nutmeg
¾ ounces unsalted butter
¼ tbsp AP flour

CHEF SECRETS (CONTINUED)

"I'm sure you can buy coconut custard filling at the store, BUT it will never be the same as making your own. If you really want to make something special, don't shortchange yourself on any of the ingredients. You just can't believe how making almost ANY ingredient not only makes the difference between an okay dish and a special WOW moment but also is usually much healthier."

"As an added benefit, you can also use your coconut custard recipe to make a coconut custard pie!"

"My family's double bake process is unique to baking a crumb cake. It assures that the fillings and crumbs topping will remain on the top of the cake and not drift into the cake mix."

Chef J Stephen

Continued on next page

Crumbs Topping
Melt your unsalted butter in a microwave or sauce pan on low heat. DO NOT BOIL

Combine your granulated white sugar, dark brown Muscovado sugar, kosher salt, and Saigon cinnamon into a mixing bowl and then mix with a paddle, on slow speed speed until ALL lumps have been removed. Add your melted butter and Madagascar bourbon vanilla and then mix with a paddle on slow speed speed until fully incorporated. Add your cake flour into the mix and mix on slow speed until fully incorporated

"When finished, your crumbs won't look like crumbs. Don't worry, you will pull them apart and form your crumbs when you make your cake."

Cake Preparation
Preheat your oven to 300°

CREATE YOUR DRY MIX
Sift your cake flour into a mixing bowl and add your castor sugar, kosher salt, baking powder, and baking soda. Combine to create your dry mix

CREATE YOUR WET MIX
Separate your large eggs, placing the yolks in a bowl. (You will not be using your egg whites). Add your Madagascar bourbon vanilla to your egg yolks

Continued on next page

AUSTRIA

COCONUT CUSTARD CRUMB CAKE

CHEF SECRETS

"My crumb cake recipe is an updated version of my family's 400-year-old recipe from Austria (to bake my family's original recipe, see my Old World Style Crumb Cake recipe). The crumbs and streusel used in all my crumb cake recipe's are exactly as they were from the original recipe. The only change to the original recipe is the use of a golden cake versus a yeast dough cake base. The reason for this change is due to spoilage. I ship my cakes worldwide and because yeast cakes only retain their freshness for 3-4 days (without preservatives), I was faced with a dilemma. I NEVER use any artificial flavors, chemicals, colorants or preservatives in any of my cakes. The average time a client would receive my shipped cakes in the States is 2-4 days, just as they were started to reach their freshness limits. Properly wrapped, a golden cake will retain its freshness for 7-10 days. The choice was simple and that is why, all of my crumb cakes (except for my Old World Style Crumb Cake recipe) feature a golden cake recipe."

"It's important that you use they type of ingredients specified without substitution. Cinnamon - Most cinnamon sold in the States is an inferior Cassia cinnamon that provides overpowering spikes in taste. The subtle complexity of flavor and texture of Ceylon cinnamon from Vietnam, is far superior."

Continued on next page

CONTINUED

COMBINE MIXES
Cut your unsalted butter into ⅛" thick pieces

Add your cut unsalted butter to your dry mix

Add ¾ (only) of the sour cream to your dry mix

Mix with a paddle for 1 minute 30 seconds (start slow, progress to med/high speed)

Add your remaining ¼ of your sour cream and the your egg yolk, vanilla wet mix to the dry mix

Mix for 1 minute (start slow, progress to med/high speed)

CREATE YOUR CAKE
Preheat your oven to 300°

With pan spray, spray a 10" cake pan (include sides) and pour your combined cake mix into your sprayed cake pan

Top your cake mix with <u>half</u> of your coconut custard filling

Bake at 300° for approx. 30 minutes (your cake should be partially cooked but firm enough to hold your topping and crumbs)

Remove your cake from the oven and top your partially baked cake with the rest of your coconut custard filling

Continued on next page

AUSTRIA

COCONUT CUSTARD CRUMB CAKE

CONTINUED

CHEF SECRETS (CONTINUED)

"It builds gradually into a complex symphony of rich floral flavors and aromas that compliment rather than overwhelm as Cassia does. Although expensive and often hard to find, Ceylon cinnamon also known as Saigon cinnamon should be a vital part of your basic ingredient set."

"Vanilla - NEVER use imitation vanilla. The chemical composition of imitation vanilla is different than 'real' vanilla and interacts differently with creations. The finest vanilla is Madagascar bourbon vanilla, pure vanilla extract. I use Nielson-Massey because of their cold extraction process, which draws out over 300 flavor compounds from the vanilla bean. You can find it online at My Spice Sage."

"Castor Sugar - Also known as superfine sugar produces a finer, lighter, more delicate cake which is what you're looking for here. You can find castor sugar at some grocers and online at India Tree."

"Cake Flour - Although you can use AP (all purpose) flour for most of your baking needs, it's always better to use the specific flour designed for the task. Cake Flour is a low protein, low gluten flour that is perfect for cakes, muffins, biscuits and most other baked goods. That's why you'll always see it specified in my cake recipe's. You can find cake flour at most of your grocery stores. I believe that Swans Down is the best and you can find it at Walmart."

Chef J Stephen

Create Cake (continued)
Break up, with your hands, your crumb topping to form crumbs. Top your coconut custard filling layer with your crumbs

Place your cake back in your oven at 300° for an additional 30 minutes

Check your cake with a toothpick in the center. When your cake is done, remove from oven. Place your cake on a cooling rack to cool

Using your squeeze bottle, top your cake with your coconut custard topping in a zig-zag pattern

As an option, you can choose to further top your cake with confectioners sugar

You can refrigerate for 10 days or freeze for 120 days

AUSTRIA

EGG NOG CRUMB CAKE

Serves 12, Prep 45min, Total 1hr 45min

Ingredients

Cake
¾ cup sour cream (room temperature)
4 large eggs separated; (room temperature)
1 ½ tsp Madagascar bourbon vanilla
6 ounces unsalted butter (room temperature)
¾ cup cake flour (sifted)
¾ cup castor sugar
¼ tsp kosher salt
½ tsp baking powder
½ tsp baking soda

Crumb Topping (serves 1 cake)
1 cup unsalted butter
½ cup white granulated sugar
½ cup dark brown Muscovado sugar
1 ½ tbsp Saigon cinnamon
½ tsp kosher salt
1 ½ tbsp Madagascar bourbon vanilla
1 ⅓ cups cake flour (no substitute)

Egg Nog Cheesecake Filling/Topping
16 ounces cream cheese
2 large eggs
½ tbsp Madagascar bourbon vanilla
6 ounces white granulated sugar
1 ounce AP (all purpose) flour
4 ounces sour cream
6 ounces egg nog
½ tbsp Saigon cinnamon
¼ tsp fresh ground nutmeg
1 ½ tsp Tuaca liqueur

See Chef Secrets on next page

Instructions

Egg Nog Cheesecake Filling/Topping
Place your cream cheese in a plastic bowl and place in your microwave foe 30 seconds (or until smooth)

Combine in a mixer bowl, with paddle, your cream cheese and white granulated sugar for approx. 30 seconds on medium speed

Add your egg nog, Tuaca and large eggs. Mix for approx. 1 minute on medium speed

Add your sour cream, Madagascar bourbon vanilla, fresh ground nutmeg, Saigon cinnamon, and AP flour. Mix for approx. 15 seconds on medium speed. Put aside

Crumbs Topping
Melt your unsalted butter in a microwave or sauce pan on low heat. DO NOT BOIL

Combine your granulated white sugar, dark brown Muscovado sugar, kosher salt, and Saigon cinnamon into a mixing bowl and then mix with a paddle, on slow speed speed until ALL lumps have been removed.

Add your melted butter and Madagascar bourbon vanilla and then mix with a paddle on slow speed speed until fully incorporated.

Add your cake flour into the mix and mix on slow speed until fully incorporated

"When finished, your crumbs won't look like crumbs. Don't worry, you will pull them apart and form your crumbs when you make your cake."

Continued on next page

AUSTRIA

EGG NOG CRUMB CAKE

CONTINUED

Cake Preparation
Preheat your oven to 300°

CREATE YOUR DRY MIX
Sift your cake flour into a mixing bowl and add your castor sugar, kosher salt, baking powder, and baking soda. Combine to create your dry mix

CREATE YOUR WET MIX
Separate your large eggs, placing the yolks in a bowl. (You will not be using your egg whites). Add your Madagascar bourbon vanilla to your egg yolks

COMBINE YOUR MIXES
Cut your unsalted butter into ⅛" thick pieces

Add your cut unsalted butter to your dry mix

Add ¾ (only) of the sour cream to your dry mix

Mix with a paddle for 1 minute 30 seconds (start slow, progress to med/high speed)

Add your remaining ¼ of your sour cream and the your egg yolk, vanilla wet mix to the dry mix

Mix for 1 minute (start slow, progress to med/high speed)

Continued on next page

CHEF SECRETS (CONTINUED)

"My family's double bake process is unique to baking a crumb cake. It assures that the fillings and crumbs topping will remain on the top of the cake and not drift into the cake mix."

"My crumb cake recipe is an updated version of my family's 400-year-old recipe from Austria (to bake my family's original recipe, see my Old World Style Crumb Cake recipe). The crumbs and streusel used in all my crumb cake recipe's are exactly as they were from the original recipe. The only change to the original recipe is the use of a golden cake versus a yeast dough cake base. The reason for this change is due to spoilage. I ship my cakes worldwide and because yeast cakes only retain their freshness for 3-4 days (without preservatives), I was faced with a dilemma. I NEVER use any artificial flavors, chemicals, colorants or preservatives in any of my cakes. The average time a client would receive my shipped cakes in the States is 2-4 days, just as they were started to reach their freshness limits. Properly wrapped, a golden cake will retain its freshness for 7-10 days. The choice was simple and that is why, all of my crumb cakes (except for my Old World Style Crumb Cake recipe) feature a golden cake recipe."

"It's important that you use they type of ingredients specified without substitution. Cinnamon - Most cinnamon sold in the States is an inferior Cassia cinnamon that provides overpowering spikes in taste. The subtle complexity of flavor and texture of Ceylon cinnamon from Vietnam, is far superior."

Continued on next page

AUSTRIA

EGG NOG CRUMB CAKE

CONTINUED

CHEF SECRETS

"It builds gradually into a complex symphony of rich floral flavors and aromas that compliment rather than overwhelm as Cassia does. Although expensive and often hard to find, Ceylon cinnamon also known as Saigon cinnamon should be a vital part of your basic ingredient set."

"Vanilla - NEVER use imitation vanilla. The chemical composition of imitation vanilla is different than 'real' vanilla and interacts differently with creations. The finest vanilla is Madagascar bourbon vanilla, pure vanilla extract. I use Nielson-Massey because of their cold extraction process, which draws out over 300 flavor compounds from the vanilla bean. You can find it online at My Spice Sage."

"Castor Sugar - Also known as superfine sugar produces a finer, lighter, more delicate cake which is what you're looking for here. You can find castor sugar at some grocers and online at India Tree."

"Cake Flour - Although you can use AP (all purpose) flour for most of your baking needs, it's always better to use the specific flour designed for the task. Cake Flour is a low protein, low gluten flour that is perfect for cakes, muffins, biscuits and most other baked goods. That's why you'll always see it specified in my cake recipe's. You can find cake flour at most of your grocery stores. I believe that Swans Down is the best and you can find it at Walmart."

Chef J Stephen

CREATE YOUR CAKE
Preheat your oven to 300°

With pan spray, spray a 10" cake pan (include sides) and pour your combined cake mix into your sprayed cake pan

Top your cake mix with <u>half</u> of your coconut custard filling

Bake at 300° for approx. 30 minutes (your cake should be partially cooked but firm enough to hold your topping and crumbs)

Remove your cake from the oven and top your partially baked cake with half of your Egg Nog Cheesecake Filling/Topping

Break up, with your hands, your crumb topping to form crumbs. Top your Egg Nog Cheesecake Filling/Topping layer with your crumbs

Place your cake back in your oven at 300° for an additional 30 minutes

Check your cake with a toothpick in the center. When your cake is done, remove from oven. Place your cake on a cooling rack to cool

Using your squeeze bottle, top your cake with the remaining half of your Egg Nog Cheesecake Filling/Topping in a zig-zag pattern

As an option, you can choose to further top your cake with confectioners sugar

You can refrigerate for 10 days or freeze for 120 days

AUSTRIA

Hot Butter Toffee Rum Crumb Cake

SERVES 12, PREP 1HR 15MIN, TOTAL 2HR 15MIN

INGREDIENTS

Cake
¾ cup sour cream (room temperature)
4 large eggs separated; (room temperature)
1 ½ tsp Madagascar bourbon vanilla
6 ounces unsalted butter (room temperature)
¾ cup cake flour (sifted)
¾ cup castor sugar
¼ tsp kosher salt
½ tsp baking powder
½ tsp baking soda

Crumb Topping (serves 1 cake)
1 cup unsalted butter
½ cup white granulated sugar
½ cup dark brown Muscovado sugar
1 ½ tbsp Saigon cinnamon
½ tsp kosher salt
1 ½ tbsp Madagascar bourbon vanilla
1 ⅓ cups cake flour (no substitute)

Hot Butter Toffee Rum Filling/Topping
8 ounces heavy mixing cream
1 ounce unsalted butter (*room temp*)
1 ¾ ounces dark Karo syrup
2 ounces white granulated sugar
3 ounces water
2 ounces Jamaican dark rum
2 ounces milk chocolate toffee bits
¼ tsp corn starch
¾ tbsp Tuaca liqueur

See Chef Secrets on next page

INSTRUCTIONS

Hot Butter Toffee Rum Filling/Topping
Pour your water into a medium sauce pan
Add your white granulated sugar. Dissolve your sugar in the water stirring for approx. 30 seconds (NO FLAME)
Cook on high flame to continue to dissolve. Bring to a low boil
Boil for approx. 5 minutes
Add your milk chocolate toffee bits. Stir until fully incorporated (melted)
Add your unsalted butter and stir until fully incorporated (melted)
Add your dark Karo syrup. Incorporate
Add your Jamaican spiced rum and Tuaca Liqueur
Reduce your flame to a simmer
Add your heavy cream
FILLING
Stir your mixture until reduced to a thin nape. Pour out half your mixture into a bowl. When cool (but still pourable), pour into plastic pour container. (*A nap is when your liquid thickens but still slowly slides off your ladle.*)
TOPPING
Add your corn starch to the remaining mix. Stir over a medium flame to reduce (approx. 25 min.) to a nap, stirring occasionally

Crumbs Topping
Melt your unsalted butter in a microwave or sauce pan on low heat. DO NOT BOIL

Combine your granulated white sugar, dark brown Muscovado sugar, kosher salt, and Saigon cinnamon into a mixing bowl and then mix with a paddle, on slow speed speed until ALL lumps have been removed.

Continued on next page

AUSTRIA

HOT BUTTER TOFFEE RUM CRUMB CAKE

CONTINUED

CHEF SECRETS (CONTINUED)

"My family's double bake process is unique to baking a crumb cake. It assures that the fillings and crumbs topping will remain on the top of the cake and not drift into the cake mix."

"My crumb cake recipe is an updated version of my family's 400-year-old recipe from Austria (to bake my family's original recipe, see my Old World Style Crumb Cake recipe). The crumbs and streusel used in all my crumb cake recipe's are exactly as they were from the original recipe. The only change to the original recipe is the use of a golden cake versus a yeast dough cake base. The reason for this change is due to spoilage. I ship my cakes worldwide and because yeast cakes only retain their freshness for 3-4 days (without preservatives), I was faced with a dilemma. I NEVER use any artificial flavors, chemicals, colorants or preservatives in any of my cakes. The average time a client would receive my shipped cakes in the States is 2-4 days, just as they were started to reach their freshness limits. Properly wrapped, a golden cake will retain its freshness for 7-10 days. The choice was simple and that is why, all of my crumb cakes (except for my Old World Style Crumb Cake recipe) feature a golden cake recipe."

"It's important that you use they type of ingredients specified without substitution. Cinnamon - Most cinnamon sold in the States is an inferior Cassia cinnamon that provides overpowering spikes in taste. The subtle complexity of flavor and texture of Ceylon cinnamon from Vietnam, is far superior."

Continued on next page

Crumbs Topping (continued)
Add your melted butter and Madagascar bourbon vanilla and then mix with a paddle on slow speed speed until fully incorporated. Add your cake flour into the mix and mix on slow speed until fully incorporated

"When finished, your crumbs won't look like crumbs. Don't worry, you will pull them apart and form your crumbs when you make your cake."

Cake Preparation
Preheat your oven to 300°

CREATE YOUR DRY MIX
Sift your cake flour into a mixing bowl and add your castor sugar, kosher salt, baking powder, and baking soda. Combine to create your dry mix

CREATE YOUR WET MIX
Separate your large eggs, placing the yolks in a bowl. (You will not be using your egg whites). Add your Madagascar bourbon vanilla to your egg yolks

COMBINE YOUR MIXES
Cut your unsalted butter into ⅛" thick pieces

Add your cut unsalted butter to your dry mix

Add ¾ (only) of the sour cream to your dry mix. Mix with a paddle for 1 minute 30 seconds (start slow, progress to med/high speed)

Add your remaining ¼ of your sour cream and your egg yolk, vanilla wet mix to the dry mix. Mix for 1 minute (start slow, progress to med/high speed)

Continued on next page

AUSTRIA

HOT BUTTER TOFFEE RUM CRUMB CAKE

CONTINUED

CHEF SECRETS

"It builds gradually into a complex symphony of rich floral flavors and aromas that compliment rather than overwhelm as Cassia does. Although expensive and often hard to find, Ceylon cinnamon also known as Saigon cinnamon should be a vital part of your basic ingredient set."

"Vanilla - NEVER use imitation vanilla. The chemical composition of imitation vanilla is different than 'real' vanilla and interacts differently with creations. The finest vanilla is Madagascar bourbon vanilla, pure vanilla extract. I use Nielson-Massey because of their cold extraction process, which draws out over 300 flavor compounds from the vanilla bean. You can find it online at [My Spice Sage.](#)"

"Castor Sugar - Also known as superfine sugar produces a finer, lighter, more delicate cake which is what you're looking for here. You can find castor sugar at some grocers and online at [India Tree.](#)"

"Cake Flour - Although you can use AP (all purpose) flour for most of your baking needs, it's always better to use the specific flour designed for the task. Cake Flour is a low protein, low gluten flour that is perfect for cakes, muffins, biscuits and most other baked goods. That's why you'll always see it specified in my cake recipe's. You can find cake flour at most of your grocery stores. I believe that Swans Down is the best and you can find it at [Walmart.](#)"

Chef J Stephen

CREATE YOUR CAKE
Preheat your oven to 300°

With pan spray, spray a 10" cake pan (include sides) and pour your combined cake mix into your sprayed cake pan

Top your cake mix with <u>half</u> of your coconut custard filling

Bake at 300° for approx. 30 minutes (your cake should be partially cooked but firm enough to hold your topping and crumbs)

Remove your cake from the oven and top your partially baked cake with hot butter toffee filling

Break up, with your hands, your crumb filling to form crumbs. Top your hot butter toffee filling layer with your crumbs

Place your cake back in your oven at 300° for an additional 30 minutes

Check your cake with a toothpick in the center. When your cake is done, remove from oven. Place your cake on a cooling rack to cool

Using your squeeze bottle, top your cake with your hot butter toffee topping in a zig-zag pattern

You can refrigerate for 10 days or freeze for 120 days

AUSTRIA

KEY LIME PIE CRUMB CAKE

SERVES 12, PREP 45MIN, TOTAL 1HR 45MIN

INGREDIENTS

Key Lime Pie Filling & Topping
The zest of 2 Key Limes
⅔ cup fresh Key Lime juice
1 cup white granulated sugar
2 large egg yolks
2 large eggs
3 ounces unsalted butter
⅛ tbsp sea salt

Cheesecake Filling & Topping
7 ½ ounces unsalted butter
¾ cup white granulated sugar
16 ounces cream cheese
½ cup sour cream
3 ounces whole milk
2 large eggs
½ tbsp Madagascar bourbon vanilla
1 ounce AP (all purpose) flour

Cake
¾ cup sour cream (room temperature)
4 large eggs separated; (room temperature)
1 ½ tsp Madagascar bourbon vanilla
6 ounces unsalted butter (room temperature)
¾ cup cake flour (sifted)
¾ cup castor sugar
¼ tsp kosher salt
½ tsp baking powder
½ tsp baking soda
8 ounces crumbled Graham Crackers

Crumb Topping (serves 1 cake)
1 cup unsalted butter
½ cup white granulated sugar
½ cup dark brown Muscovado sugar
1 ½ tbsp Saigon cinnamon
½ tsp kosher salt
1 ½ tbsp Madagascar bourbon vanilla
1 ⅓ cups cake flour (no substitute)

See See Chef Secrets on next page

INSTRUCTIONS

Key Lime Curd
In a large mixing bowl, add your butter and sugar and whisk for approx. 2 minutes. Slowly add your eggs and yolks. Whisk for 1 minute. Add your Key Lime juice. Don't worry about curdled look, it will smooth into a curd as it cooks. In a medium saucepan, cook your curd over low heat until it becomes smooth. Raise the heat to medium and cook, stirring continually, until the curd thickens, approx. 15 minutes (should hold to the back of a spoon) **DO NOT BOIL**. Remove your curd from the heat and stir in your Key Lime zest. Transfer your curd to a bowl. Cover with plastic wrap on the surface of the curd and chill in the refrigerator. The curd will thicken further as it cools

Cheesecake Filling & Topping
Bring your cream cheese to room temperature (Must be room temperature, don't cheat). Combine in a mixer bowl, with paddle, your cream cheese, pumpkin pie spice, and granulated sugar for approx. 30 seconds on medium speed. Add your whole milk and large eggs. Mix for 1 minute
Add your sour cream, Madagascar bourbon vanilla, and AP flour. Mix on medium speed for 15 seconds

Crumbs Topping
Melt your unsalted butter in a microwave or sauce pan on low heat. **DO NOT BOIL** Combine your granulated white sugar, dark brown Muscovado sugar, kosher salt, and Saigon cinnamon into a mixing bowl. Mix with a paddle, on slow speed until ALL lumps have been removed. Add your melted butter and Madagascar bourbon vanilla. Mix with a paddle on slow speed until fully incorporated. Add your cake flour into the mix and mix on slow speed until fully incorporated.
"When finished, your crumbs won't look like crumbs. Don't worry, you will pull them apart and form your crumbs when you make your cake"

Continued on next page

AUSTRIA

KEY LIME PIE CRUMB CAKE

CONTINUED

Cake Preparation
Preheat your oven to 300°

CREATE YOUR DRY MIX
Sift your cake flour into a mixing bowl and add your castor sugar, kosher salt, baking powder, and baking soda. Combine to create your dry mix

CREATE YOUR WET MIX
Separate your large eggs, placing the yolks in a bowl. (You will not be using your egg whites)

Add your Madagascar bourbon vanilla to your egg yolks

Place your sour cream in a medium deli container

COMBINE YOUR MIXES
Cut your unsalted butter into ⅛" thick pieces

Add your cut unsalted butter to your dry mix

Add ¾ (only) of the sour cream to your dry mix

Mix with a paddle for 1 minute 30 seconds (start slow, progress to med/high speed)

Add your remaining ¼ of your sour cream and the your egg yolk, vanilla wet mix to the dry mix

Mix for 1 minute (start slow, progress to med/high speed)

CREATE YOUR GRAHAM CRACKER LAYER
Place your graham crackers in a food processor on high until uniformly fine

CHEF SECRETS

"Don't substitute with regular lime juice. If you can't find real Key Limes, you can find the what I consider the best Key West lime juice (Nellie & Joe's) on Amazon*."*

"My crumb cake recipe is an updated version of my family's 400-year-old recipe from Austria (to bake my family's original recipe, see my Old World Style Crumb Cake recipe). The crumbs and streusel used in all my crumb cake recipe's are exactly as they were from the original recipe. The only change to the original recipe is the use of a golden cake versus a yeast dough cake base. The reason for this change is due to spoilage. I ship my cakes worldwide and because yeast cakes only retain their freshness for 3-4 days (without preservatives), I was faced with a dilemma. I NEVER use any artificial flavors, chemicals, colorants or preservatives in any of my cakes. The average time a client would receive my shipped cakes in the States is 2-4 days, just as they were started to reach their freshness limits. Properly wrapped, a golden cake will retain its freshness for 7-10 days. The choice was simple and that is why, all of my crumb cakes (except for my Old World Style Crumb Cake recipe) feature a golden cake recipe."

"My family's double bake process is unique to baking a crumb cake. It assures that the fillings and crumbs topping will remain on the top of the cake and not drift into the cake mix. It's important that you use the type of ingredients specified."

Continued on next page

Continued on next page

AUSTRIA

KEY LIME PIE CRUMB CAKE

CONTINUED

CHEF SECRETS (CONTINUED)

"Cinnamon - Most cinnamon sold in the States is an inferior Cassia cinnamon that provides overpowering spikes in taste. The subtle complexity of flavor and texture of Ceylon cinnamon from Vietnam, is far superior. It builds gradually into a complex symphony of rich floral flavors and aromas that compliment rather than overwhelm as Cassia does. Although expensive and hard to find, Ceylon cinnamon also known as Saigon cinnamon should be a vital part of your basic ingredients"

"Vanilla - NEVER use imitation vanilla. The chemical composition of imitation vanilla is different than 'real' vanilla and interacts differently with creations. The finest vanilla is Madagascar bourbon vanilla, pure vanilla extract. I use Nielson-Massey because of their cold extraction process, which draws out over 300 flavor compounds from the vanilla bean. You can find it online at [My Spice Sage.](#)"

"Castor Sugar - Also known as superfine sugar produces a finer, lighter, more delicate cake which is what you're looking for here. You can find castor sugar at some grocers and online at [India Tree.](#)"

"Cake Flour - Although you can use AP (all purpose) flour for most of your baking needs, it's always better to use the specific flour designed for the task. Cake Flour is a low protein, low gluten flour that is perfect for cakes, muffins, biscuits and most other baked goods. That's why you'll always see it specified in my cake recipe's. You can find cake flour at most of your grocery stores. I believe that Swans Down is the best and you can find it at [Walmart.](#)"

Chef J Stephen

CREATE YOUR CAKE
With pan spray, spray a 10" cake pan (include sides)

Pour your cake mix into your sprayed cake pan

Top your cake mix with your pre-made graham cracker crumbs (fully cover cake filling)

Top your graham cracker layer with half of your Cheesecake Topping/Filling

Swirl into your Cheesecake Topping/Filling layer half of your Key Lime curd

Bake at 300° for approx. 30 minutes (your cake should be partially cooked but firm enough to hold your topping and crumbs)

Break up, with your hands, your crumb topping to form crumbs. Top your cake with your crumbs

Mix the remaining Key Lime curd with your remaining Cheesecake Topping/Filling. Using a squeeze bottle or pastry bag, top your crumbs with your combined mix in an irregular pattern

Place your cake back in your oven at 300° for an additional 30 minutes

Check your cake with a toothpick in the center. When your cake is done, remove from oven. Place your cake on a cooling rack to cool

You can refrigerate for 10 days or freeze for 120 days

AUSTRIA

OLD WORLD STYLE CRUMB CAKE

SERVES 12, PREP 35MIN, TOTAL 1HR 35MIN

INGREDIENTS

Cake
6 ounces whole milk
1 large egg
2 ½ cups AP (all purpose) flour
3 ounces unsalted butter (room temperature)
2 ¾ tsp rapid rise yeast
1 ¾ ounces white granulated sugar
¾ tsp kosher salt

Crumb Topping
11 ounces unsalted butter
5 ¼ ounces white granulated sugar
5 ¼ ounces dark brown Muscovado sugar
1 ½ tsp Saigon cinnamon
½ tsp kosher salt
2 ounces confectioners sugar
3 ½ cups cake flour (no substitute)

CHEF SECRETS

"This is my family's original 400-year-old receipt from Austria. It is unlike all my other crumb cakes because it is a yeast based cake. I don't ship my yeast based cake due to spoilage. I ship my cakes worldwide and because yeast cakes only retain their freshness for 3-4 days (without preservatives), and I NEVER use any artificial flavors, chemicals, colorants or preservatives in any of my cakes, I switched to a golden cake for all my shipped cakes. By making it at home, you have the benefit of enjoying the actual original recipe cake in your own home. If you're worried about spoilage, don't worry, I assure you it won't last long enough to spoil."

Continued on next page

INSTRUCTIONS

Cake
Preheat your oven to 275°F.

Grease a 13 x 9-inch baking pan

Cut your unsalted butter into 24 pieces

Warm your whole milk in a sauce pan LUKE WARM

Combine in a mixer bowl with dough hook, your purpose flour, whole milk, white granulated sugar, large egg, rapid rise yeast, and kosher salt

Knead on low speed for approx. 2 minutes or until your dough comes together

With your mixer running, add your unsalted butter 1 piece at a time

Increase the speed of your mixer to medium-high and continue to knead until your dough forms stretchy, web-like strands on the sides of your bowl (approx. 6 minutes) your dough should be soft and sticky

Press your dough into an even layer out to the edges of your pan

Cover your pan tightly with plastic wrap and let the dough rise at room temperature until slightly puffy, approx. 1 hour.

Continued on next page

AUSTRIA

OLD WORLD STYLE CRUMB CAKE

CONTINUED

Crumbs Topping
Ten minutes before dough has finished rising, in a mixing bowl, whisk, your melted butter, white granulated white sugar, dark brown Muscovado sugar, Saigon cinnamon, and kosher salt

Add your cake flour and stir by hand until mixture forms a thick, cohesive dough

Let your dough sit for 10 minutes to allow the flour to hydrate

NOTE: If dough has pulled away from sides of bowl after rising, gently pat it back into place

Break by hand, your crumb mixture into rough 1/2-inch pieces

Distribute in an even layer over the dough in your pan

Place in your pre-heated oven for approx. 18 minutes

NOTE: Bake until your crumbs are light brown. Check the center of your cake with a tooth pick to assure it comes out clean

Remove your cake from oven and place on cooling rack to cool

SERVING
Cut your cake into 12 squares. Dust the squares with confectioners' sugar and serve

You can refrigerate for 10 days or freeze for 120 days

CHEF SECRETS (CONTINUED)

"Don't substitute ingredients because of cost or convenience. Using the right ingredients often makes the difference between a good cake and a great cake."

"Cinnamon - Most cinnamon sold in the States is an inferior Cassia cinnamon that provides overpowering spikes in taste. The subtle complexity of flavor and texture of Ceylon cinnamon from Vietnam, is far superior. It builds gradually into a complex symphony of rich floral flavors and aromas that compliment rather than overwhelm as Cassia does. Although expensive and hard to find, Ceylon cinnamon also known as Saigon cinnamon should be a vital part of your basic ingredients."

"Vanilla - NEVER use imitation vanilla. The chemical composition of imitation vanilla is different than 'real' vanilla and interacts differently with creations. The finest vanilla is Madagascar bourbon vanilla, pure vanilla extract. I use Nielson-Massey because of their cold extraction process, which draws out over 300 flavor compounds from the vanilla bean. You can find it online at My Spice Sage."

"Cake Flour - Although you can use AP (all purpose) flour for most of your baking needs, it's always better to use the specific flour designed for the task. Cake Flour is a low protein, low gluten flour that is perfect for cakes, muffins, biscuits and most other baked goods. That's why you'll always see it specified in my cake recipe's. You can find cake flour at most of your grocery stores. I believe that Swans Down is the best and you can find it at Walmart."

Chef J Stephen

AUSTRIA

PEACHES & CREAM CRUMB CAKE

SERVES 12, PREP 45MIN, TOTAL 1HR 45MIN

INGREDIENTS

Peaches & Cream Filling & Topping
6 ounces white granulated sugar
16 ounces cream cheese
4 ounces sour cream
3 ounces whole milk
2 large eggs
½ tsp Madagascar bourbon vanilla
1 ounce AP (all purpose) flour
1 tsp natural peach extract
3 large fresh peaches

Cake
¾ cup sour cream (room temperature)
4 large eggs separated; (room temperature)
1 ½ tsp Madagascar bourbon vanilla
6 ounces unsalted butter (room temperature)
¾ cup cake flour (sifted)
¾ cup castor sugar
¼ tsp kosher salt
½ tsp baking powder
½ tsp baking soda
8 ounces crumbled graham crackers

Crumb Topping (serves 1 cake)
1 cup unsalted butter
½ cup white granulated sugar
½ cup dark brown Muscovado sugar
1 ½ tbsp Saigon cinnamon
½ tsp kosher salt
1 ½ tbsp Madagascar bourbon vanilla
1 ⅓ cups cake flour (no substitute)

See See Chef Secrets on next page

INSTRUCTIONS

Peaches & Cream Filling & Topping
Place your cream cheese in plastic bowl in your microwave for approx. 30 seconds (or until smooth)

Combine in a mixer bowl, with paddle, the your cream cheese and white granulated sugar for approx. 30 seconds on medium speed

Add your whole milk and large eggs. Mix for approx. 1 minute

Add your sour cream, Madagascar bourbon vanilla, natural peach extract, and AP flour. Mix for approx. 15 seconds on medium speed

Crumbs Topping
Melt your unsalted butter in a microwave or sauce pan on low heat. DO NOT BOIL

Combine your granulated white sugar, dark brown Muscovado sugar, kosher salt, and Saigon cinnamon into a mixing bowl

Mix with a paddle, on slow speed until ALL lumps have been removed

Add your melted butter and Madagascar bourbon vanilla

Mix with a paddle on slow speed until fully incorporated

Add your cake flour into the mix and mix on slow speed until fully incorporated

"When finished, your crumbs won't look like crumbs. Don't worry, you will pull them apart and form your crumbs when you make your cake"

Continued on next page

AUSTRIA

PEACHES & CREAM CRUMB CAKE

CHEF SECRETS

"ALWAYS use fresh peaches and 'natural' peach extract. You can find a good 'natural' peach extract online at Olive Nation."

"When it comes to your apricot filling, you can use apricot jam, BUT it won't taste near as good as apricot filling. What you traditionally find in the grocery store are Turkish apricots and they don't come close to the robust flavor of Blenheim apricots. Blenheim apricots come from California and I use Blenheim apricot topping on all my apricot cakes and you can find it at the same place we buy ours online at: B&R Farms . Their topping beats all others."

"My crumb cake recipe is an updated version of my family's 400-year-old recipe from Austria (to bake my family's original recipe, see my Old World Style Crumb Cake recipe). The crumbs and streusel used in all my crumb cake recipe's are exactly as they were from the original recipe. The only change to the original recipe is the use of a golden cake versus a yeast dough cake base. The reason for this change is due to spoilage. I ship my cakes worldwide and because yeast cakes only retain their freshness for 3-4 days (without preservatives), I was faced with a dilemma. I NEVER use any artificial flavors, chemicals, colorants or preservatives in any of my cakes. The average time a client would receive my shipped cakes in the States is 2-4 days, just as they were started to reach their freshness limits. Properly wrapped, a golden cake will retain its freshness for 7-10 days. The choice was simple and that is why, all of my crumb cakes (except for my Old World Style Crumb Cake recipe) feature a golden yellow cake recipe."

Continued on next page

CONTINUED

Cake Preparation
Preheat your oven to 300°

CREATE YOUR DRY MIX
Sift your cake flour into a mixing bowl and add your castor sugar, kosher salt, baking powder, and baking soda. Combine to create your dry mix

CREATE YOUR WET MIX
Separate your large eggs, placing the yolks in a bowl. (You will not be using your egg whites)

Add your Madagascar bourbon vanilla to your egg yolks

Place your sour cream in a medium deli container

COMBINE YOUR MIXES
Cut your unsalted butter into ⅛" thick pieces

Add your cut unsalted butter to your dry mix

Add ¾ (only) of the sour cream to your dry mix

Mix with a paddle for 1 minute 30 seconds (start slow, progress to med/high speed)

Add your remaining ¼ of your sour cream and the your egg yolk, vanilla wet mix to the dry mix

Mix for 1 minute (start slow, progress to med/high speed)

CREATE YOUR GRAHAM CRACKER LAYER
Place your graham crackers in a food processor on high until uniformly fine

Slice your peaches into ½" slices

Continued on next page

234

AUSTRIA

PEACHES & CREAM CRUMB CAKE
CONTINUED

CHEF SECRETS (CONTINUED)

"My family's double bake process is unique to baking a crumb cake. It assures that the fillings and crumbs topping will remain on the top of the cake and not drift into the cake mix. It's important that you use the type of ingredients specified. Cinnamon - Most cinnamon sold in the States is an inferior Cassia cinnamon that provides overpowering spikes in taste. The subtle complexity of flavor and texture of Ceylon cinnamon from Vietnam, is far superior. It builds gradually into a complex symphony of rich floral flavors and aromas that compliment rather than overwhelm as Cassia does. Although expensive and hard to find, Ceylon cinnamon also known as Saigon cinnamon should be a vital part of your basic ingredients Vanilla.

NEVER use imitation vanilla. The chemical composition of imitation vanilla is different than 'real' vanilla and interacts differently with creations. The finest vanilla is Madagascar bourbon vanilla, pure vanilla extract. I use Nielson-Massey because of their cold extraction process, which draws out over 300 flavor compounds from the vanilla bean. You can find it online at [My Spice Sage.](#) Castor Sugar - Also known as superfine sugar produces a finer, lighter, more delicate cake which is what you're looking for here. You can find castor sugar at some grocers and online at [India Tree](#). Cake Flour - Although you can use AP (all purpose) flour for most of your baking needs, it's always better to use the specific flour designed for the task. Cake Flour is a low protein, low gluten flour that is perfect for cakes, muffins, biscuits and most other baked goods. That's why you'll always see it specified in my cake recipe's. You can find cake flour at most of your grocery stores. I believe that Swans Down is the best and you can find it at [Walmart](#)."

Chef J Stephen

CREATE YOUR CAKE

With pan spray, spray a 10" cake pan (include sides)

Pour your cake mix into your sprayed cake pan

Top your cake mix with your pre-made graham cracker crumbs (fully cover cake filling)

Top your graham cracker layer with half of your peaches & cream topping/filling

Top your peaches and cream topping/filling layer with half of your sliced fresh peaches

Bake at 300° for approx. 30 minutes (your cake should be partially cooked but firm enough to hold your topping and crumbs)

Break up, with your hands, your crumb topping to form crumbs. Top your peaches and cream topping/filling layer with your crumbs

Using a squeeze bottle or pastry bag, top your crumbs with your remaining peaches and cream topping/filling layer in an irregular pattern

Place your cake back in your oven at 300° for an additional 30 minutes

Check your cake with a toothpick in the center. When your cake is done, remove from oven. Place your cake on a cooling rack to cool

You can refrigerate for 10 days or freeze for 120 days

AUSTRIA

PECAN PIE CRUMB CAKE

Serves 12, Prep 45min, Total 1hr 45min

INGREDIENTS

Pecan Pie Filling & Topping
7 ounces white granulated sugar
6 ounces pecan halves
2 ounces unsalted butter
8 ounces dark corn syrup
2 large eggs
1 tbsp Madagascar bourbon vanilla
2 large eggs
1 tbsp Tuaca liqueur

Cake
¾ cup sour cream (room temperature)
4 large eggs separated; (room temperature)
1 ½ tsp Madagascar bourbon vanilla
6 ounces unsalted butter (room temperature)
¾ cup cake flour (sifted)
¾ cup castor sugar
¼ tsp kosher salt
½ tsp baking powder
½ tsp baking soda

Crumb Topping (serves 1 cake)
1 cup unsalted butter
½ cup white granulated sugar
½ cup dark brown Muscovado sugar
1 ½ tbsp Saigon cinnamon
½ tsp kosher salt
1 ½ tbsp Madagascar bourbon vanilla
1 ⅓ cups cake flour (no substitute)

See Chef Secrets on next page

INSTRUCTIONS

Pecan Pie Filling & Topping
Place your unsalted butter in a microwavable container and microwave for approx. 15 seconds (or until melted)

In a mixing bowl, place your melted butter, dark corn syrup, white granulated sugar, large eggs, Madagascar bourbon vanilla, and Tuaca liqueur
Mix on slow speed until thoroughly incorporated

Add your pecan halves (fold in)
Put aside

Crumbs Topping
Melt your unsalted butter in a microwave or sauce pan on low heat. DO NOT BOIL

Combine your granulated white sugar, dark brown Muscovado sugar, kosher salt, and Saigon cinnamon into a mixing bowl

Mix with a paddle, on slow speed until ALL lumps have been removed

Add your melted butter and Madagascar bourbon vanilla

Mix with a paddle on slow speed until fully incorporated

Add your cake flour into the mix and mix on slow speed until fully incorporated

"When finished, your crumbs won't look like crumbs. Don't worry, you will pull them apart and form your crumbs when you make your cake"

Continued on next page

AUSTRIA

PECAN PIE CRUMB CAKE

CONTINUED

Cake Preparation
Preheat your oven to 300°

CREATE YOUR DRY MIX
Sift your cake flour into a mixing bowl and add your castor sugar, kosher salt, baking powder, and baking soda. Combine to create your dry mix

CREATE YOUR WET MIX
Separate your large eggs, placing the yolks in a bowl. (You will not be using your egg whites).

Add your Madagascar bourbon vanilla to your egg yolks

Place your sour cream in a medium deli container

COMBINE YOUR MIXES
Cut your unsalted butter into ⅛" thick pieces

Add your cut unsalted butter to your dry mix

Add ¾ (only) of the sour cream to your dry mix

Mix with a paddle for 1 minute 30 seconds (start slow, progress to med/high speed)

Add your remaining ¼ of your sour cream and the your egg yolk, vanilla wet mix to the dry mix.

Mix for 1 minute (start slow, progress to med/high speed)

Continued on next page

CHEF SECRETS

"Try to find fresh pecans if possible. There are many online companies that offer them. I have the fortune to live in Dallas, where fresh pecans are always available. If you can't find them, packaged, although not as tasty, will work."

"My crumb cake recipe is an updated version of my family's 400-year-old recipe from Austria (to bake my family's original recipe, see my Old World Style Crumb Cake recipe). The crumbs and streusel used in all my crumb cake recipe's are exactly as they were from the original recipe. The only change to the original recipe is the use of a golden cake versus a yeast dough cake base. The reason for this change is due to spoilage. I ship my cakes worldwide and because yeast cakes only retain their freshness for 3-4 days (without preservatives), I was faced with a dilemma. I NEVER use any artificial flavors, chemicals, colorants or preservatives in any of my cakes. The average time a client would receive my shipped cakes in the States is 2-4 days, just as they were started to reach their freshness limits. Properly wrapped, a golden cake will retain its freshness for 7-10 days. The choice was simple and that is why, all of my crumb cakes (except for my Old World Style Crumb Cake recipe) feature a golden cake recipe."

"My family's double bake process is unique to baking a crumb cake. It assures that the fillings and crumbs topping will remain on the top of the cake and not drift into the cake mix. It's important that you use the type of ingredients specified."

Continued on next page

AUSTRIA

PECAN PIE CRUMB CAKE
CONTINUED

CHEF SECRETS (CONTINUED)

"Cinnamon - Most cinnamon sold in the States is an inferior Cassia cinnamon that provides overpowering spikes in taste. The subtle complexity of flavor and texture of Ceylon cinnamon from Vietnam, is far superior. It builds gradually into a complex symphony of rich floral flavors and aromas that compliment rather than overwhelm as Cassia does. Although expensive and hard to find, Ceylon cinnamon also known as Saigon cinnamon should be a vital part of your basic ingredients."

"Vanilla - NEVER use imitation vanilla. The chemical composition of imitation vanilla is different than 'real' vanilla and interacts differently with creations. The finest vanilla is Madagascar bourbon vanilla, pure vanilla extract. I use Nielson-Massey because of their cold extraction process, which draws out over 300 flavor compounds from the vanilla bean. You can find it online at [My Spice Sage.](#)"

"Castor Sugar - Also known as superfine sugar produces a finer, lighter, more delicate cake which is what you're looking for here. You can find castor sugar at some grocers and online at [India Tree](#)."

"Cake Flour - Although you can use AP (all purpose) flour for most of your baking needs, it's always better to use the specific flour designed for the task. Cake Flour is a low protein, low gluten flour that is perfect for cakes, muffins, biscuits and most other baked goods. That's why you'll always see it specified in my cake recipe's. You can find cake flour at most of your grocery stores. I believe that Swans Down is the best and you can find it at [Walmart](#)."

Chef J Stephen

CREATE YOUR CAKE
With pan spray, spray a 10" cake pan (include sides)

Pour your cake mix into your sprayed cake pan

Bake at 300° for approx. 30 minutes (your cake should be partially cooked but firm enough to hold your topping and crumbs)

Top your partially baked cake with half of your Pecan Pie Filling & Topping making sure your pecans are spread evenly across your cake

Break up, with your hands, your crumb topping to form crumbs. Top your Pecan Pie Filling & Topping layer with your crumbs

Top your crumbs with your remaining Pecan Pie Filling & Topping in an irregular pattern

Place your cake back in your oven at 300° for an additional 30 minutes

Check your cake with a toothpick in the center. When your cake is done, remove from oven. Place your cake on a cooling rack to cool

You can refrigerate for 10 days or freeze for 120 days

AUSTRIA

PUMPKIN CHEESECAKE CRUMB CAKE

SERVES 12, PREP 45MIN, TOTAL 1HR 45MIN

INGREDIENTS

Pumpkin Cheesecake Filling & Topping
7 ½ ounces unsalted butter
¾ cup white granulated sugar
16 ounces cream cheese
½ cup sour cream
3 ounces whole milk
2 large eggs
½ tbsp Madagascar bourbon vanilla
1 ounce AP (all purpose flour)
15 ounces pumpkin pie filling
¼ tbsp pumpkin pie spice

Cake
¾ cup sour cream (room temperature)
4 large eggs separated; (room temperature)
1 ½ tsp Madagascar bourbon vanilla
6 ounces unsalted butter (room temperature)
¾ cup cake flour (sifted)
¾ cup castor sugar
¼ tsp kosher salt
½ tsp baking powder
½ tsp baking soda
8 ounces crumbled Graham Crackers

Crumb Topping (serves 1 cake)
1 cup unsalted butter
½ cup white granulated sugar
½ cup dark brown Muscovado sugar
1 ½ tbsp Saigon cinnamon
½ tsp kosher salt
1 ½ tbsp Madagascar bourbon vanilla
1 ⅓ cups cake flour (no substitute)

See Chef Secrets on next page

INSTRUCTIONS

Pumpkin Cheesecake Filling & Topping
Bring your cream cheese to room temperature (Must be room temperature, don't cheat)

Combine in a mixer bowl, with paddle, your cream cheese, pumpkin pie spice, and granulated sugar for approx. 30 seconds on medium speed

Add your whole milk and large eggs. Mix for 1 minute

Add your sour cream, Madagascar bourbon vanilla, and AP flour. Mix on medium speed for 15 seconds. Put aside

Crumbs Topping
Melt your unsalted butter in a microwave or sauce pan on low heat. DO NOT BOIL

Combine your granulated white sugar, dark brown Muscovado sugar, kosher salt, and Saigon cinnamon into a mixing bowl

Mix with a paddle, on slow speed until ALL lumps have been removed

Add your melted butter and Madagascar bourbon vanilla

Mix with a paddle on slow speed until fully incorporated

Add your cake flour into the mix and mix on slow speed until fully incorporated

"When finished, your crumbs won't look like crumbs. Don't worry, you will pull them apart and form your crumbs when you make your cake."

Continued on next page

AUSTRIA

PUMPKIN CHEESECAKE CRUMB CAKE

CONTINUED

CHEF SECRETS

"You can make your own pumpkin filling if you choose, and that's what I usually do , but except for around the holidays, pumpkin's are hard to find and that's why I include pre-mades in this recipe."

"My crumb cake recipe is an updated version of my family's 400-year-old recipe from Austria (to bake my family's original recipe, see my Old World Style Crumb Cake recipe). The crumbs and streusel used in all my crumb cake recipe's are exactly as they were from the original recipe. The only change to the original recipe is the use of a golden cake versus a yeast dough cake base. The reason for this change is due to spoilage. I ship my cakes worldwide and because yeast cakes only retain their freshness for 3-4 days (without preservatives), I was faced with a dilemma. I NEVER use any artificial flavors, chemicals, colorants or preservatives in any of my cakes. The average time a client would receive my shipped cakes in the States is 2-4 days, just as they were started to reach their freshness limits. Properly wrapped, a golden cake will retain its freshness for 7-10 days. The choice was simple and that is why, all of my crumb cakes (except for my Old World Style Crumb Cake recipe) feature a golden cake recipe."

"My family's double bake process is unique to baking a crumb cake. It assures that the fillings and crumbs topping will remain on the top of the cake and not drift into the cake mix. It's important that you use the type of ingredients specified."

Continued on next page

Cake Preparation
Preheat your oven to 300°

CREATE YOUR DRY MIX
Sift your cake flour into a mixing bowl and add your castor sugar, kosher salt, baking powder, and baking soda. Combine to create your dry mix

CREATE YOUR WET MIX
Separate your large eggs, placing the yolks in a bowl. (You will not be using your egg whites).

Add your Madagascar bourbon vanilla to your egg yolks

Place your sour cream in a medium deli container

COMBINE YOUR MIXES
Cut your unsalted butter into ⅛" thick pieces

Add your cut unsalted butter to your dry mix

Add ¾ (only) of the sour cream to your dry mix

Mix with a paddle for 1 minute 30 seconds (start slow, progress to med/high speed)

Add your remaining ¼ of your sour cream and the your egg yolk, vanilla wet mix to the dry mix.

Mix for 1 minute (start slow, progress to med/high speed)

Continued on next page

240

AUSTRIA

Pumpkin Cheesecake Crumb Cake

Chef Secrets (continued)

"Cinnamon - Most cinnamon sold in the States is an inferior Cassia cinnamon that provides overpowering spikes in taste. The subtle complexity of flavor and texture of Ceylon cinnamon from Vietnam, is far superior. It builds gradually into a complex symphony of rich floral flavors and aromas that compliment rather than overwhelm as Cassia does. Although expensive and hard to find, Ceylon cinnamon also known as Saigon cinnamon should be a vital part of your basic ingredients."

"Vanilla - NEVER use imitation vanilla. The chemical composition of imitation vanilla is different than 'real' vanilla and interacts differently with creations. The finest vanilla is Madagascar bourbon vanilla, pure vanilla extract. I use Nielson-Massey because of their cold extraction process, which draws out over 300 flavor compounds from the vanilla bean. You can find it online at [My Spice Sage](#)."

"Castor Sugar - Also known as superfine sugar produces a finer, lighter, more delicate cake which is what you're looking for here. You can find castor sugar at some grocers and online at [India Tree](#)."

"Cake Flour - Although you can use AP (all purpose) flour for most of your baking needs, it's always better to use the specific flour designed for the task. Cake Flour is a low protein, low gluten flour that is perfect for cakes, muffins, biscuits and most other baked goods. That's why you'll always see it specified in my cake recipe's. You can find cake flour at most of your grocery stores. I believe that Swans Down is the best and you can find it at [Walmart](#)."

Chef J Stephen

CONTINUED

CREATE YOUR CAKE
With pan spray, spray a 10" cake pan (include sides)

CREATE YOUR GRAHAM CRACKER LAYER
Place your graham crackers in a food processor on high until uniformly fine

Pour your cake mix into your sprayed cake pan.

Top your cake mix with your pre-made graham cracker crumbs (fully cover cake filling).

Top your graham cracker layer with half of your Cheesecake Topping/Filling & pumpkin pie spice mix.

Swirl in your pumpkin pie filling

Bake at 300° for approx. 30 minutes (your cake should be partially cooked but firm enough to hold your topping and crumbs)

Break up, with your hands, your crumb topping to form crumbs. Top your cake with your crumbs

Top your crumbs with your remaining Cheesecake Topping/Filling & pumpkin pie spice mix in an irregular pattern

Place your cake back in your oven at 300° for an additional 30 minutes

Check your cake with a toothpick in the center. When your cake is done, remove from oven. Place your cake on a cooling rack to cool

AUSTRIA

Ruby Red Raspberry Crumb Cake

Serves 12, Prep 45min, Total 1hr 45min

Ingredients

Cake
- ¾ cup sour cream (room temperature)
- 4 large eggs separated; (room temperature)
- 1 ½ tsp Madagascar bourbon vanilla
- 6 ounces unsalted butter (room temperature)
- ¾ cup cake flour (sifted)
- ¾ cup castor sugar
- ¼ tsp kosher salt
- ½ tsp baking powder
- ½ tsp baking soda

Crumb Topping (serves 1 cake)
- 1 cup unsalted butter
- ½ cup white granulated sugar
- ½ cup dark brown Muscovado sugar
- 1 ½ tbsp Saigon cinnamon
- ½ tsp kosher salt
- 1 ½ tbsp Madagascar bourbon vanilla
- 1 ⅓ cups cake flour (no substitute)

Ruby Red Raspberry Filling/Topping
- 12 ounces Hungarian Lekvar preserves

Chef Secrets

"When it comes to your raspberry filling, you can use raspberry jam, BUT although it may be a challenge to find, try to find Hungarian Lekvar. It's what I use because it has the most robust raspberry flavor and has no fillers or sugars. If you can't find Hungarian Lekvar, use a raspberry preserve that is made from all fruit with no sugar added."

Continued on next page

Instructions

Crumbs Topping
Melt your unsalted butter in a microwave or sauce pan on low heat. DO NOT BOIL

Combine your granulated white sugar, dark brown Muscovado sugar, kosher salt, and Saigon cinnamon into a mixing bowl

Mix with a paddle, on slow speed until ALL lumps have been removed

Add your melted butter and Madagascar bourbon vanilla

Mix with a paddle on slow speed until fully incorporated

Add your cake flour into the mix and mix on slow speed until fully incorporated

"When finished, your crumbs won't look like crumbs. Don't worry, you will pull them apart and form your crumbs when you make your cake."

Cake Preparation
Preheat your oven to 300°

CREATE YOUR DRY MIX
Sift your cake flour into a mixing bowl and add your castor sugar, kosher salt, baking powder, and baking soda. Combine to create your dry mix

Continued on next page

AUSTRIA

Ruby Red Raspberry Crumb Cake

CONTINUED

CHEF SECRETS (CONTINUED)

"My crumb cake recipe is an updated version of my family's 400-year-old recipe from Austria (to bake my family's original recipe, see my Old World Style Crumb Cake recipe). The crumbs and streusel used in all my crumb cake recipe's are exactly as they were from the original recipe. The only change to the original recipe is the use of a golden cake versus a yeast dough cake base. My family's double bake process is unique to baking a crumb cake. It assures that the fillings and crumbs topping will remain on the top of the cake and not drift into the cake mix."

"It's important that you use they type of ingredients specified without substitution."

"Cinnamon - Most cinnamon sold in the States is an inferior Cassia cinnamon that provides overpowering spikes in taste. The subtle complexity of flavor and texture of Ceylon cinnamon from Vietnam, is far superior. It builds gradually into a complex symphony of rich floral flavors and aromas that compliment rather than overwhelm as Cassia does. Although expensive and often hard to find, Ceylon cinnamon also known as Saigon cinnamon should be a vital part of your basic ingredient set."

Continued on next page

Cake Preparation (continued)

CREATE YOUR WET MIX

Separate your large eggs, placing the yolks in a bowl. (You will not be using your egg whites).

Add your Madagascar bourbon vanilla to your egg yolks

Place your sour cream in a medium deli container

COMBINE YOUR MIXES

Cut your unsalted butter into $\frac{1}{8}$" thick pieces

Add your cut unsalted butter to your dry mix

Add $\frac{3}{4}$ (only) of the sour cream to your dry mix

Mix with a paddle for 1 minute 30 seconds (start slow, progress to med/high speed)

Add your remaining $\frac{1}{4}$ of your sour cream and the your egg yolk, vanilla wet mix to the dry mix.

Mix for 1 minute (start slow, progress to med/high speed)

Continued on next page

AUSTRIA

RUBY RED RASPBERRY CRUMB CAKE

CONTINUED

CHEF SECRETS (CONTINUED)

"Vanilla - NEVER use imitation vanilla. The chemical composition of imitation vanilla is different than 'real' vanilla and interacts differently with creations. The finest vanilla is Madagascar bourbon vanilla, pure vanilla extract. I use Nielson-Massey because of their cold extraction process, which draws out over 300 flavor compounds from the vanilla bean. You can find it online at [My Spice Sage](#)."

"Castor Sugar - Also known as superfine sugar produces a finer, lighter, more delicate cake which is what you're looking for here. You can find castor sugar at some grocers and online at [India Tree](#)."

"Cake Flour - Although you can use AP (all purpose) flour for most of your baking needs, it's always better to use the specific flour designed for the task. Cake Flour is a low protein, low gluten flour that is perfect for cakes, muffins, biscuits and most other baked goods. That's why you'll always see it specified in my cake recipe's. You can find cake flour at most of your grocery stores. I believe that Swans Down is the best and you can find it at [Walmart](#)."

Chef J Stephen

Create Cake
Preheat your oven to 300°
With pan spray, spray a 10" cake pan (include sides)

Pour your cake mix into your sprayed cake pan

Bake at 300° for approx. 30 minutes (your cake should be partially cooked but firm enough to hold your topping and crumbs)

Remove your cake from oven and using a spatula, top your cake with a thin layer (approx. 6 ounces) of your red raspberry preserve. Make sure your cake is completely covered with your layer of preserve

Break up, with your hands, your crumb topping to form crumbs. Top your red raspberry preserve layer with your crumbs

Using a squeeze bottle or pastry bag, top your crumbs with an additional topping of your red raspberry preserve (approx. 6 ounces) in an irregular pattern (see photo)

Place your cake back in your oven at 300° for an additional 30 minutes

Check your cake with a toothpick in the center. When your cake is done, remove from oven. Place your cake on a cooling rack to cool

You can refrigerate for 10 days or freeze for 120 days

AUSTRIA

Strawberry Cheesecake Crumb Cake

Serves 12, Prep 45min, Total 1hr 45min

INGREDIENTS

Strawberry Cheesecake Filling & Topping
7 ½ ounces unsalted butter
¾ cup white granulated sugar
16 ounces cream cheese
½ cup sour cream
3 ounces whole milk
2 large eggs
½ tbsp Madagascar bourbon vanilla
1 ounce AP (all purpose flour)
7 ½ ounces strawberry pie filling
7 ½ ounces strawberry jam (natural no-sugar)

Cake
¾ cup sour cream (room temperature)
4 large eggs separated; (room temperature)
1 ½ tsp Madagascar bourbon vanilla
6 ounces unsalted butter (room temperature)
¾ cup cake flour (sifted)
¾ cup castor sugar
¼ tsp kosher salt
½ tsp baking powder
½ tsp baking soda
8 ounces crumbled Graham Crackers

Crumb Topping (serves 1 cake)
1 cup unsalted butter
½ cup white granulated sugar
½ cup dark brown Muscovado sugar
1 ½ tbsp Saigon cinnamon
½ tsp kosher salt
1 ½ tbsp Madagascar bourbon vanilla
1 ⅓ cups cake flour (no substitute)

See Chef Secrets on next page

INSTRUCTIONS

Strawberry Cheesecake Filling & Topping
Bring your cream cheese to room temperature (Must be room temperature, don't cheat)

Combine in a mixer bowl, with paddle, your cream cheese, and granulated sugar for approx. 30 seconds on medium speed

Add your whole milk and large eggs. Mix for 1 minute

Add your sour cream, Madagascar bourbon vanilla, and AP flour. Mix on medium speed for 15 seconds. Put aside

Crumbs Topping
Melt your unsalted butter in a microwave or sauce pan on low heat. DO NOT BOIL

Combine your granulated white sugar, dark brown Muscovado sugar, kosher salt, and Saigon cinnamon into a mixing bowl

Mix with a paddle, on slow speed until ALL lumps have been removed

Add your melted butter and Madagascar bourbon vanilla

Mix with a paddle on slow speed until fully incorporated

Add your cake flour into the mix and mix on slow speed until fully incorporated

"When finished, your crumbs won't look like crumbs. Don't worry, you will pull them apart and form your crumbs when you make your cake."

Continued on next page

AUSTRIA

STRAWBERRY CHEESECAKE CRUMB CAKE

CONTINUED

CHEF SECRETS

"You can make your own strawberry filling and jam if you choose, and that's what I usually do, but in this case, I found that there really wasn't much of a difference in taste or texture and that's why I include pre-mades in this recipe."

"My crumb cake recipe is an updated version of my family's 400-year-old recipe from Austria (to bake my family's original recipe, see my Old World Style Crumb Cake recipe). The crumbs and streusel used in all my crumb cake recipe's are exactly as they were from the original recipe. The only change to the original recipe is the use of a golden cake versus a yeast dough cake base. The reason for this change is due to spoilage. I ship my cakes worldwide and because yeast cakes only retain their freshness for 3-4 days (without preservatives), I was faced with a dilemma. I NEVER use any artificial flavors, chemicals, colorants or preservatives in any of my cakes. The average time a client would receive my shipped cakes in the States is 2-4 days, just as they were started to reach their freshness limits. Properly wrapped, a golden cake will retain its freshness for 7-10 days. The choice was simple and that is why, all of my crumb cakes (except for my Old World Style Crumb Cake recipe) feature a golden cake recipe."

"My family's double bake process is unique to baking a crumb cake. It assures that the fillings and crumbs topping will remain on the top of the cake and not drift into the cake mix. It's important that you use the type of ingredients specified."

Continued on next page

Cake Preparation
Preheat your oven to 300°

CREATE YOUR DRY MIX
Sift your cake flour into a mixing bowl and add your castor sugar, kosher salt, baking powder, and baking soda. Combine to create your dry mix

CREATE YOUR WET MIX
Separate your large eggs, placing the yolks in a bowl. (You will not be using your egg whites)

Add your Madagascar bourbon vanilla to your egg yolks

Place your sour cream in a medium deli container

COMBINE YOUR MIXES
Cut your unsalted butter into ⅛" thick pieces

Add your cut unsalted butter to your dry mix

Add ¾ (only) of the sour cream to your dry mix

Mix with a paddle for 1 minute 30 seconds (start slow, progress to med/high speed)

Add your remaining ¼ of your sour cream and the your egg yolk, vanilla wet mix to the dry mix

Mix for 1 minute (start slow, progress to med/high speed)

Continued on next page

AUSTRIA

STRAWBERRY CHEESECAKE CRUMB CAKE

CONTINUED

CHEF SECRETS (CONTINUED)

"Cinnamon - Most cinnamon sold in the States is an inferior Cassia cinnamon that provides overpowering spikes in taste. The subtle complexity of flavor and texture of Ceylon cinnamon from Vietnam, is far superior. It builds gradually into a complex symphony of rich floral flavors and aromas that compliment rather than overwhelm as Cassia does. Although expensive and hard to find, Ceylon cinnamon also known as Saigon cinnamon should be a vital part of your basic ingredients."

"Vanilla - NEVER use imitation vanilla. The chemical composition of imitation vanilla is different than 'real' vanilla and interacts differently with creations. The finest vanilla is Madagascar bourbon vanilla, pure vanilla extract. I use Nielson-Massey because of their cold extraction process, which draws out over 300 flavor compounds from the vanilla bean. You can find it online at My Spice Sage."

"Castor Sugar - Also known as superfine sugar produces a finer, lighter, more delicate cake which is what you're looking for here. You can find castor sugar at some grocers and online at India Tree".

"Cake Flour - Although you can use AP (all purpose) flour for most of your baking needs, it's always better to use the specific flour designed for the task. Cake Flour is a low protein, low gluten flour that is perfect for cakes, muffins, biscuits and most other baked goods. That's why you'll always see it specified in my cake recipe's. You can find cake flour at most of your grocery stores. I believe that Swans Down is the best and you can find it at Walmart."

Chef J Stephen

CREATE YOUR CAKE
With pan spray, spray a 10" cake pan (include sides)

CREATE YOUR GRAHAM CRACKER LAYER
Place your graham crackers in a food processor on high until uniformly fine

Pour your cake mix into your sprayed cake pan.

Top your cake mix with your pre-made graham cracker crumbs (fully cover cake filling)

Top your graham cracker layer with half of your Cheesecake Topping/Filling

Swirl in your and your strawberry pie filling

Bake at 300° for approx. 30 minutes (your cake should be partially cooked but firm enough to hold your topping and crumbs)

Break up, with your hands, your crumb topping to form crumbs. Top your cake with your crumbs

Top your crumbs with your strawberry jam in an irregular pattern

Place your cake back in your oven at 300° for an additional 30 minutes

Check your cake with a toothpick in the center. When your cake is done, remove from oven. Place your cake on a cooling rack to cool

You can refrigerate for 10 days or freeze for 30 days

AUSTRIA

Villafranca Lemon Crumb Cake

Serves 12, Prep 50min, Total 1hr 50min

Ingredients

Lemon Curd Filling & Topping
the zest of 1 lemon Villafranca lemon (if available)
⅔ cup fresh lemon juice Villafranca lemon (if available)
1 cup white granulated sugar
2 large egg yolks
2 large eggs
3 ounces unsalted butter
⅛ tbsp sea salt

Cake
¾ cup sour cream (room temperature)
4 large eggs separated; (room temperature)
1 ½ tsp Madagascar bourbon vanilla
6 ounces unsalted butter (room temperature)
¾ cup cake flour (sifted)
¾ cup castor sugar
¼ tsp kosher salt
½ tsp baking powder
½ tsp baking soda

Crumb Topping (serves 1 cake)
1 cup unsalted butter
½ cup white granulated sugar
½ cup dark brown Muscovado sugar
1 ½ tbsp Saigon cinnamon
½ tsp kosher salt
1 ½ tbsp Madagascar bourbon vanilla
1 ⅓ cups cake flour (no substitute)

See Chef Secrets on next page

Instructions

Lemon Curd Filling & Topping
In a large mixing bowl, add your unsalted butter, and white granulated sugar. Whisk for approx. 2 minutes

Slowly add your eggs and yolks. Whisk for 1 minute. Add your lemon juice. Don't worry about curdled look, it will smooth into a curd as it cooks

In a medium saucepan, cook your curd over low heat until it becomes smooth. Raise the heat to medium and cook, stirring continually, until the curd thickens, approx. 15 minutes (should hold to the back of a spoon) (do not boil)

Remove your curd from the heat; stir in your lemon zest. Transfer your curd to a bowl. Cover with plastic wrap on the surface of the curd and chill in the refrigerator. The curd will thicken further as it cools

Crumbs Topping
Melt your unsalted butter in a microwave or sauce pan on low heat. DO NOT BOIL

Combine your granulated white sugar, dark brown Muscovado sugar, kosher salt, and Saigon cinnamon into a mixing bowl. Mix with a paddle, on slow speed until ALL lumps have been removed

Add your melted butter and Madagascar bourbon vanilla.Mix with a paddle on slow speed until fully incorporated

Continued on next page

AUSTRIA

VILLAFRANCA LEMON CRUMB CAKE

CHEF SECRETS

"Yes you can buy lemon curd at the store BUT… there is a big difference in taste and texture when you make it yourself. If you want your dish to stand out, you need to go the extra mile. Not easy, but try to find Villafranca lemons. They are from Italy. They are much more tart than a traditional lemon and will add a really robust zing to your cake."

"My crumb cake recipe is an updated version of my family's 400-year-old recipe from Austria (to bake my family's original recipe, see my Old World Style Crumb Cake recipe). The crumbs and streusel used in all my crumb cake recipe's are exactly as they were from the original recipe. The only change to the original recipe is the use of a golden cake versus a yeast dough cake base. The reason for this change is due to spoilage. I ship my cakes worldwide and because yeast cakes only retain their freshness for 3-4 days (without preservatives), I was faced with a dilemma. I NEVER use any artificial flavors, chemicals, colorants or preservatives in any of my cakes. The average time a client would receive my shipped cakes in the States is 2-4 days, just as they were started to reach their freshness limits. Properly wrapped, a golden cake will retain its freshness for 7-10 days. The choice was simple and that is why, all of my crumb cakes (except for my Old World Style Crumb Cake recipe) feature a golden cake recipe."

"My family's double bake process is unique to baking a crumb cake. It assures that the fillings and crumbs topping will remain on the top of the cake and not drift into the cake mix. It's important that you use the type of ingredients specified."

Continued on next page

CONTINUED

Add your cake flour into the mix and mix on slow speed until fully incorporated

"When finished, your crumbs won't look like crumbs. Don't worry, you will pull them apart and form your crumbs when you make your cake."

Cake Preparation
Preheat your oven to 300°

CREATE YOUR DRY MIX
Sift your cake flour into a mixing bowl and add your castor sugar, kosher salt, baking powder, and baking soda. Combine to create your dry mix

CREATE YOUR WET MIX
Separate your large eggs, placing the yolks in a bowl. (You will not be using your egg whites)

Add your Madagascar bourbon vanilla to your egg yolks

Place your sour cream in a medium deli container

COMBINE YOUR MIXES
Cut your unsalted butter into 1/8" thick pieces

Add your cut unsalted butter to your dry mix

Add 3/4 (only) of the sour cream to your dry mix

Mix with a paddle for 1 minute 30 seconds (start slow, progress to med/high speed)

Add your remaining 1/4 of your sour cream and the your egg yolk, vanilla wet mix to the dry mix

Mix for 1 minute (start slow, progress to med/high speed)

Continued on next page

AUSTRIA

Villafranca lemon Crumb Cake

Chef Secrets (continued)

"Cinnamon - Most cinnamon sold in the States is an inferior Cassia cinnamon that provides overpowering spikes in taste. The subtle complexity of flavor and texture of Ceylon cinnamon from Vietnam, is far superior. It builds gradually into a complex symphony of rich floral flavors and aromas that compliment rather than overwhelm as Cassia does. Although expensive and hard to find, Ceylon cinnamon also known as Saigon cinnamon should be a vital part of your basic ingredients."

"Vanilla - NEVER use imitation vanilla. The chemical composition of imitation vanilla is different than 'real' vanilla and interacts differently with creations. The finest vanilla is Madagascar bourbon vanilla, pure vanilla extract. I use Nielson-Massey because of their cold extraction process, which draws out over 300 flavor compounds from the vanilla bean. You can find it online at [My Spice Sage.](#)"

"Castor Sugar - Also known as superfine sugar produces a finer, lighter, more delicate cake which is what you're looking for here. You can find castor sugar at some grocers and online at [India Tree.](#)"

"Cake Flour - Although you can use AP (all purpose) flour for most of your baking needs, it's always better to use the specific flour designed for the task. Cake Flour is a low protein, low gluten flour that is perfect for cakes, muffins, biscuits and most other baked goods. That's why you'll always see it specified in my cake recipe's. You can find cake flour at most of your grocery stores. I believe that Swans Down is the best and you can find it at [Walmart](#)."

CONTINUED

CREATE YOUR CAKE

With pan spray, spray a 10" cake pan (include sides)

Pour your cake mix into your sprayed cake pan

Top your cake mix with half of your pre-made lemon curd

Bake at 300° for approx. 30 minutes (your cake should be partially cooked but firm enough to hold your topping and crumbs)

Break up, with your hands, your crumb topping to form crumbs. Top your cake with your crumbs

Top your crumbs with your remaining lemon curd in an irregular pattern

Place your cake back in your oven at 300° for an additional 30 minutes

Check your cake with a toothpick in the center. When your cake is done, remove from oven

Place your cake on a cooling rack to cool

You can refrigerate for 10 days or freeze for 120 days

Chef J Stephen

CHILDREN'S RECIPE'S

"Although many of the recipes in my recipe book are clearly children friendly. the recipes in this section are only found in my Happy Veggies series of children's books (available online at jstephensgarden.com). My 'Happy' Garden™ Happy Veggies™ books are designed to teach children that there are vegetable dishes that even they will like. Healthy eating explained in a way that kids will enjoy is at the core of every one of my books."

"Each book is about an adventure of a specific vegetable and features a recipe using that vegetable. By reading the books children identify with the characters and are anxious, to not only try the characters very own dish but also help make the dish! Every featured characters dish is designed to be easy to make and fun to do, and most of all, you'll find your children asking for a healthy 'vegetable' dish."

"You'll find a Tanya Tomato, Homemade Pizza; Bubba Broccoli Tater Tots; Colinda Cauliflower Mashed Potatoes; Chuckie Carrot Muffins; Eddie Eggplant Brownies, Paulina Potato French Fries, Sidney String Bean Casserole and Sammy Spinach Pineapple & Spinach Popsicles."

"I hope you and your children enjoy making and eating these healthy, child-friendly recipes as they learn that even vegetables can be, not only fun to read about, but also delicious to eat as well."

Chef J Stephen

UNITED STATES

Bubba Broccoli Tater Tots

Serves 6, Prep 20min, Total 40min

Instructions

Preheat your oven to 400°

Line with parchment or grease a baking sheet

Fill a medium sized pan with enough water to cover the broccoli and bring to a boil

Fill a medium sized bowl with cold tap water and set aside

Blanch (not cook) your broccoli by placing it in the boiling water for approx. 1 minute

Remove and place broccoli in your bowl of cold tap water (This will stop the cooking process) Drain well. Dab with a paper towel to assure your broccoli is not too wet and then finely chop

Add your large egg, diced yellow onions, shredded cheddar cheese, panko bread crumbs, Italian bread crumbs, chopped parsley, table salt, black pepper, and mix throughly

Scoop about 1 ½ tbsp of your mix and gently press between your hands into a firm ball. Once you have a firm ball, shape into a tater-tot. (You might want to wash your hands after every few tots to keep the mix from sticking to your hands)

Place on your prepared baking sheet and place in your pre-heated oven

Bake until golden brown and crispy, usually around 20 minutes, turning your tot's at the half way mark to assure they brown on all sides

Your now good to go. Provide a dip of your choice and enjoy

Ingredients

12 ounces fresh or frozen broccoli
1 large egg
¼ cup diced yellow onion
⅓ cup shredded cheddar cheese
⅓ cup panko breadcrumbs
⅓ cup Italian breadcrumbs
2 tbsp chopped parsley
½ tsp table salt
½ tsp black pepper

UNITED STATES

COLINDA CAULIFLOWER MASHED POTATOES

SERVES 4, PREP 10MIN, TOTAL 20MIN

INGREDIENTS

2 heads of fresh cauliflower
4 ounces of sour cream
2 tbsp of fresh chives
3 ounces of shredded cheddar cheese
1 tsp black pepper
2 tsp table salt
2 ½ tsp unsalted butter
2 ounces of heavy cream

INSTRUCTIONS

Cut your 2 heads of fresh cauliflower into florets

Chop your chives

Place your cut cauliflower florets into a plastic bowl

Cover the bowl with clear wrap

Place into your microwave and steam until your cauliflower are fork tender

Cool your cauliflower and squeeze out all the water with a towel

Place your fully drained cauliflower in a food processor

Add your sour cream, shredded sharp cheddar, black pepper, chopped chives, table salt, unsalted butter, and heavy cream

Mix in your food processor until creamy smooth

Warm in the microwave to your desired temperature and top with gravy or butter

You now have the healthiest and tastiest mashed potatoes you can make. Enjoy!

UNITED STATES

CHUCKIE CARROT MUFFINS

Serves 4, Prep 25min, Total 45min

Instructions

Preheat your oven to 400°

Line a muffin tin with paper liners or spray

In a large bowl, add your flour, sugar, cinnamon, dark brown Muscovado sugar, fresh ground nutmeg, fresh ground ginger, baking powder, and table salt. Stir

Add your grated carrots and unsweetened coconut

Mix - and then set this dry-mix aside

In a separate bowl, add your Greek yogurt, large eggs, coconut oil, and milk

Stir well until completely incorporated

Add your wet mix to your dry mix and stir until fully incorporated. You have now created your batter

Spread your batter into your lined or sprayed muffin tins

Bake for 15-20 minutes

Ingredients

- 2 cups AP flour
- ⅔ cup dark brown Muscovado sugar
- 2 tsp Saigon cinnamon
- ¼ tsp fresh ground nutmeg
- ¼ tsp fresh ground ginger
- 2 tsp baking powder
- ½ tsp table salt
- 2 cups fresh carrots (grated)
- ⅓ cup unsweetened coconut (shredded)
- 6-ounce pineapple Greek yogurt
- 2 large eggs
- ⅓ cup coconut oil
- ¼ cup milk (any milk of your choice)

UNITED STATES

Eddie Eggplant Brownies

Serves 4, Prep 20min, Total 40min

Instructions

Preheat your oven to 350°

Peel and slice your 1 medium sized fresh eggplant

Break into little pieces your 5 oz of dark chocolate

Remove pits and dice your 2 oz of soft dates

If you can't find almond meal, grind your almonds in a food processor

Place your sliced eggplant in a large mixing bowl and microwave until soft (approximately 5 minutes). Use your spatula to break up your eggplant slices into smaller pieces

Add your 5 oz of dark chocolate and your 2 oz of coconut oil. Stir until the chocolate and oil melts and all your ingredients are combined

Add your 2 oz of diced dates and your ¾ tsp of table salt

Place your ingredients in a table top blender or a food processor. Mix until smooth

Add your 3 large eggs, 1 tsp of baking powder and 2.5 oz of ground almond meal and mix again for approximately 1 minute

Spread the mixture into a 9" square glass baking dish. Bake for approx. 20 minutes

Check with a knife or tooth pick. When it comes out clean you're good to go

Let cool (if possible) and watch them fly off the dish

Ingredients

1 medium fresh eggplant
5 ounces dark chocolate (70% cocoa)
2 ounces coconut oil
2 ounces soft pitted dates
¾ tsp table salt
3 packets Stevia (Truvia)
3 large eggs
1 tsp baking powder
2 ½ ounces almond meal (can substitute with almonds crushed in blender)

UNITED STATES

Sammy Spinach Pineapple & Spinach Popsicles

SERVES 6, PREP 10MIN, TOTAL 15MIN

Ingredients

1 cup fresh spinach
1 ripe banana (black skin ok)
½ cup whole milk (any milk of your choice will work)
1 cup pineapple chunks

Instructions

Blend your fresh spinach, ripe banana, pineapple chunks, and whole milk in a blender until smooth

Pour into popsicle molds (You can get inexpensive BPA free moulds at Walmart)

Place your popsicles in the freezer overnight

"The banana will sweeten your popsicles (without any sugar) and because the pineapple will override all the other flavors, your kids will never taste the spinach, BUT you can now show them that even a healthy 'SPINACH' vegetable popsicle actually tastes great!"

United States

Tanya Tomato Pizza

SERVES 4, PREP 20MIN, TOTAL 60MIN

Ingredients

Sauce
2 tbsp virgin olive oil
1 small white onion, peeled and chopped
1 clove garlic, peeled and sliced
2 cans crushed tomatoes (Heinz Heirloom are the healthiest)
¾ tbsp granulated sugar
2 tsp kosher salt
1 tsp fresh oregano (dried is ok if you can't get fresh)

Dough
¼ ounce active dry yeast (1 packet)
1 tsp white granulated sugar
1 cup warm water (must be 110 degrees)
2 ½ cups bread flour
2 tbsp virgin olive oil
1 tsp kosher salt

Toppings
1 cup fresh mozzarella cheese (shredded)
¼ cup fresh basil

Instructions

Sauce
Heat your virgin oil in a small saucepan over medium heat and then add your onion and garlic. Cook for 3–4 minutes or until the onions take on a bit of a golden color. Reduce the heat to medium-low and add the your crushed tomatoes, granulated sugar, kosher salt, and fresh oregano. Simmer for 20 minutes. (Make sure you keep the heat low enough so that the sauce barely bubbles). Remove the sauce from the range and allow to cool. Transfer the sauce to a blender or food processor and process until smooth. Check to see if your sauce tastes a bit too acidic. If it does, add ¼ tsp granulated sugar

Dough
"If you're not up to making your own dough at home, you can buy a pre-made frozen crust at your local grocery store, BUT a home-made crust is much healthier and more fun to do when you use my simple to make recipe"

Preheat your oven to 450°

In a medium bowl, dissolve your active yeast and granulated sugar in your warm (not hot) water. Let stand until creamy, about 10 minutes

Stir in your bread flour, kosher salt, and virgin olive oil. With a whisk, beat until smooth. Let it rest for 5 minutes

Turn your dough out onto a lightly floured surface and pat or roll into a round pizza size crust and then transfer your crust to a lightly greased pizza pan dusted with some cornmeal

Spread with your homemade sauce, add some shredded mozzarella cheese and some fresh basil toppings and bake in your preheated oven for 15 to 20 minutes, or until golden brown

Let your pizza cool for 5 minutes before serving

UNITED STATES

PAULINA POTATO FRENCH-FRIES

Serves 4, Prep 15min, Total 55min

Ingredients

- 3 russet potatoes
- 3 tablespoons of avocado oil
- 2 teaspoons kosher salt

Instructions

Preheat your oven to 445°

Peel and slice your potatoes into ½ inch French-fry sticks

Rinse your sliced potatoes in a colander under cold water

Pat completely dry with a towel

Place potatoes on a sheet pan, drizzle with your avocado oil and kosher salt, and toss to make sure you coat the entire sides of each potato

Bake for 25 minutes and toss to assure your potatoes brown on all sides, and then bake for an additional 15 minutes (for a total of 40 minutes)

"You and your children have now made your own, home-made, deliciously 'healthy' French-fries!"

Enjoy!

UNITED STATES

SIDNEY STRING BEAN CASSEROLE

SERVES 4, PREP 20MIN, TOTAL 60MIN

INGREDIENTS

Sauce
1 can of 10 ½ oz Campbells® Cream of Mushroom Soup
¾ cup whole milk
⅛ tsp black pepper
4 cups cooked cut string beans
1 ⅓ cups FRENCH'S® Crispy Fried Onions

Dough
¼ ounce active dry yeast (1 packet)
1 tsp white granulated sugar
1 cup warm water (must be 110 degrees)
2 ½ cups bread flour
2 tbsp virgin olive oil
1 tsp kosher salt

Toppings
1 cup fresh mozzarella cheese (shredded)
¼ cup fresh basil

INSTRUCTIONS

Mix your soup, milk, and black pepper in a 1 ½ quart baking dish

Stir in your cooked string beans

Add ⅔ cup of Crispy Fried Onions

Bake at 350° for 30 minutes or until hot

Stir

Top with your remaining Crispy Fried Onions

Bake for 5 minutes or until the Onions are crispy and golden

Remove from oven and serve

"Cooking is all about people. Food is maybe the only universal thing that really has the power to bring everyone together. No matter what culture, everywhere around the world, people eat together."

Guy Fieri

Index of Recipes

APPETIZERS	p.23	**BREADS & BISCUITS**	p.47
Brie - Baked Honey Almond	p.28	Biscuits - Buttermilk	p.51-52
Camembert with Pistachio Crust	p.24	Bread - Baguette's, Toasted	p.50
Crab Cakes - Belizean	p.31-32	Bread - Banana Nut	p.55
Cucumber Vases	p. 27	Bread - Cranberry Nut	p.54
Nochalette's	p.25	Bread - Escargot	p.49
Scallops - Streusel & Bacon Wrapped	p.29-30	Croutons - Parmesan	p.48
Toast - śmietanka	p.26	Pudding - Yorkshire	p.53

INDEX OF RECIPES (CONTINUED)

BREAKFAST & BRUNCH — p.57

Bacon - Ontario Candied Bacon	p.88
Biscuits - Jalapeño Sausage Gravy & Biscuits	p.85-86
Cereal - Oatmeal - Parisian Style Oatmeal	p.80
Eggs - Corned Beef Hash & Eggs	p.78-79
Eggs - Quiche - Ham & Asparagus	p.60-61
Eggs - Quiche - Jalapeño Bacon & Broccolini	p.62-63
Eggs - Quiche - Mushroom Spinach	p.58-59
Eggs - Soufflé - Blue Lump Crab	p.64-65
Eggs - Soufflé - Gruyère Cheese	p.66-67
Eggs - Catalina Isles Eggs Benedict	p.83-84
Eggs - Salmon Eggs Benedict	p.81-82
French Toast - Grand Mariner	p.68-69
French Toast - Jamaican Rum	p.70-71
Pancakes - Gamberaia Blueberry Ricotta	p.74-75
Pancakes - Japanese	p.72-73
Sausage - Jalapeño Sausage	p.87
Waffles - Gaufre Liege	p.76-77

CHILDREN'S DISHES — p.252

Bubba Broccoli Tater Tots	p.253
Colinda Cauliflower Mashed Potatoes	p.254
Chuckie Carrot Muffins	p.255
Eddie Eggplant Brownies	p.256
Sammy Spinach Pineapple & Spinach Popsicles	p.257
Tanya Tomato Pizza	p.258
Paulina Potato French Fries	p.259
Sidney String Bean Casserole	P.260

INDEX OF RECIPES (CONTINUED)

DESSERTS — p.179

Cakes - Apple Strudel Crumb Cake	p.197-199
Cakes - Blenheim Apricot Crumb Cake	p.200-202
Cakes - Banana's Foster Crumb Cake	p.203-205
Cakes - Caramel Sea Salt Crumb Cake	p.206-208
Cakes - Carrot Cake Crumb Cake	p.209-212
Cakes - Chocolate de la Terre Crumb Cake	p.213-215
Cakes - Cinnamon Streusel Crumb Cake	p.216-218
Cakes - Coconut Custard Crumb Cake	p.219-222
Cakes - Egg Nog Crumb Cake	p.223-225
Cakes - Hot Toffee Buttered Rum Crumb Cake	p.226-228
Cakes- Key Lime Pie Crumb Cake	p.229-231
Cakes - Old World Style Crumb Cake	p.232-233
Cakes - Peaches & Cream Crumb Cake	p.234-236
Cakes - Pecan Pie Crumb Cake	p.237-239
Cakes - Pumpkin Cheesecake Crumb Cake	p.240-242
Cakes - Ruby Red Raspberry Crumb Cake	p.243-245
Cakes - Strawberry Cheesecake Crumb Cake	p.246-248
Cakes - Villafranca Lemon Crumb Cake	p.249-251
Cakes - Tiramisu	p.189
Cookies - Almond Biscotti	p.182
Cookies - Chocolate Chip	p.180
Cookies - Chocolate Chip - Nestle Tollhouse Tips	p.181
Cookies - Linzer Torte	p.184-185
New Orleans Bread Pudding	p.192
Pastries - Cranberry Orange Scones	p.186
Pastries - Cannoli's	p.187-188
Pastries - Danish Pancake Puffs	p.183
Pastries - Eclairs	p.190-191
Pies- Banana Cream	p.193-194
Pies - Chocolate Cream	p.195-196

INDEX OF RECIPES (CONTINUED)

FILLINGS, FROSTINGS & TOPPINGS — p.163

Crème Anglaise — p.164

Curd - Lemon — p.164

Curd - Key Lime — p.165

Fruit Macerate — p.165

Filling - Carrot Cake — p.170

Filling - Graham Cracker — p.174

Filling/Topping - Apple Strudel — p.167

Filling/Topping - Cinnamon Streusel — p.167

Filling/Topping - Cheesecake — p.170

Filling/Topping - Chocolate — p.171

Filling - Coconut Custard — p.171

Filling/Topping - Egg Nog Cheesecake — p.172

Filling/Topping - Caramel — p.173

Filling/Topping - Hot Butter Toffee Rum — p.175

Filling/Topping - Marshmallow — p.174

Filling/Topping - Peaches & Cream — p.176

Filling/Topping - Pecan Pie — p.176

Frosting - Cream Cheese Cake — p.169

Topping - Carrot Cake — p.169

Topping - Coconut Custard — p.172

Topping - Crumb Cake Crumb Mix — p.168

Topping - Cinnamon Crumb Ice Cream — p.166

Topping - Cinnamon Streusel Ice Cream — p.166

Topping - Toasted Coconut — p.168

INDEX OF RECIPES (CONTINUED)

GRAVIES, SAUCES, DIPS & SPREADS — p.146

Aioli	p.153
Aioli - Sun-dried Tomato	p.153
Beurre Manié	p.147
Butter - Banana	p.155
Butter - Basil	p.156
Butter - Bourguignon Garlic	p.156
Butter - Lemon	p.156
Butter - Waffle	p.157
Butter - Orange	p.157
Clotted Cream	p.157
Dip - Avocado	p.155
Dip - French Moutarde	p.155
Dip - Passion Fruit	p.158
Cuban Sofrito	p.159
Gravy - Jalapeño Sausage	p.147
Gravy - Country White	p.148
Gravy - Southern Style Brown	p.151
Pesto	p.149
Sauce - Hollandaise	p.152
Sauce - Alfredo	p.152
Sauce - Pelican Bay Crêpe	p.148
Sauce - Cajun Crawfish	p.154
Sauce - Pepper jack Crawfish Cream	p.154
Sauce - Pesto Alfredo	p.149
Sauce - Classic Mornay	p.150
Sauce - Marinara (Sunday)	p.150
Sauce - French Béchamel	p.151
Sauce - Store Bought Sauce Fix	p.161
Spread - Grilled Cheese	p.158
Spread - Pesto	p.158
Misc. - Chicken Broth	p.160
Misc. - Parmesan Croutons	p.159
Misc. - Toasted Walnuts	p.160

INDEX OF RECIPES (CONTINUED)

SANDWICHES — p.137

Croque-Monsieur Provençal	p.138
Grilled Cheese	p.142-143
Impossible Burger Sliders	p.144-145
Portobello Burger	p.141
Tailor Ham & Egg	p.139
Tuscany Garden	p.140

SOUPS & SALADS — p.33

Salad - Caprese	p.34
Salad - Ceasar	p.35
Salad - Marina Bay	p.36
Salad - Spinach	p.37-38
Salad - Tuna	p.39
Soup - Cuban Black Bean	p.46
Soup - French Onion	p.42-43
Soup - Lobster Bisque	p.44-45
Soup - Tomato Basil	p.40-41

SIDE DISHES — p.127

Baked Asparagus	p.135
Baleada Jalapeño Grits	p.134
Cauliflower Mashed Potatoes	p.129
Fried Plantains	p.133
Macaroni & Cheese	p.136
Risotto	p.132
Roasted Quartered Potatoes	p.131
Rosemary Fingerling Potatoes	p.130
Southern Style Mashed Potatoes	p.128

INDEX OF RECIPES (CONTINUED)

THE MAIN COURSE — p.89

Casserole - King Ranch	p.97
Seafood. - HJ's (Kinda) Fried Clams	p.125
Seafood - New Orleans Crawfish Roll	p.92
Seafood - Pelican Cay Crep's	p.90-91
Seafood - Crawfish Vol-au-Vent	p.93
Foul - Chicken Pot Pie	p.94-95
Foul - Black Current Duck	p.102-103
Foul - Lemon Chicken	p.98
Foul - Turkey Tetrazzini	p.122
Meat - Beef - Braised Brisket & Wild Mushrooms	p.117-118
Meat - Beef - Papa Rellena	p.105
Meat - Beef - Hungarian Beef Stroganoff	p.120-121
Meat - Beef - Steak Bistecca Morsi	p.100-101
Meat - Beef - Steak Pizzaiola	p.96
Meat - Lamb - Lamb Chops & Saffron Pilaf	p.104
Meat - Pork - Spanish Pork Bites	p.126
Meat - Veal - Veal Scaloppine A La Marsala	p.119
Pasta - Homemade	p.115-116
Pasta - Nero di Seppia	p.106
Pasta - New Orleans Cajun	p.111
Pasta - Pesto Alfredo Tortellini	p.109-110
Pasta - Polish Pierogies	p.123-124
Pasta - Raviolini	p.107-108
Pasta - Squid Ink Pasta	p.112-114
Misc. - Hong Kong Egg Waffles	p.99

EQUIVALENT MEASURES

Dash	Equals	Less than ⅛ teaspoon
Pinch	Equals	⅛ teaspoon
3 teaspoons	Equals	1 tablespoon
2 tablespoons	Equals	1 liquid ounce
8 tablespoons	Equals	½ cup or 4 ounces
16 tablespoons	Equals	1 cup or 8 ounces
1 cup	Equals	½ pint or 8 ounces
2 cups	Equals	1 pint or 16 ounces
2 pints	Equals	1 quart or 32 ounces
4 quarts	Equals	1 gallon
16 (dry) ounces	Equals	1 pound
16 (fluid) ounces	Equals	2 cups
2 cups water	Equals	1 pound
1 large egg	Equals	2 ounces
8–10 large egg whites	Equals	1 cup
12–14 large egg yolks	Equals	1 cup
5 whole large eggs	Equals	1 cup
2 cups (unsifted) flour	Equals	10 ounces
2 cups granulated sugar	Equals	1 pound less 2 ounces
1 cup (packed) brown sugar	Equals	8 ounces
2 ⅔ cups (not packed) brown sugar	Equals	1 pound
3 ¾ cups (unsifted) powdered sugar	Equals	1 pound
4 cups grated cheese	Equals	1 pound
1 cup uncooked rice	Equals	2 cups

"Life is a combination of magic and pasta."

Federico Fellini

CHEF
J STEPHEN SADLER

As a restauranteur for over 40 years, Chef J Stephen Sadler has a vast well of knowledge when it comes to crafting a great dish. His bistros and cafes are recognized by those fortunate enough to have shared his unique offerings as some of the most creative dishes available in the States.

As an entrepreneurial restauranteur, Chef Sadler manages the company's Crumbzz International Bistro concept and worldwide bakery that manufactures and distributes the Crumbzz family of artisan cakes.

His travels across the world as a travel host in search of the finest culinary dishes, culminates in a unique view of the world of fine dining and street foods that is unlike any found worldwide.

As a speaker, Chef Sadler tours the world speaking on his two favorite topics. His "I Can Eat That!" children's healthy eating presentations are a popular event at schools across the country and his "The Right Ingredient Can Make a World of a Difference" presentations are extremely popular at clubs and organizations.

An accomplished, best selling author, Chef Sadler's books cover the gamut from his "Quest For The Best" series of books including, "The Story Of An Unlikely Chef Who Built An Improbable Empire From A Lost Family Recipe", his memoir of his worldwide quest in search of the roots of his 400-year-old family recipe artisan crumb cake; "Bringing Fine Dining To Small Town America" which dives into the challenges faced as a restauranteur in opening his international bistro, and his series of Happy Gardens™ children's books which highlight healthy eating "Kid Style" through individual garden character storytelling.

And finally, there is Chef Sadler's third book in the "Quest For The Best series, "The World On My Plate" recipe book. This much anticipated book features over 200 recipe's gathered through his world travel, with many of the very same dishes offered at his bistros and cafes. Most importantly, "The World On My Plate" features his never before offered, gold standard recipe for his family's 400-year-old artisan crumb cake.

www.ingramcontent.com/pod-product-compliance
Lightning Source LLC
Chambersburg PA
CBHW061354010526
44107CB00011B/935